W9-BXO-121

The Communicator's Commentary

John

THE COMMUNICATOR'S COMMENTARY SERIES

Lloyd J. Ogilvie

———— General Editor ————

The Communicator's Commentary

John

Roger L. Fredrikson

WORD BOOKS, PUBLISHER • WACO, TEXAS

Library of Congress Cataloging in Publication Data
Main entry under title:

The Communicator's commentary

   Includes bibliographical references.
   Contents: v. 4. John/Roger L. Fredrikson
     1. Bible. N.T.—Commentaries—Collected works.
I. Ogilvie, Lloyd John. II. Fredrikson, Roger L.
BS2341.2.C65   225.7'7   81–71764
ISBN 0–8499–0157-X (v. 4) regular edition   AACR2
ISBN 0–8499–3803–1 (v. 4) deluxe edition

Printed in the United States of America

To three congregations

The First Baptist Churches
of
Ottawa, Kansas
Sioux Falls, South Dakota
and
Wichita, Kansas

who have nurtured and loved
Ruth and me
and taught us

*"By this all will know
that you are My disciples,
if you have love
for one another."*
John 13:35

Contents

Editor's Preface

God has called all of His people to be communicators. Everyone who is in Christ is called into ministry. As ministers of "the manifold grace of God," all of us—clergy and laity—are commissioned with the challenge to communicate our faith to individuals and groups, classes and congregations.

The Bible, God's Word, is the objective basis of the truth of His love and power that we seek to communicate. In response to the urgent, expressed needs of pastors, teachers, Bible study leaders, church school teachers, small group enablers, and individual Christians, the Communicator's Commentary is offered as a penetrating search of the Scriptures of the New Testament to enable vital personal and practical communication of the abundant life.

Many current commentaries and Bible study guides provide only some aspects of a communicator's needs. Some offer in-depth scholarship but no application to daily life. Others are so popular in approach that biblical roots are left unexplained. Few offer impelling illustrations that open windows for the reader to see the exciting application for today's struggles. And most of all, seldom have the expositors given the valuable outlines of passages so needed to help the preacher or teacher in his or her busy life to prepare for communicating the Word to congregations or classes.

This Communicator's Commentary series brings all of these elements together. The authors are scholar-preachers and teachers outstanding in their ability to make the Scriptures come alive for individuals and groups. They are noted for bringing together excellence in biblical scholarship, knowledge of the original Greek and Hebrew, sensitivity to people's needs, vivid illustrative material from biblical, classical, and contemporary sources, and lucid communication by the use of clear outlines of thought. Each has been selected to contribute to this series because of his Spirit-empowered ability to help people live in the skins of biblical characters and provide a "you-are-there" intensity to the drama of events of the Bible which have so much to say about our relationships and responsibilities today.

The design for the Communicator's Commentary gives the reader an overall outline of each book of the New Testament. Following the introduction, which reveals the author's approach and salient background on the book, each chapter of the commentary provides the Scripture to be exposited. The New King James Bible has been chosen for the Communicator's Commentary because it combines with integrity the beauty of language, underlying Greek textual basis, and thought-flow of the 1611 King James Version, while replacing obsolete verb forms and other archaisms with their everyday contemporary counterparts for greater readability. Reverence for God is preserved in the capitalization of all pronouns referring to the Father, Son, or Holy Spirit. Readers who are more comfortable with another translation can readily find the parallel passage by means of the chapter and verse reference at the end of each passage being exposited. The paragraphs of exposition combine fresh insights to the Scripture, application, rich illustrative material, and innovative ways of utilizing the vibrant truth for his or her own life and for the challenge of communicating it with vigor and vitality.

It has been gratifying to me as Editor of this series to receive enthusiastic progress reports from each contributor. As they worked, all were gripped with new truths from the Scripture—God-given insights into passages, previously not written in the literature of biblical explanation. A prime objective of this series is for each user to find the same awareness: that God speaks with newness through the Scriptures when we approach them with a ready mind and a willingness to communicate what He has given; that God delights to give communicators of His Word "I-never-saw-that-in-that-verse-before" intellectual insights so that our listeners and readers can have "I-never-realized-all-that-was-in-that-verse" spiritual experiences.

The thrust of the commentary series unequivocally affirms that God speaks through the Scriptures today to engender faith, enable adventuresome living of the abundant life, and establish the basis of obedient discipleship. The Bible, the unique Word of God, is unlimited in its resource for Christians in communicating our hope to others. It is our weapon in the battle for truth, the guide for ministry, and the irresistible force for introducing others to God. In the New Testament we meet the divine Lord and Savior whom we seek to communicate to others. What He said and did as God with us has been faithfully recorded under the inspiration of the Spirit of God. The cosmic implications of the Gospels are lived out in Acts and spelled out in the Epistles. They have stood the test of time because the eternal Communicator, God Himself, communicates through them to those who would be communicators of grace. His essential nature is exposed, the plan of salvation is explained, and the Gospel for all of life, now and for eternity, is proclaimed.

A biblically rooted communication of the Gospel holds in unity and oneness what divergent movements have wrought asunder. This commentary series courageously presents personal faith, caring for individuals, and social responsibility as essential, inseparable dimensions of biblical Christianity. It seeks to present the quadrilateral Gospel in its fullness which calls us to unreserved commitment to Christ, unrestricted self-esteem in His grace, unqualified love for others in personal evangelism, and undying efforts to work for justice and righteousness in a sick and suffering world.

A growing renaissance in the church today is being led by clergy and laity who are biblically rooted, Christ-centered, and Holy Spirit-empowered. They have dared to listen to people's most urgent questions and deepest needs and then to God as He speaks through the Bible. Biblical preaching is the secret of growing churches. Bible study classes and small groups are equipping the laity for ministry in the world. Dynamic Christians are finding that daily study of God's Word allows the Spirit to do in them what He wishes to communicate through them to others. These days are the most exciting time since Pentecost. The Communicator's Commentary is offered to be a primary resource of new life for this renaissance.

In our efforts to grow as effective communicators we all long to find truly authentic leaders to emulate. We want to read commentaries written by people who have proven, seasoned skills of biblical exposition, illustration, and application, coupled with an ability to preach with power, warmth, and vision. At the same time we'd like to sense that, in leading a group or congregation, the person has faced the same challenges and problems that we have faced. When we discover the evidence of the same struggles we experience in seeking to be faithful and obedient disciples in personal evangelism, church renewal, and social responsibility, we take that person's exposition of the Scripture all the more seriously. We search for models who combine impelling preaching and teaching with a profound understanding of people and therefore are able to communicate the Gospel with sensitivity and love.

Dr. Roger Fredrikson, Pastor of the First Baptist Church of Wichita, is that kind of preacher, leader, and counselor. There is one word that comes to my mind when I think of this outstanding communicator: authentic. I define the word *authentic* to mean that which is of indisputable origin, original, consistent with the facts, congruent with reality, trustworthy, and true. The source of Dr. Fredrikson's authenticity is Christ. The Lord's indwelling power in his life is evident in all that he does and in the way he communicates. His zest for life and his empathy with people is the Master's love reaching out through his personality. This explains the freshness of his style and content as a communicator. As you listen to him preach, you know you are hearing a person who knows the Lord and spends quality time with Him in his own personal devotions and in prolonged study of the Scriptures. But you also sense something else—that this is a person who lives in depth, who is able to laugh and cry, hope and hurt. You feel he has lived what he communicates.

What Phillips Brooks said about his relationship with Christ is what I have observed in Roger Fredrikson when I've heard him speak or have enjoyed leisurely times of sharing personally as friends. Brooks said, "All experience comes to be but more and more the presence of Christ's life upon ours. I cannot tell how personal this grows to me. He is here. He knows me and I know Him. It is no figure of speech; it is the realest thing in the world."

That's the quality of awe, wonder, and gratitude for Christ that you find in this volume. Roger Fredrikson's love for Christ and the power of Christ in his life and ministry caused me to feel he was the person who should write this commentary on John's Gospel. I was convinced that it had to be done by a person who was distinguished both as a preacher and teacher, but also one who was committed to ministry to people in the frontline trenches of human suffering. Roger Fredrikson pastors an inner-city congregation that is seeking to be a caring community of faith. He preaches to a congregation representing the broad spectrum of social and economic backgrounds. As a leader in his denomination, he has been on the cutting edge of church renewal. He is in constant demand as a speaker and conference leader. Revered and admired by clergy and church leaders, he has been a pivotal person in pressing the church in America forward in discovering new life and vitality. All the congregations he has served have become dynamic laboratories of new life in which people meet Christ, become involved in the ministry of the laity, and make an impact on their city as responsible servants.

In this volume you will experience a fine blend of scholarship in exposition and communication skills in the vivid use of metaphors, contemporary parables, and stories of people. You will appreciate the new insights into the biblical text, but also the utilization of the great wealth of classical and more recent studies of the Fourth Gospel. You will share the process as Dr. Fredrikson grapples with John's account of Christ's life, message, death, and resurrection. Added to that you will be enriched in your own efforts to preach and teach as you are challenged to dig deeper in both understanding and experience of Christ as eternal Logos, Master, Friend of the lost and lonely, Savior of the world, reigning, resurrected Lord, and indwelling Power.

Keats said, "Nothing is ever real until it is expressed—even a proverb is no proverb to you till your life has illustrated it. Call the world, if you please, 'the vale of soul-making.' " The same is true for biblical exposition. It is real as we live it and then communicate the excitement and power we have discovered and experienced in our own spiritual adventure. Roger Fredrikson helps us live the Gospel of John in a new way. The result will be that our own preaching and teaching of Christ as revealed in John will be all the more gripping and life-changing. I commend this volume to you with gratitude to the author for his faithful friendship through the years and for his consistently dynamic preaching of Christ.

LLOYD OGILVIE

Acknowledgments

None of us ever lives to himself, particularly in the struggle to write a book. We are surrounded by fellow believers, encouragers, and critics who call forth the best in us. And to some of these, I give thanks.

Lloyd Ogilvie, a dear friend and the general editor of the Communicator's Commentary, was either foolhardy or daring enough to ask if I would be one of the contributors to this series. I had no concept of what I was getting into when I reluctantly told Lloyd I would accept the challenge. This turned out to be a much longer journey than I anticipated. The writing took place in the midst of the joys and burdens and excitement of an inner-city congregation struggling to be reborn and too much in snatches on days off and in places like Tribune, Kansas; Toronto, Canada; our cabin at Lobster Lake in Minnesota; and the American Baptist Assembly in Wisconsin. But here it is finally, hopefully to the glory of God. I am thankful now that Lloyd called on me, and grateful for his patience and gentle encouragement, all of which I have needed, for I am a man who struggles to put words on paper.

And I am indebted to Floyd Thatcher, editor-in-chief, Word Books, for his long-suffering support and kind nudges.

And how can I ever thank my beloved wife, Ruth, who at the beginning said, "Do you really think you can do this, Roger?" She was my staunchest human source of support and strength, as she has always been. She has lovingly given up the days off that we usually spend together and kept the coffeepot warm on many, many of these long writing days. But most of all she has prayed.

To our children, three beautiful, challenging people, with their families; and to my vibrant, eighty-eight-year-old mother. They have all been a part of this project in spirit.

To LeeDel Howard, a faithful, devoted secretary and helper for more than seventeen years. She has typed and retyped every word of this manuscript, offered helpful suggestions, and "cleaned up" sentences, while carrying on her other work.

And I have a deepened appreciation for our whole church staff—a great team—for their understanding and prayer, and for covering for me now and then at critical times.

And thanks to a loving, caring congregation who became more involved in this project than they may realize. When they got word of what was going on, particularly in these last months, many, many of these people have spoken words of encouragement and quietly said they were praying. And a number of these people have allowed their names to be used in this volume.

Perhaps the best evidence of this prayerful support came in an unexpected visit I had one Monday morning near the end of the project when I was trying to meet all kinds of deadlines. The doorbell rang and here stood one of our lovely, strong, faithful women who simply said, "I felt the Lord wanted me to come and pray with you." We knelt at the coffee table for a moment, then she went her way. This woman may never know how timely her visit was—which illustrates again how He is with us to strengthen and encourage us in all our times of weakness.

Introduction

Let me be frank. Wrestling with this remarkable Gospel has been a love-hate relationship. There have been times when I have almost run to the den to write, eager for what I felt I would find. Now and then I have literally sung and danced because the truth has broken through in some fresh, new way. While these insights have sometimes come from commentaries, more often the most rewarding illumination has come from the One who has been sent to be our Teacher. Here I claim no special revelation, but offer only gratitude that the Spirit is willing to open the Scripture and continually lead us into more truth.

On the other hand, there have also been those times when I have almost given up in despair, when I have struggled with a passage for hours, and its meaning has seemed more elusive and hidden than when I began. Some of these places still seem "locked" for me. I can well understand Sir Edwyn Hoskyns, who wrote, after spending much of a lifetime with John's Gospel, "He will not be true to the book he is studying if, at the end, the Gospel does not still remain strange, restless, and familiar."[1]

Here is a Gospel so humanly simple a child can quote many of its verses with understanding. How well I remember as a boy in Daily Vacation Bible School being expected to memorize all thirty-one verses of the fourteenth chapter. But it is also a Gospel so profound and mysterious that its hidden meanings challenge the keenest students of Scripture. It has been well said that John's Gospel is like "a pool in which a child may wade and an elephant can swim."[2]

In the end, I am grateful for the discipline and the joy of attempting to search out its meaning, and am chastened and renewed by the

One who dominates its pages. I can only cry out with Thomas, "My Lord and my God!"

The Purpose

This Gospel is first and foremost a message of evangelism, carefully and creatively written, that men may come to have life in the name of Jesus, the Christ, the Son of God. This is John's declared purpose (John 20:31), so the constant question throughout is the identity of the man Jesus. By what authority does He speak and minister? At the outset the writer makes the awesome theological affirmation that this man is the eternal Word who has been with God and who is God and who has now become flesh. In saying that Jesus is the *Word,* John is appealing with great imagination and force to both Jews and Greeks. For both, this concept had a unique and powerful meaning.

Throughout the Gospel this Word, Jesus, is illuminated and defined through His deeds and teachings. Men have the opportunity to behold the very glory of God through the signs of Jesus, mighty works which called men to understand and believe. And this glory breaks forth in unlikely, fleshly places—at a wedding or a funeral, among a hungry crowd, or with a man blind from birth. The climax in this revelation comes in Jesus' final hour. It is in the hushed anguish of Jesus' death on the cross that the Father's glory is fully revealed in the Son. Here is the strange, wondrous paradox of Jesus' ministry. Abundant fruit will come forth only if a grain of wheat falls into the ground and dies.

Through it all, men ponder and argue about who this is that has come. Jesus uses a whole cluster of images to define His identity and mission. He is "Living Water" and "Bread that comes down from heaven," the "Good Shepherd" and the "Resurrection and the Life." But finally He speaks of Himself as *ego eimi,* "I AM." He uses the most sacred, mysterious name the Hebrews had for deity, Yahweh. He is the creative, eternal One who has been sent by the Father— uniquely dependent upon Him, seeking only to give glory to Him through every act of obedience and finally insisting He would return to His Father and send another Paraclete.

Only a handful of those who see and hear really understand. They are drawn to believe and "remain." The rest either come near for a time and then fall away or angrily reject Him, calling Him a blasphemer, shouting for His death, because they are "children of the devil." No one can remain neutral about Jesus. He precipitates conflict between light and darkness, life and death.

This Gospel also tells the story of a new community. Jesus chooses a few ordinary men and shares His life with them so deeply that they will manifest the glory and love of the Father. They are called to love one another as Jesus loves them. That loving unity will reflect the intimate relationship between the Father and the Son, which both call and judge the world. They will be a people bearing "the name"; for the mission which the Son has been given by the Father is now given to His disciples.

And it is the Spirit, the other Paraclete, who will continue this ministry of Jesus within and among these disciples. He will come alongside to call out and encourage and guide these men as He witnesses through them, convicting the world of its sin.

John also wrote to encourage new Jewish believers who had been cast out of their synagogues and ostracized by their families. The blind man, who is healed by Jesus, is a good illustration of this. Even though he does not know who Jesus is until the climax of the account, he stubbornly continues to speak a good word for Him in the face of growing hostility. This man is welcomed by his Healer after being put out of the synagogue. There is also encouragement for new believers. Here they can see the rich, eternal meaning of being a part of Jesus' company, children of God, as contrasted with being in the old, dead Israel.

The Writer

I am convinced that the writer of this Gospel is John, the beloved disciple, who was the son of Zebedee, even though I am fairly aware of most of the reasons for questioning his authorship.

There are two overwhelming reasons for accepting the beloved disciple as the author of this Gospel. One is the way natural, intimate details are almost casually included in the whole account. Only a person living with Jesus on a day-to-day basis could easily include this kind of personal detail. Someone writing "from the outside" would have included more contrived, obvious details. Furthermore, we must take quite seriously the writer's conscious inclusion of himself in speaking of his own witness. "We beheld His glory" (John 1:14), and "He who has seen has testified, and his testimony is true" (John 19:35), illustrate John's own involvement as a firsthand witness.

The second reason is that the early church fathers, those who lived closest to the time when the New Testament was written, are almost unanimous in their claim that John the Beloved is the writer of the Gospel that bears his name. Westcott voices the understanding of a number of commentators: "But it is most significant that Eusebius, who had access to many works which are now lost, speaks without reserve of the Fourth Gospel as the unquestioned work of John, no less than those three great representative Fathers who sum up the teaching of the century."[3] These were Irenaeus, Clement of Alexandria, and Tertullian. And it is almost certain that John had been living in Ephesus, a great Hellenistic center, for a considerable time when this Gospel was written. Surely in this inquisitive, sophisticated, cosmopolitan culture John had been opened up, had been internationalized, so that he saw the history of Jesus through the eyes of the larger world. He would always be a fisherman from Galilee, but he also had become a citizen of a city influenced by Greek culture. The Lord had schooled John for the writing of this particular Gospel.

I recall some young men I had in class when I taught New Testament Life and Literature at Ottawa University in Ottawa, Kansas. They were simple, honest farm boys—naive and unspoiled. More than twenty years later, as I have had the opportunity to see some of these former students, I have discovered among them a brilliant atomic scientist in Washington and a well-known professor in economics, a Phi Beta Kappa, teaching at his alma mater. Who is to say that this fisherman, the son of Zebedee, could not be the writer of this sophisticated, yet simple, Gospel?

It is almost too easily assumed this Gospel was written near the end of the first century or early in the second. However, I have begun to wonder about that and almost "feel" in living and working with John that his Gospel might have been written much earlier. The detail he has included, which is so fresh, and the strong encouragement he is giving to new Jewish Christians who would have been shunned and persecuted early in the Christian era, could be reasons for dating the Gospel earlier. I was intrigued to discover that Earl Palmer, a thoughtful pastor, has indicated the Gospel may have been written near the time of the fall of Jerusalem in A.D. 70. He substantiated this by quoting Dr. W. F. Albright, "All the concrete arguments for a late date for the Johannine literature have now been dissipated."[4]

It is evident that John is aware of much of the material in the synoptic Gospels that tells us a great deal about Jesus' Galilean ministry. However, most of the events and teachings in the Fourth Gospel are centered in Judea. John has his own reasons for giving us that part of the story. And much of this account is woven into the rich meaning of the national feast days which Jesus enjoyed attending. Here is where the issues of faith and rejection were joined, where the chasm between light and darkness became so dramatically clear. For it was in Jerusalem that Jesus had His sharpest conflict with the Jewish leaders, who totally rejected Him, and finally crucified Him.

I have deliberately not attempted to work out a comparison of John's chronology of Jesus' ministry with the other three Gospels. That is a long, technical undertaking which W. B. Westcott[5] in earlier times and Raymond Brown[6] more recently have given us in their tremendously helpful studies of this Gospel.

This volume is a result of a dialogue between the Scripture given us by the Spirit through the Apostle John and my own life among a people I seek to serve, some of whom have been "breathed on" and know they have a mission, others who seek and wonder, and a few who may even be hostile. The communication that has been opened in this effort has blessed and strengthened my own faith.

NOTES

1. Sir Edwyn Hoskyns, *The Fourth Gospel*, ed. F. N. Davey (London: Faber and Faber Limited, 1947), p. 20.

2. Leon Morris, *The Gospel According to John* (Grand Rapids: Wm. B. Eerdmans, 1971), p. 7.

3. W. B. Westcott, *The Gospel According to John* (Grand Rapids: Wm. B. Eerdmans, reprint 1981), p. xxviii.

4. Earl F. Palmer, *The Intimate Gospel* (Waco, TX: Word Books, 1978), p. 12.

5. See n. 3.

6. Raymond E. Brown, *The Gospel According to John I–XII* and *XIII–XXI*, Vols. 29 and 29A, *The Anchor Bible* (New York: Doubleday & Company, Inc., 1966).

An Outline of John

C. He Himself Believed and His Whole Household: 4:51–54
D. A Cripple Walking Home: "Do You Want to Be Made Well?": 5:1–8
E. The Controversy: "Who Is the Man?": 5:9–15
F. The Issue: The Relation of Father and Son: 5:16–20
G. Life and Judgment Are in the Son: 5:21–30
H. The Witnesses Who Surround Him: 5:31–39
I. The Tragic Rejection: 5:40–47
VII. A Costly Meal: 6:1–71
A. Jesus Spreads a Feast: 6:1–15
B. The Assurance of His Presence: 6:16–21
C. Dialogue and Decision: 6:22–59
D. Those Who Finally Remain: 6:60–71
VIII. Conflict at the Feast: Whose Descendants?: 7:1—8:59
A. His Time, Not His Brothers': 7:1–9
B. Going up to the Feast: Confusion—A Good Man or a Deceiver?: 7:10–13
C. His Open Teaching: Doctrine from God: 7:14–24
D. Seeking, but Not Finding Him: 7:25–36
E. Rivers of Living Water: 7:37–39
F. Rejection, but a Cautious Defense: 7:40–52
G. The Merciful Judge: 7:53—8:11
H. The Open Witness: 8:12–20
I. The Infinite Chasm: 8:21–29
J. Not Children of Abraham: 8:30–47
K. His Majestic Identity: 8:48–59
IX. New Eyes for Old: 9:1–38
A. The Healing: 9:1–7
B. The Witness: 9:8–12
C. He Is a Prophet: 9:13–17
D. Questioning His Parents: 9:18–23
E. This Man Must Be from God: 9:24–34
F. Belief and Worship: 9:35–38
X. The Shepherd's Last Appeal: 9:39—10:42
A. Judgment: "Your Sin Remains": 9:39–41
B. Truth Hidden in a Parable: 10:1–6
C. The Only Door: 10:7–10
D. The Good Shepherd: 10:11–16
E. Laying Down His Life: 10:17–21
F. The Sheep Hear and Follow: 10:22–30

CHAPTER ONE

The Prologue: The Divine Overture

John 1:1–18

Is there any way one can plumb the depths of John's prologue to his Gospel? Such intense power in so few words! After brooding over the meaning of these short verses for months, I am more reluctant than ever to put my thoughts on paper. Yet, strangely, I am eager and compelled to do so. I can readily understand why both Augustine and Chrysostom are reported as saying, "It is beyond the power of man to speak as John does in his prologue." John Calvin has written of the prologue, "Rather should we be satisfied with this heavenly oracle, knowing that it says much more than our minds can take in."[1]

Living with this prologue is like standing in the foothills of an awesome mountain range catching a breathtaking glimpse of massive, snowcapped peaks reaching up through the haze. Or it is like being overwhelmed by haunting melodies that introduce the themes of a mighty symphony. I had such a moment recently when I found myself being swept along by the sheer beauty and power of Shostakovich's Eighth Symphony. I came to the concert tired and unexpectant, but left lifted and fulfilled. In the midst of this surprising, spiritual experience my eye caught the words in the program notes, "His [Shostakovich's] symphonies combine somber tragedy, mordant wit, expressive melody, dramatic development and profound emotion, all under a brilliantly orchestrated surface." I almost shouted, "Why, that could have been written about John's prologue."

John has caught the sweep and wonder of the history of salvation and shared it in hymnic form. All through the prologue he is setting forth the career of the Incarnate Word in simple, powerful phrases—"the light shining in the darkness," "became flesh and dwelt among us," "full of grace and truth," "declaring the Father," some "did not receive Him," but others were "born of God." The prologue is far more than an introduction to the Gospel. It is really a dramatic summary, a revelation, of all that will take place throughout the earthly ministry of our Lord.

But John cannot speak of His career without asking about its Source. When did the story of our salvation really begin? This drives him back to or into the heart of Reality. He must plumb the mystery of his Source if he is to make plain the identity and vocation of the Word dwelling among us. This is like discovering that the refreshing, healing water, which gives life to all around it, comes from a hidden, limitless spring in the bowels of the earth.

THE SPEECH OF GOD: WORD AND LOGOS

1 In the beginning was the Word, and the Word was with God, and the Word was God.

2 He was in the beginning with God.

3 All things were made through Him, and without Him nothing was made that was made.

4 In Him was life, and the life was the light of men.

5 And the light shines in the darkness, and the darkness did not comprehend it.

6 There was a man sent from God, whose name was John.

7 This man came for a witness, to bear witness of the Light, that all through him might believe.

8 He was not that Light, but was sent to bear witness of that Light.

John 1:1–8

Eternal, Coexistent, Yet God (vv. 1–2). John begins with a disarmingly simple phrase, *"In the beginning was the Word."* Here is the central theme, the grand motif, of the symphony which will come pouring forth with such glory throughout the Gospel narrative. The "Speech of God" John Calvin called it. What a wonder that God should speak. Here is a mystery, not unlike speech among us humans, that unique capacity to use signs and symbols, sounds and touch, and even silence, to communicate with one another.

Think of the power words have among us. It was said of John

Knox, the fiery Scottish reformer, "When he preached his words were more powerful than ten thousand trumpets." And who of us in this generation can forget Martin Luther King crying out in the shadow of the Lincoln Memorial, "I have a dream"? Words can fulfill or hurt or bless. They can build up or tear down. There are those tender, healing, affirming words, "Welcome home." "Congratulations, it's a girl." "I love you." Or those angry, destructive, cutting words, "Divorce is granted." "I hate you." "She's dead." What meaning they carry—far more than mere sounds hanging in the air.

But when John speaks of *"the Word,"* he is taking us far beyond the meaning it has for us in general. He is a Hebrew speaking to his own people, and for them, the Word had unique power. For these people, there was a precious quality, a living reality, about words, so they were used sparingly. There were only ten thousand words in Hebrew speech and only two hundred thousand words in the Greek language. The Semitic root for "word," *dabar,* also meant "thing," "affair," "event," or "action." A word spoken was a happening. Once it had been uttered, it could not be torn from the event that it evoked. Thus, when Isaac had blessed Jacob and then later discovered that Jacob had cleverly stolen his twin brother Esau's birthright, he could not recall his words of blessing, even though Esau pleaded with his aged father to do this. The words had gone forth and the blessing stood (Gen. 27:32–38).

But when God spoke, that was a creative, awesome moment! Thus all creation was called into existence by the word of the Lord. "Then God said, 'Let there be light'; and there was light" (Gen. 1:3). He also spoke at the climax of the creation event, "Then God said, 'Let Us make man in Our image, according to Our likeness. . . .' So God created man in His own image; in the image of God He created him; male and female He created them" (Gen. 1:26–27).

So the Scripture celebrates over and over again the power of God's creative word.

> For as the rain comes down, and the snow from heaven,
> And do not return there,
> But water the earth,
> And make it bring forth and bud,
> That it may give seed to the sower
> And bread to the eater,
> So shall My word be that goes forth from My mouth;

It shall not return to Me void,
But it shall accomplish what I please,
And it shall prosper in the thing for which I sent it (Isa. 55:10–11).

It was this Word that had called Abraham to leave his familiar, safe surroundings for the insecurity of a far country to become the father of a mighty people. Generations later this same Word broke the shackles of Egyptian bondage and set Israel free to enter into their promised destiny. And in the ebb and flow of later history, the Word came again and again through the prophets—"Thus saith the Lord," calling a wandering, whoring people back to their first love and vocation.

Little wonder then that when John wrote, *"In the beginning was the Word,"* he evoked a whole cluster of memories among his Hebrew readers and touched a nerve of understanding.

But John was also reaching out beyond his Hebrew countrymen to a vast Gentile audience dominated by Greek thought. William Barclay has pointed out that by A.D. 60 "there must have been a hundred thousand Greeks in the church for every Jew who was a Christian."[2] And for this audience, the Word, for them *Logos,* was charged with a unique meaning.

As far back as 560 B.C., Heraclitus had asked if there was anything permanent and lasting in the flux of constant change that was all about. His answer was that the *Logos,* the Reason of God, controlled and guided this stream of change. Later the Stoics held that *Logos* was the "mind of God," the eternal principle of order in the universe, that which makes the chaos of the world a cosmos. If John had begun his Gospel by declaring that the Messiah had come it would have had little, if any, meaning for the Greeks. It was the *Logos* that became the point of contact, and opened the door for a hearing of the Gospel.

So in using *"the Word,"* the *Logos,* John was speaking to both the Jewish and Greek worlds—those two widely divergent cultures. The Greeks were sophisticated, inquisitive, and philosophic; the Jews righteous, traditional, and struggling to be faithful to the Law. How amazing that John could share the Gospel narrative with these two cultures at the same time, using a single, simple concept that carried such profound meaning for both.

John understood and empathized with the Hellenistic world. He was aware of the nuances and subtleties of Greek thought and tried constantly to help his Greek audience understand the ways of the

Jewish people that they might understand the Gospel more clearly. For example, in telling of Jesus' encounter with the Samaritan woman, he adds simply, "For Jews have no dealings with Samaritans" (John 4:9b), and thus helps his Greek readers understand how radical Jesus had been in reaching out toward this needy woman. All through the Gospel, John shares helpful insights for his Greek audience. Here is a true evangelist establishing rapport and trust. John did not try to force his Greek readers into an alien point of view, but rather sought to lead them into investigating seriously who Jesus was. This is why that simple invitation Jesus gave the first disciples, "Come and see," is an opportunity for all readers to check out the evidence. How could the *Logos* and "the Lamb of God who takes away the sin of the world" be one and the same? Surely that kind of honest invitation would appeal to the Greek mind.

John, the writer, was the son of Zebedee, a fairly prosperous Galilean fisherman, through and through a Jew. Nourished on the Law and Prophets, all the Jewish customs and traditions had shaped John's deepest inner life. There is no way he can shake off or dismiss those roots, nor should he. This is why his appeal to this Gentile audience is so remarkable. Adolf Schlatter has argued persuasively in *Der Evangelist Johannes* (1930) that "the writer thought in Semitic idiom while he wrote in Greek."[3]

Those of us who are eager to be authentic witnesses have much to learn from John. We have been so domesticated and institutionalized within the ghetto of the religious establishment that we have been cut off and alienated from the very people we have been eager to reach. There is no way we can enter into honest dialogue with either the Hebrew or Greek of our day if we hide within our "churchly" groups using the "in" jargon of the initiated. How often I have heard, "Oh, I couldn't show up there; I don't know the right words," or "I don't have the right clothes," or "If you only knew what terrible things I've done," in response to an invitation to some church affair.

It is only when we are in a vulnerable, open posture, if we hear the disturbing questions of uprooted, secular man or understand the bankruptcy of his chaotic value system, that we can discover a language that is fresh and alive and true to the Gospel. That language can become a bridge and enter into the mind and heart of our confused, seeking, and often angry generation. How else can we share the Gospel story? John has done this. His Gospel is a passionate evangelistic confession, carefully written that "men may believe." *"The Word"* is the cutting edge of that confession.

"In the beginning was the Word." But what beginning? At creation? When light came and the chaos became cosmos? No, not that beginning, although John's phrase surely comes from the Genesis account. There are words throughout the prologue that recall the creation event—life, light, darkness.

But John reaches back further and plunges deeper than the beginning of created existence. He is speaking of a new creation, of what God has done in His new dispensation, of salvation history, asking, "When did the story of Jesus really begin?" This takes us beyond our dependent, contingent world of space and time to the wonder and sweep of the "One who inhabits eternity." Here we are brought to the Source, the Origin of all things, to the "root of the universe," to use William Temple's phrase. This is an eternal Gospel.

"The Word" of which John speaks is uncreated. There has never been a time when it was not. Here is existence beyond time, that which was when time and finite being began its course. So created existence can only be understood in the light of this uncreated Word.

But this Word does not dwell in lonely isolation. *"And the Word was with God."* The literal translation could be "the Word was towards God." The whole existence of the Word is oriented toward the Father and is in eternal, active communion with Him. The Word is in the presence of God, face to face with Him. This living intercourse is revealed in the words and deeds of Jesus throughout His earthly existence. "Then Jesus answered and said to them, 'Most assuredly, I say to you, the Son can do nothing of Himself, but what He sees the Father do; for whatever He does, the Son also does in like manner' " (John 5:19). " 'Do you not believe that I am in the Father, and the Father in Me? The words that I speak to you I do not speak on My own authority; but the Father who dwells in Me does the works' " (John 14:10).

"The Word" and the Father are not identical, yet They are One. There is a creative fullness within God's being, a wondrous unity, yet a rich diversity, revealed in all that He is and does. Early in Scripture this "mode of being," this intimacy, is spoken of in the act of creation. " 'Let Us make man in Our image, according to Our likeness' " (Gen. 1:26). It is as if a family decision is made within the very life of God. Little wonder then that the most common name for the Deity in Hebrew is *Elohim*, a plural form.

It is this reality, the Word being with God, that is the source of and power for all authentic Christian community. It is not worthwhile action projects, nor common goals, nor geographic or ethnic homogeneity, nor a particular theological language that holds us together as believers. Much of our so-called "Christian fellowship" has waded in a shallows of human effort and organization rather than swimming in the deeps of God's reality. No, it is abiding in the intimate, loving relationship of the Word turned toward the Father that creates our life together.

Every healing of broken relationships within the body of believers is always a new acceptance of that reality. In recent months I have seen two churches, after twenty years of alienation and separation, set free to let God do His new thing through them when they finally dared come together to worship our wondrous God. This did not come to pass without pain and much searching of heart in both congregations. But who in those two congregations can ever forget the power and release that swept through the people that night as they sang the first hymn, "Great Is Thy Faithfulness"? The people reached out to greet one another, with joy and tears. They joined together in holy, cleansing prayer. I know, because I am the pastor of one of these churches. The good news of this healing moved out on the streets, and people wondered what happened. And there was a new openness to believe that the Father had sent the Son because there was new love among God's people after all these years of misunderstanding and hurt.

"And the Word was God." Here is the climactic statement in John's speaking of the Word and God. All that can be said about God can be said about the Word. That Word partakes of the innermost being of God. It is only the One "who is in the bosom of the Father" who can declare Him.

John is saying far more than that "the Word was divine," as Moffatt and Goodspeed and others have translated this phrase. That is to dilute the high Christology so evident throughout the whole of this Gospel. The believing cry of Thomas, "My Lord and my God," when he met the risen Christ is but a later testimony of the true identity of the Word.

John came from a people who were fiercely monotheistic. Their faith in one holy living God was no academic affair; it was a life and death matter which no amount of social pressure or cruel persecution could stamp out. So the confession, "the Word was God," was a startling affirmation of faith that could only be made by one who had accepted the invitation of Jesus to "come and see" and had ended up beholding His glory, which could only have been the glory of "the only begotten of the Father." John had moved beyond the monotheism of the Law into the rich wonder of the Incarnate Word's being very God.

Yet the Word is not identical to God. The Greek grammatical construction of this phrase underlines this. Ordinarily the definite article *ho* is used before *Theos*, God. Had John done so here, he would have been saying the Word is identical with God. But he says the Word was *Theos*, with no definite article. Thus the noun, God, almost becomes an adjective. So John is saying that the Word was of the very essence, the very character, of God, while not being identical with God.

"He was in the beginning with God." John is an excellent teacher. So He continues to underline these crucial facts that are basic to the Gospel. The history of salvation is from eternity, and the intimate, loving relationship between God and the Word is at the heart of all that takes place—forever. This whole Gospel is really a beautiful illustration of that.

But here a new, beautiful fact is introduced. *"He was in the beginning."* The Word is personal. We are not dealing with an "it" or an abstraction.

Salvation does not come in concepts, but through the Living Word, who is personal. God's move toward us is wondrously human and understandable. This Gospel is an account of His intimate dealing with persons—Nicodemus, Mary of Magdala, a lad with loaves and fish, a woman at a well, and at the end, His mother whom He cares for from a cross—how deeply personal!

How desperately we cry out for that personal Word in the midst of TV sets, technological gimmicks, and religion that becomes slick and manipulative and marketable.

The Word That Creates (v. 3). Out of that amazing relationship— "the Word with God"—flowed creation. This is God's work through His personal Word. God is the Source, but the Word is the living Agent, the Vehicle, through Whom He creates. Paul has clearly stated the same truth. "For by Him all things were created that are in heaven and that are on earth, visible and invisible, whether thrones or dominions or principalities or powers. All things were created through Him and for Him" (Col. 1:16). This Word which has been hidden in the eternal sanctuary of God now is made known. "The Evangelist's plan is to show that the Word of God came forth to outward action immediately from the creation of the world. For having previously been incomprehensible in His essence, He was then openly known by the effect of His power."[4] And Jesus testifies to this continuing "working" relationship throughout His earthly ministry. "But Jesus answered them, 'My Father has been working until now, and I have been working'" (John 5:17).

Everything owes its existence to the Word. Not just the whole, but separately—the birds that are singing outside my window just now, the child happily skipping home from school, the vastness of the universe we are now attempting to explain—all these were made by Him. Throughout the Gospel, John often states a truth in negative terms as well as positive, as he does here: *"without Him nothing was made that was made."* The form of the verb is the perfect tense. Here is the Word's continuing creative activity in that which we see all around.

How wonderfully creation becomes the arena of God's salvation. All through this Gospel, creation and salvation are intertwined. At the time of John's writing there was a growing school of thought which insisted that all matter was inherently evil. Salvation then really became a denial of creation, a deliverance from all fleshly entanglements. Or at best, it meant a perfect God could approach creation only at a distance, through a series of downward steps or emanations by emissaries or angels, to avoid besmirching His perfection.

But this is a denial of a Gospel that is very earthy and fleshly. For, if God created "all things" through His personal Word and continues to communicate with this creation, then even a fallen, alienated creation is His and ultimately becomes the historical arena for His saving acts. The cross was really driven into the ground. Here He lays claim to His whole creation. There will be in the end not only a new heaven, but a new earth (Isa. 65:17, Rev. 21:1).

In Him: Life and Light (vv. 4–5). Here John introduces the fresh, great theme of life in God's unfolding song. This word "life," *zoe* in Greek, is used thirty-five times in this Gospel and the word "to live" or "to have life," *zin,* fifteen times. It is this uncreated, everlasting Life that both creates and redeems. Nothing can exist without that Life. Every leaf that comes forth after the long night of winter and every cry at birth and every step toward healing in a psychiatric ward is evidence of that Life.

But His Life also redeems, as an eternal gift, through His Word.

Instead of life that merely goes on and on—how tedious that would be—His gift is a quality of existence that is secure in knowing that the Word is eternal. Here is peace and joy, power and love. *"The life,"* John called it. And Jesus spoke of this gift repeatedly. " 'I have come that they may have life, and that they may have it more abundantly' " (John 10:10). "Whoever eats My flesh and drinks My blood has eternal life" (John 6:54). "I am the way, the truth, and the life" (John 14:6).

This *"life was the light of men."* At creation God said, " 'Let there be light'; and there was light" (Gen. 1:3). Out of the very life of God, light shines forth to dispel the chaos and darkness. That light is in man in a particular way. The Lord God has breathed into him His own breath of life. An intimate, personal act which sets man apart, making him uniquely responsible to his Maker. That breath is the source of reason, conscience, and the longing to love and worship— the light that makes us human.

But in that life there is also the light of salvation. The Word has come to give us life and open our eyes. As Jesus gave life to Lazarus (John 11) so He gave sight to the man born blind (John 9). He is the light of the world and whoever follows Him "shall not walk in darkness, but have the light of life" (John 8:12).

Now we are suddenly and unexpectedly introduced to darkness, an alien force, the environment into which all men are born. It is a somber, negative theme, *"light shines in the darkness."* The song now takes on the tragic dimension of struggle and hostility. If the light unmasks and reveals the darkness for what it is, then the darkness will not remain passive, but will fight back. It is the nature of darkness to try to quench the light. This darkness is never explained, but is accepted as a fact, a strong, but minor, theme in the total symphony. Here there is a change in the verb form, "the light shines," indicating a continuous action. The light is constantly showing up the darkness for what it is—ignorance, unbelief, rebellion. This struggle is a constant, recurring theme throughout the Gospel. "For everyone practicing evil hates the light and does not come to the light, lest his deeds should be exposed" (3:20).

The darkness cannot *"comprehend"* or overcome the light. The light is always a mystery to darkness. There is a hardness, a stubborn rebellion, which makes it impossible for the darkness to understand or open up to the light. The Pharisees began by refusing to understand, thus their minds were darkened and their hearts were hardened. Finally their rejection of the light was ultimate, and they cried, "Crucify Him!"

But neither can the darkness overcome the light. That single penetrating shaft of light is more powerful than the utter blackness of rejection. Over and over again, this Gospel makes that clear. A simple act, stooping to wash the feet of the confused, worried disciples or a quiet word to a guilt-ridden adulterous woman, "Neither do I condemn you; go and sin no more" (John 8:11), is mightier than the anger and violence of His enemies.

The Witness to That Light (vv. 6–8). In a moment we have moved from the vast stretches of eternity to a simple, solitary person in time. Here the earthiness, the humanity of the whole story begins at a particular place in history. The writer simply calls this witness John without designating him as the Prophet as do the synoptic Gospels. He evidently knew John well, for he had been one of his followers. The writer also must have had a deep sense of gratitude that John had introduced him to Jesus.

The writer was aware of John's greatness—the last of the prophets, standing between the old and the new, a blazing, courageous spokesman calling men to repentance and righteousness. He refers to John's being a baptizer only in passing, but emphasizes repeatedly his faithfulness as a witness, identifying and pointing to the One Who was Light and "the Lamb of God who takes away the sin of the world" (John 1:29).

But John the Apostle is also keenly aware of the danger of followers clinging to a powerful figure like John the Baptist and making him the center of their focus. And there may have been a John the Baptist sect at the time this Gospel was written. At least the church in Ephesus had to contend with this. For when Paul asked the disciples there if they had received the Holy Spirit, their response was they had never heard of the Holy Spirit. "And he said to them, 'Into what then were you baptized?' So they said, 'Into John's baptism.' " After they heard the whole Gospel from Paul, they were then baptized in the name of the Lord Jesus (Acts 19:1–7). And the gifted preacher, Apollos, "spoke and taught accurately the things of the Lord, though he knew only the baptism of John" (Acts 18:25).

So John makes it clear throughout his writing that the Baptist stands in the shadow of Jesus. He is a witness to Him, but is in no way to be confused with the Christ. So the contrasts are made plain in the prologue. Jesus was "in the beginning." John *"came for a witness."*

Jesus is "the Word." John was "a man." This Word was "with God." John was *"sent from God."* John is a witness to the Light, but is not the Light. In our time of super churches and ecclesiastical super stars with booking agents and all the rest, one wonders if the witness and the Light do not often become confused.

There is an awesome power in John's mission. He has been sent from God, a great calling with divine credentials. He is to be a *"witness,"* another key word in this Gospel. The noun form of "witness" is used fourteen times and the verb form thirty-three times. There is a seriousness, a burden, in being a witness. He is committed all the way—even when doubts tear at him in prison—which finally means his head on a platter at Herod's party. Here the aorist tense in the Greek is used for the verb "to bear witness," which means he finished his work.

Do we understand what this means in the church? So often we are in the stands, but not on the playing field. We are an evangelical church, but not a witnessing church. In Hitler's Germany, the "evangelical church" somehow survived by sticking to an emasculated Gospel. But the "confessional church" made its costly declaration that Jesus was Lord even over *der Führer,* and Dietrich Bonhoeffer was executed, but not before he had written *The Cost of Discipleship* in which he made it so clear that there is always a costly grace in being a witness.

The end of John's witness is that *"all through him might believe."* The witness is to bring men to the place where they must decide, where they take a definite step of faith. And the witness comes that all may believe. How universal! The invitation is sent out to all creation. Water is turned into wine at a wedding; a cripple is told to pick up his bed and go home after thirty-eight years by the pool; a respectable member of the Council is told his only hope is to be born again; and the Samaritan woman with a bad reputation drinks of everlasting water and hurries away to let her village know whom she has met. All are included.

REJECTED, BUT ALSO RECEIVED

9 That was the true Light which gives light to every man who comes into the world.

10 He was in the world, and the world was made through Him, and the world did not know Him.

11 He came to His own, and His own did not receive
Him.

12 But as many as received Him, to them He gave
the right to become children of God, even to those
who believe in His name:

13 who were born, not of blood, nor of the will
of the flesh, nor of the will of man, but of God.

John 1:9–13

The True Light (v. 9). The Light to which the witness points is the
"true" or real Light. There is nothing unreal or shadowy about it.
By contrast all other lights are imperfect, transitory, and flickering,
only partial rays or reflections.

No man is destitute of the illumination of this light, for God has
revealed something of Himself to all men. This is the common light
of nature. Paul has also spoken of this light for all men. "For since
the creation of the world His invisible attributes are clearly seen,
being understood by the things that are made, even His eternal power
and Godhead" (Rom. 1:20). While this light is universal, for *"every
man,"* yet it is personal. Each one has this gift of light, however faint
it may be.

Laurie is a friendly, twenty-four-year-old young lady who had
been asked to serve as a ring bearer at the wedding of our son, Joel,
and Jeanne Anne. She sat in the front pew with Jeanne Anne's folks
during the early part of the ceremony until I mentioned that a very
special friend of Jeanne Anne's would step forward with the rings.
At this point she clapped joyously and with a broad grin gingerly
moved forward with the rings.

Our son, Randy, the best man, stepped down to meet her. Then,
proud as a peacock, she presented the rings for that part of the service.
According to the script, she was then to go back down. But she
was enjoying herself too much to leave now, standing there between
the groom and the best man. So Randy gently and quite naturally
put his arm over her shoulder and every once in awhile she would
gently tap Joel and grin as if to say, "Don't forget me. I'm still here."
Laurie brought an unexpected tenderness, a gift of grace, to the rest
of the service, which most people now followed through tear-filled
eyes.

Humanly speaking, Laurie is a badly retarded young lady, abused
much of her early life. She is now a precious student of Jeanne Anne's.
Jeanne Anne lovingly teaches retarded adults. And having no one

in the world to claim her, Laurie has spent much time at Jeanne Anne's home. Can any one of us measure the gift of God-given light in Laurie that blessed us all that day?

This true Light is always coming into the world, continuously in action, never static, but alive and dynamic, penetrating all existence, surprising us under microscopes or in libraries, in the exploration of space or in the quiet, honest conversation of friends. And our restless search for further light, at whatever level, always leads us to Him—that personal, living Presence, always with us.

In the World, but Not Known (v. 10). *"He was in the world."* The Light is with us. He has not paid us a fleeting visit, dropped in and then gone on. But stayed with us in this world which owes its existence to Him. So Professor Westcott has written, "The Word acts by his Presence as well as by His special Advent."[5]

"And the world did not know Him." Now there is a subtle shift in the use of "world." It no longer means simply creation; now a sense of indifference, ignorance, and alienation is introduced. Specifically, man is addressed here rather than the whole of creation, including inanimate objects. John often uses "world" with this negative connotation throughout the Gospel. Here is the darkness and disobedience of mankind, a rebellion which affects the whole of the cosmos. This rebellion does not consist of isolated acts of ignorance and unbelief here and there, but an organized, cosmic unwillingness to recognize the Light. The music has become strange and dissonant.

So this rebellious world did not know Him. Not in that personal, believing, saving way, for it had chosen the darkness, not knowing Him.

Not Received by His Own (v. 11). This phrase brings us nearer home, and the tragedy deepens. Note how John moves in, becomes more personal, as He speaks of the coming of the Word. At first, the "Light was," then "He was in the world," and finally *"He came to His own."* He did not come as an outsider, but as One Who belonged. The phrase *"to His own"* is the same one that is used in John 19:27, "And from that hour that disciple took her to his own home" when from the cross, Jesus commits His mother to John.

He came to His own particular people and dwelled in their own land. These were a people who had been prepared for His coming for centuries. They had been schooled and taught through the law and the prophets and through God's gracious acts of deliverance and provision. Surely these people would *"receive"* Him! The Greek word used for "receive" here is an intimate, relational word like that expressed when Joseph "took" Mary to be his wife in obedience to the command of the Lord (Matt. 1:24). But then He was not received by His own in that tender, loving way. Anything but!

For rather than welcoming Him, His people refused to understand Him, then became more and more suspicious, and finally rejected Him in blind anger, even accusing Him of being the child of a devil. Then they killed Him. All through the Gospel there are angry, suspicious accusations made by the very religious leaders who should have received Him with great joy.

But Some Received (vv. 12–13). However, there were some who received Him, who took that which was within reach. Those first eager disciples joined Him and remained with Him—Nicodemus making His cautious defense before the Council, then becoming His disciple; that stubbornly independent blind man, who after being healed refused to change his confession one iota, discovering that his Healer was the Son of God. What surprising acceptances!

And to these *"He gave."* Here is God's grace of giving. *"The right"* is the full authority to have one's status changed to that exalted place of being adopted into the heavenly family. *"To become children of God."* Incredibly, those who received Him shared His divine nature. Notice the plural—children. This is a community of those who share in God's very nature.

These are the ones *"who believe in His name."* In antiquity, the name given to someone was not the result of a casual choice, as it often is today, because the name revealed the person's character. Thus, when God gives *"His name"* to His people, He graciously allows them to know who He is. "Let those also who love Your name be joyful in You" (Ps. 5:11).

Throughout the Gospel of John, the verb "believe" is emphasized as an activity, something men do. There is also the idea of possession in belief. When we believe, we yield ourselves up to be possessed by the One in whom we believe. The New English Bible makes this clear. "To those who have yielded him their allegiance, he gave the right to become children of God" (John 1:12, NEB).

Now John uses an earthy, highly suggestive word, *"born."* There is a richness, a depth, in sharing in the nature of God—first *"received,"* then *"believe,"* and now *"born."*

However, when John speaks of being "born of God," he eliminates all possibility of this happening by human initiative or achievement.

"Not of blood," he says. The ancients held that the power of birth was in the intermingling of blood or bloods, the activity of life in the blood of the father and mother. But this is not the source of spiritual birth. Nor could this birth come through the Jewish blood line, even though there was a sense of pride among them in being a chosen people, the children of Abraham.

Neither is this birth by the *"will of the flesh,"* the sexual desire that comes out of our bodily constitution. This desire may often reveal our frailty and weakness, but also manifests the creative goodness of God. But no one can be "born of God" by the flesh.

Nor is this birth by the *"will of man."* No human decision to be "born of God" can bring us into His family. Neither can man-centered planning or ingenuity or urgent attempts to "build the kingdom" produce a single divine birth.

No, this birth is a sheer miracle of God's sovereign grace who gives birth to His own children. John has used a bold, earthy verb here to make unmistakably clear the unique meaning of being "born of God." It is the sexual action of the male that begets children; likewise, we are born in response to God's initiative.

Again there is the plural, *"who were born."* While each birth is personal and unique, these children are of one family, members of a new community.

THE WORD BECAME FLESH

14 And the Word became flesh and dwelt among us, and we beheld His glory, the glory as of the only begotten of the Father, full of grace and truth.

15 John bore witness of Him and cried out, saying, "This was He of whom I said, 'He who comes after me is preferred before me, for He was before me.'"

16 And of His fullness we have all received, and grace for grace.

17 For the law was given by Moses, but grace and truth came by Jesus Christ.

18 No one has seen God at any time. The only begotten Son, who is in the bosom of the Father, He has declared Him.

John 1:14–18

We Beheld His Glory (v. 14). Here is God's greatest surprise. John now makes the bold, sweeping declaration that the *"Word became flesh."* This is the major theme of the overture. A deepening intensity of movement throughout the prologue has finally brought us to this climax. The Word that was, the Word that was with God, and the Word that was God—that Word has become flesh.

John does not say He became man or even body, but *"flesh"*—a crude, blunt word for sophisticated Greeks who assumed that the body would eventually be cast aside. The living God has made His great, decisive move in coming among us in the flesh! Salvation did not come through "intermediaries" or "emanations" as the early Gnostic sect, the Docetists, insisted it must. To them, the humanity of Jesus was an illusion. He only "seemed" to have a real body. Thus, John answers them boldly, *"And the Word became flesh."* In this act of incarnation, eternity and time, the divine and the human, salvation and creation, are reconciled. No longer can we divide the sacred and the secular. God has proclaimed His rightful ownership of all that He has created.

However, in becoming flesh, the Word did not cease to be God. There is a unity in His person before and after the Incarnation. He is divine. Yet He became flesh. By this act, He became subject to all the conditions of human existence—the weakness, dependence, and mortality which is our common lot. He was subject to temptation, and He could have sinned. His humanity is real and complete. All through this Gospel, we see both His human weakness and His divine majesty. The eternal Word and the Jesus of history are one. There is a mystery here beyond which we cannot go. Suffice it to say that our only hope of sharing in the life of God is that the Word has really become flesh.

A contemporary illustration of all this may well be found in that remarkable motion picture *Chariots of Fire.* How well I recall praising God when it was announced that this film had been chosen to receive the Academy Award as the "Best Picture of the Year" for 1981. Who would have thought that a book with the dry, unappealing title of *The Official History of the Olympics* could become the basis for a thrilling, sensitive film? But this was the only book David Puttnam, an imaginative British producer, could find while he was rummaging through the big, empty house he had just rented in Los Angeles. Something clicked in Puttnam when he came on the story of Eric Liddell, a gifted, dedicated Scottish runner, who had won the 400-meter gold medal in the 1924 Olympic games—a race in which he had never competed before. But this became his only opportunity to participate, after years of training, because he stubbornly refused to run trial heats for his regular 100-meter distance on a Sunday. He would not yield to any pressure, including requests from the Prince of Wales.

As Puttnam read of Liddell's untarnished convictions, memories of his own childhood stirred—days of simpler values of right and wrong. Would people respond to this kind of a story on film? Well, it was worth a try.

He gathered a rather amazing assortment of people to finance, produce, and distribute this picture—Dodi Fayed, an Arab shipping magnate; Alan Ladd, Jr., son of the actor, Alan Ladd, Sr., and a film distributor; officials from Twentieth Century Fox and Warner Brothers; Colin Welland, the writer who had written the script for "Straw Dogs"; and a host of others. The picture was put together not to be a moral preachment, but because this was a good story to tell, and there was hope it might make some money.

Many of us know what happened. Running all through this "non-Christian" film was a shining integrity and the winsome beauty of a quiet Christian witness that struck a responsive chord deep in our seeking, secular society, so jaded by sex and violence on the screen. People lined up at theaters all across the country and left grateful because they had seen and heard the truth. Surely in some wondrous way, God had been at work in all this, right in the middle of an industry that multitudes of good people have written off as a hopeless cause. Dare we not believe that the Word had once again been revealed in flesh in a place where people least expected it?

We in the church, the "religious people," have taken far too lightly, or turned our backs on, great areas of real, fleshly life. We have said by attitude and style of life that the care of the earth, the intimacy of human sexuality, those artistic impulses expressed in painting and music and dance, or the meaning and significance of work, and all the other great human ventures, are really not our concern. We have more "spiritual" things to look after. So the false gods of the secularists, really demonic forces, move into the vacuum that we have left in vital areas, and life becomes cheapened and vulgarized, a barren wasteland.

The Orthodox Church in Russia during the rule of the czars is a tragic case in point. Rich and powerful, but callously unconcerned about injustice and poverty, its leaders debated the color of the clerical vestments while Kerensky and Lenin planned the Marxist revolution to "liberate the people." In our own country, vast church buildings, TV programs, and burgeoning statistics could blind us from accepting the reality and implications of the Word that has become flesh. But the presence of the Living God in flesh opens endless possibilities for all creation.

And in our time there are illustrations of that Word becoming flesh in many differing places—Bob Dylan writing gospel songs that challenge our false values; John Perkins establishing an economic base for the powerless people of Mississippi; the dream of Millard Fuller becoming Habitat for Humanity, personally owned housing giving new dignity to the desperately poor; Bill Leslie and his LaSalle Street congregation offering free legal help for the dispossessed of Cabrini Green in Chicago; Sojourners Community of Washington challenging the whole war-making madness of our times. The list goes on and on—those who "recover lost provinces," who reclaim the earth, in the name of Jesus who has come in flesh.

"And dwelt among us." John is speaking of the historical life of the Incarnate Word. He has literally dwelt among us as God dwelt among His people in their wanderings through the wilderness, particularly in the tent which housed the Ark of the Covenant and the tablets of the commandments (Exod. 40:34). Here His special presence was known; this presence is different from his omnipresence. But even then He could be known at best in a partial, mystical way, and this could pass away if the Tabernacle, and later the temple, were destroyed.

But now God has come to dwell among His people, in His Living Word. Not at the edge of life, for a passing time, but at the center of everything, in the flesh of Jesus, for all time. Those who believe become the abiding place for the Living Word. The company of believers now become the tabernacle, the body in which the Living Word can dwell through His Spirit. God has guaranteed His presence, His settling down permanently in one place, as the Word dwells in us.

There is a glory in the Word dwelling among us. This is the visible presence of God among men—the same majestic splendor and power that appeared in the cloud when God heard the murmuring of His people (Exod. 16:10) or when that glory of the Lord settled "like a consuming fire on the top of the mountain in the eyes of the children of Israel" as Moses received the instruction at Sinai for the building of the Tabernacle (Exod. 24:16–17) or when His glory "filled the tabernacle" (Exod. 40:34). This was His Shekinah, His visible Presence among His people. But even then, the glory was partial, unfulfilled, and even sporadic. The final tabernacle, the ultimate place of God's dwelling, became the flesh of Jesus. And here His glory is fulfilled!

John has "beheld" that glory with his physical eyes. He is reporting events he has seen. The word "beheld" is the same as used elsewhere in the Gospel when people see with the bodily eye. "Look at the fields, for they are already white for harvest!" (John 4:35). This is the way John has seen a specific Man involved in concrete, day-to-day events. There is the ring of historical validity in his testimony. He is not reporting visions of mystical insights.

It is in unexpected happenings in the midst of life that John sees glory break forth in the ministry of the Word, such as the turning of water into wine at the wedding feast in Cana. "This beginning of signs Jesus did in Cana of Galilee, and manifested His glory; and His disciples believed in Him" (John 2:11). Or in the powerful, climactic sign of Jesus calling Lazarus forth from his grave. "Did I not say to you that if you would believe you would see the glory of God?" (John 11:40). But it is in Jesus accepting the shame and death of the cross that John sees the glory revealed most profoundly. "The hour has come that the Son of Man should be glorified" (John 12:33).

John is not the only one who has seen and believed. There is a company of apostolic witnesses, a community of believers, who have seen that glory revealed in the earthly career of the Word. When John writes *"we beheld,"* He is speaking out of that community.

Now this is the glory of the *"only begotten of the Father."* The *"only begotten"* is the unique One, the beloved One. Abraham offered up Isaac, his beloved son, "his only begotten son" (Heb. 11:17). The glory seen in the Son is the glory of the Father, yet it is uniquely His own. This is one of the great themes of the Gospel.

John and the other disciples saw *"grace and truth"* in the ministry of Jesus. They saw *"grace"* in His dealing with people, for there was compassion and uncalculating love revealed in all that He did. But the *"truth"* seen in His words and teaching was intertwined with these acts of mercy. We have in the ministry of Jesus perfect redemption in His *"grace"* and perfect revelation in His *"truth."*[6] His grace comes from the One who is Life. And the Truth revealed in Jesus comes from the One who is Light. Here is the character of the Incarnate Word, the fullness of *"grace and truth"!* How urgently we need the whole of this. An emphasis on grace by itself can dissipate into a shallow and sentimental fellowship, and stressing truth alone can become hardened dogma. But in the Living Word there is both grace and truth.

Law by Moses, but Grace and Truth by Jesus Christ (vv. 15–17). The identity of John the Baptist in relation to this One who is full of grace and truth is crucial. We are reminded throughout the prologue that John is "a witness," "a voice," that he came to "bear witness." He declares with a loud, clear voice that the One who comes after him in time is preferred before him in position. Only He can take center stage—not the Baptist—because only He is the only begotten of the Father, the One of superior power.

This is a costly and a humbling act, for surely there burned within John the Baptist natural ambitions. Were not "greater opportunities," as we call them, larger crowds and an increase in baptisms perfectly legitimate? After all, he had much at stake. But no, the Baptizer knows his place and the limitations of his ministry. He is not the one who will usher in God's kingdom. His calling is to point to that One, and this he does with faithfulness and integrity.

How much we so-called "spiritual leaders" have to learn from John the Baptist. We have so many clever, camouflaged ways of keeping ourselves in the middle of things and have so often forgotten who we are and who it is that is to have the glory!

But it is not only Christ's position of preeminent authority which makes Him central to everything. He is the One who supplies all the needs of His people. *"And of His fullness."* Here John uses the Greek word *pleroma,* "that which fills," "full to overflowing," a term that is common in Paul's writings. All the fullness of God is found in Him, and all that is in Him is available for all believers. Notice again, *"we have all received."* This fullness is for all the children of God, for Christ's whole family. Here the riches of Christ are shared freely with the new community.

This is not a one-time sharing of His fullness or a now-and-then experience, but "grace for grace." Each blessing is the foundation for a greater blessing. God's grace is given to His people continuously and is never exhausted. Every wonder leads to a new discovery, differing gifts of grace for differing times in life.

There is a great contrast between the law and the new age of grace. John makes it clear at the outset that Someone vastly superior to Moses has come. This is important, for all through the Gospel the Jews insist that Moses has the last word. They repeatedly attempt to downgrade Jesus by claiming that He is a flagrant blasphemer, constantly breaking the law of Moses. Yes, John says, the law was given by Moses, although it really came through him from God, the true Author. But it came for a special purpose. It was a "shadowy form," an image of that divine reality which was to come. It was a "school teacher" which would eventually bring us to grace.

As a matter of fact, Moses anticipated the coming of One who would be superior to the law. John emphasizes this in the way he quotes Jesus: "For if you believed Moses, you would believe Me; for he wrote about Me" (John 5:46).

Now that new era has come, a time in which *"grace and truth"* are brought in their fullness by *"Jesus Christ."* Here the name of the Word Incarnate is given for the first time. How central, how wondrous is that name! *"Jesus,"* the earthly name for the Word in our midst was used 237 times in this Gospel, and *"Christ,"* "the Anointed, Chosen One," was used 19 times in this Gospel always at significant junctures.

And grace and truth came by Him. This is the last time the word "grace" is used in this Gospel, although we see its real meaning in all of Jesus' ministry—so full of beauty and winsomeness. However, "truth" is mentioned twenty-five times throughout the Gospel.

He Has Declared the Father (v. 18). The prologue comes to a beautiful conclusion by stressing again the close, intimate relationship between the Father and the Son. Only the One *"who is in the bosom of the Father"* can make Him known. One tender, human image that this brings to mind is a husband and a wife clinging to each other in love (Deut. 13:6). The Son lives in that state all during His earthly ministry as He has done throughout all eternity. It is only the One who lives in intimate fellowship with the Father who can make Him known.

And Christ has *"declared"* Him. He has given us a full account of the Father. The revelation He has shared with us is altogether adequate, and therefore, we can have confidence in Him. "Declare" is a technical word used in the mystery religions meaning the revelation of divine secrets. And the Word, who has come from the Father, even His only begotten Son, has declared to us the inmost heart and character of God. This is the only way we can know the Father.

It is impossible for us humans, however, to use our *natural capacities* to see God as God—whether through theophanies, or visions, or reasoned concepts. At best they are only fleeting and partial. But praise God that in Jesus we can know Him!

NOTES

1. John Calvin, *The Gospel According to St. John, Part One, 1–10,* trans. T. H. L. Parker (Grand Rapids: Wm. B. Eerdmans Publishing Company, 1961), p. 10.

2. William Barclay, *The Gospel of John, Vol. I* (Philadelphia: The Westminster Press, revised ed. 1975), p. 26.

3. Quoted in Earl F. Palmer, *The Intimate Gospel,* p. 16.

4. John Calvin, *The Gospel According to St. John, Part One, 1–10,* p. 10.

5. W. B. Westcott, *The Gospel According to John,* p. 8.

6. Ibid., p. 13.

CHAPTER TWO

The Beginnings

John 1:19–51

NOT THE CHRIST, NOR ELIJAH, NOR THE PROPHET, BUT A VOICE, CRYING IN THE WILDERNESS

19 Now this is the testimony of John, when the Jews sent priests and Levites from Jerusalem to ask him, "Who are you?"

20 He confessed, and did not deny, but confessed, "I am not the Christ."

21 And they asked him, "What then? Are you Elijah?" He said, "I am not." "Are you the Prophet?" And he answered, "No."

22 Then they said to him, "Who are you, that we may give an answer to those who sent us? What do you say about yourself?"

23 He said: "I *am*

'The voice of one crying in the wilderness:
"Make straight the way of the LORD," '

as the prophet Isaiah said."

24 Now those who were sent were from the Pharisees.

25 And they asked him, saying, "Why then do you baptize if you are not the Christ, nor Elijah, nor the Prophet?"

26 John answered them, saying, "I baptize with water, but there stands One among you whom you do not know.

27 "It is He who, coming after me, is preferred

before me, whose sandal strap I am not worthy to
loose."

28 These things were done in Bethabara beyond the
Jordan, where John was baptizing.

John 1:19–28

The *"now"* at the start of this section brings us from the vast sweep
of the prologue straight into the historical narrative. In John 1:19—
2:12 is recorded a series of earthly happenings, really crucial events,
which usher in the New Creation, Jesus Christ, in a manner not
unlike the week of creation found in Genesis. John, an eyewitness
of these events, gives us a chronological account of these early beginnings: "the next day" (v. 29), "the following day" (v. 43), six days
of creative happenings if we include the wedding in Cana where
Jesus manifested His glory for the first time.

At the outset there is a confrontation between John the Baptist
and a delegation of priests and Levites sent by *"the Jews,"* a phrase
used seventy times in the Gospel, not so much to identify a racial
or religious group, as to designate the organized ecclesiastical opposition to Jesus' ministry.

There were great happenings at the river and much talk about
this dramatic new preacher who was baptizing all kinds of people
as a sign of repentance. No wonder there was much wondering and
debate about the Messiah, who had delayed His coming so long.
Both danger and expectation were in the air. Every movement and
cause had to be checked out. Could it be that something momentous
had already happened? Perhaps this John at the river had a clue to
what was going on or knew what was about to take place.

The official delegation sent to John consisted of priests and Levites.
Since John was the son of the priest Zacharias, they did not beat
around the bush. Their question was direct and to the point, "Who
are you?" The manner in which John answers is crucial. He is standing
in a place of transition, between two worlds, the old and the new.
Here there is a great opportunity to confess Christ, but also a
subtle temptation to hedge a bit on his identity, to hold back a
little, to create a false impression. But his answer is unequivocal and
decisive, *"He confessed, and did not deny, but confessed, 'I am not the Christ' "*
(v. 20). The language is strong. He has dealt with the situation
head on.

The delegation then asks about other possibilities for his identity.

51

"What then? Are you Elijah?" Elijah was popularly associated in people's thinking with the coming of the Messiah. He had been taken to heaven, mysteriously and dramatically, in a fiery chariot. Perhaps he would return in the same manner. Now John's answer is even more terse, *"I am not."* Then could he be *"the Prophet"*? There was talk of the return of Jeremiah or some other great prophet who would be a forerunner of the Messiah. The answer is even more brief, simply, *"No."* John's dialogue with the Jews has been painfully negative, a forthright declaration of who he is not, as it must be, because of the false expectation of the delegation.

But the delegation pushes on since they must give an answer to those who sent them. One senses almost a fear, a pressure, in their seeking for some kind of word they can take back— *"Who are you, that we may give an answer to those who sent us? What do you say about yourself?"* Now John quotes the great prophecy of Isaiah. He is a *"voice,"* a herald of the glory of God which is to be revealed in Jesus Christ. He is the one who points, the preacher who prepares the way.

But if John is only *"a voice,"* not one of the other men they supposed him to be, then why did he baptize? The Pharisees, also involved in sending this delegation, had a special interest in this sacred rite. After all, they spent all their time studying and interpreting the Law and the Tradition. They were well-versed in baptism, which was a cleansing act for proselytes, not for Jewish people who were already God's people. But here was John baptizing all kinds of people, including Jews, identifying them with the unwashed Gentiles and sinners. There was no privileged class; all must repent and prepare the way for the coming of the Chosen One. So the Pharisees were disturbed. How could this man take over this solemn act and claim it was a sign of preparation for a new movement?

John brushed this concern aside, saying that his baptism is only by water. While his baptism was a formal call to repentance, to turn from old ways, there was something incomplete about it. It necessitates a fulfillment, a life-giving baptism in the Spirit by One who will inaugurate God's rule.

John then announces that there is One among them whom the delegation does not know. What an indictment! Although they are seeking for the Messiah, they cannot see nor understand who He is because they bring false, self-centered expectations to John. On the one side is the Baptizer, the faithful voice who prepares the way, and the author of this Gospel, the evangelist who confesses that all may believe. On the other side is the opposition, the close-minded religious establishment. Edwyn Hoskyns says that here is the "ulti-mate gulf between faith and belief, between sight and blindness, between life and death."[1] The terror and darkness of that chasm deepens throughout the Gospel.

In verse 27 we are brought face to face with the Baptist's incredible humility. He has burned his bridges and accepted his calling all the way. For not only is this One among them preferred before him, but John says he is not even worthy to loose His sandal strap. It is an arresting statement, for this was the most menial of all tasks, one which no disciple would do regardless how much he loved his teacher. No, this was a despicable act of service done only by the slave of the house, one whose life was not his own. And John says he is not worthy to do even that. His status is lower than a slave! What task is comparable in our society? Carrying out the garbage? Emptying a bedpan? Cleaning up someone's vomit? Who of us would say we are not worthy to do that?

When we see that kind of utter selflessness shine forth, we know we are in the presence of something very precious. I will never forget how the tears of embarrassment welled up at first and then a wave of unashamed gratitude flooded over me when Gene Herr, a dear Mennonite pastor, knelt to wash my feet. It was a completely unex-pected gift given to me well over twenty years ago. It occurred at the closing celebration of a marvelous Faith at Work gathering—a movement which introduced many people to a whole new style of life—open and vulnerable, risky and hilarious, fulfilling and costly, all at the same time. The power of that moment, confronting a gentle, loving man who stooped to let me know he cared, has blessed my life all these years. It is the poor in spirit who inherit the Kingdom.

In verse 28, the writer speaks of the place of John's baptizing. He seems to be saying, "I was there. I saw it happen." It is important to learn that John was baptizing, but also that he was baptizing at a particular place and time for a particular purpose. The Gospel is history that took place in time and space. Apparently the name of this place was really Bethany.

THE ONE WHO BAPTIZES WITH THE HOLY SPIRIT: REVEALED TO JOHN

> 29 The next day John saw Jesus coming toward him,
> and said, "Behold! The Lamb of God who takes away
> the sin of the world!

30 "This is He of whom I said, 'After me comes a
Man who is preferred before me, for He was before
me.'

31 "I did not know Him; but that He should be
revealed to Israel, therefore I came baptizing with
water."

32 And John bore witness, saying, "I saw the Spirit
descending from heaven like a dove, and He remained
upon Him.

33 "I did not know Him, but He who sent me to
baptize with water said to me, 'Upon whom you see
the Spirit descending, and remaining on Him, this is
He who baptizes with the Holy Spirit.'

34 "And I have seen and testified that this is the
Son of God."

John 1:29–34

When Jesus comes toward John *"the next day,"* it is not their first
meeting. Jesus has already been baptized and passed through the
struggle of the wilderness. These are crucial events, spoken of in
some detail in the synoptic Gospels, which John assumes are common
knowledge among the believers. He goes on to deal with the wonder
of Jesus' true identity being revealed to the Baptist.

"Behold! The Lamb of God who takes away the sin of the world!" What a
mystery that John is able to make this startling announcement, so
fraught with meaning, at this stage in Jesus' ministry. This is a good
example of how the Lord opens truths to His servants that are beyond
their natural understanding. The Baptist is God's chosen vessel, and
He will make known to him whatever is necessary and appropriate
at this time. Who knows how the Almighty can move through the
memories and longings and insights of this faithful spokesman to
reveal the ultimate truth about His Son?

This was near the time of the Passover, the celebration of God's
mighty deliverance of His people from captivity. At the center of
this joyous occasion was the sacrifice of the Paschal Lamb. This must
have been in the Baptist's mind as Jesus came. Also, there may have
been flocks of lambs being driven to Jerusalem through this area to
be offered in this act of national worship. Furthermore, John was
the son of Zacharias, the priest, and he knew well the command of
the Lord to offer a lamb upon the altar every morning and evening.
"This shall be a continual burnt offering throughout your generations

at the door of the tabernacle of meeting before the Lord, where I will meet you to speak with you" (Exod. 29:42). John knew well that there could be no forgiveness without sacrifice.

We know that these words of the prophet Isaiah which speak of the suffering One, who will bear the sins of His people, were familiar to John since he had just quoted from the same prophet in speaking of his own calling. "He was led as a lamb to the slaughter, and as a sheep before its shearers is silent, so He opened not his mouth" (Isa. 53:7). John seems to be affirming here at the beginning, the consecration of Jesus as the sacrificial Lamb, who will be offered for the sin of His people.

He is the Lamb that God provides, and in this sacrifice, He takes away the sin of the world. This is a theme throughout this Gospel. The Lamb is our substitute. He takes upon Himself our infirmities. The vicarious nature of His death is made clear in the cry of John.

It is not simply our individual sins He bears, but the *"sin of the world."* We sin because our nature is sinful. How often we have been naive and superficial in our understanding of sin, minimizing its cosmic nature. It is not simply a wrongdoing now and then with which we have to contend, but a pervasive "sickness unto death" which affects all existence. Rebellious, hostile warfare is waged in all creation against its Maker. "We have been caught with the weapons in our bloody hands," as Emil Brunner said long ago. Unless this awful sickness in human existence is dealt with, there is no salvation, no hope of a new creation. John's declaration here in v. 29 makes it clear this is exactly what Jesus came to do.

John did not know this Man, as he says in verses 31 and 33. In verse 30 he calls Jesus *"a Man."* He speaks of Him with dignity underlining the richness of His humanity, again stressing that He is preferred before him in status and position. John may have known this Man in some casual way as a cousin. Surely John the Baptist knew some of the ordinary facts about Jesus' life. Mary and Elizabeth, the mothers of Jesus and John, had visited so joyfully about their sons before they were born, and they surely would not lose touch with one another completely as the destinies of their two sons unfolded. One wonders if the two—Jesus and John—ever met in their growing years.

But none of this could be enough—casual, external acquaintance. John did not know Jesus in that intimate way. It was in the act of baptism that John came to see and know who Jesus really was, the

Eternal Word in flesh. John's calling men to repentance and baptism was a preparation for Jesus' coming, and it was in the act of Jesus Himself being baptized that His true identity was revealed.

The sign of the dove made it clear that the Holy Spirit was descending upon Jesus. John saw with the physical eye, but he also saw what no physical eye could see. Here the eternal relationship between Father and Son was revealed, an intimate union that is seen all through Jesus' earthly ministry. The Son utterly depended upon the Father, and the Father abided in the Son.

Jesus was consecrated to a life of obedience and sacrifice when the Spirit came on Him. Archbishop Temple has written of this beautifully. "The dove was a poor man's sacrifice (Luke 2:24) and was commonly reputed to be the only sacrificial victim that offered its own neck to the sacrificial knife. That is the spirit that descends upon Him: that is His kingly anointing: that is what marks Him as Son of God."[2] Jesus offers Himself as a dove, the declaration of His divine vocation.

Twice John says that the Spirit remains on Him. This descent of the Spirit is no flash of inspiration for a few moments. The Spirit has taken up His permanent home in the Son. Thus, Jesus baptizes those who believe, who receive Him, and who follow Him, not with water, but with the Holy Spirit. To "baptize" means to "dip" or "submerge." So he "floods" or "saturates" our lives with the Holy Spirit. We are inaugurated through this baptism into the life of God and into His ministry in the world. We, too, are to offer ourselves as doves in obedient, sacrificial service.

THOSE WHO FOLLOWED AND REMAINED WITH HIM

35 Again, the next day John stood with two of his disciples.

36 And looking at Jesus as He walked, he said, "Behold the Lamb of God!"

37 The two disciples heard him speak, and they followed Jesus.

38 Then Jesus turned, and seeing them following, said to them, "What do you seek?" They said to Him, "Rabbi" (which is to say, when translated, Teacher), "where are You staying?"

39 He said to them, "Come and see." They came

and saw where He was staying, and remained with
Him that day (now it was about the tenth hour).

John 1:35–39

It is the *"next day,"* and now the movement begins. It is as if John
and two of his disciples were standing around waiting for something
to happen. They are not disappointed, for Jesus comes walking. (There
is an amazing timing in all this, as there always is when we are
open to God's dealings with us.) Again John declares Him to be *"the
Lamb of God!"* When the two disciples hear this, they follow Jesus.
It is almost as if John is presenting them to Jesus and saying to them,
"You are prepared. Now go! He is the One we have been waiting
for." We have much to learn from John about turning disciples over
to Jesus. So often we want to cling to them, keep them dependent
upon us. But a manipulative, self-serving game is not our business
in the church. Our calling is to introduce people to the Teacher, to
prepare the way for them, then to hand them over to Him so that
He can do His work of discipling.

The initiative is His. He chooses His disciples, which is always a
work of sovereign grace. "Therefore I have said to you that no one
can come to Me unless it has been granted to him from My Father"
(John 6:65). Jesus later prayed with loving concern for these who
have been given Him, "I have manifested Your name to the men
whom You have given Me out of the world. They were Yours, You
gave them to Me, and they have kept Your word" (John 17:6). Surely
we need to continually evaluate our style of calling forth disciples
in church life.

When Jesus sees these two following Him, He speaks His first
words recorded in this Gospel. *"What do you seek?"* What a penetrating
question. "Are you seeking for security or a new cause?" he was
asking. "Do you really have any idea of what I'm about? Who I
really am? Do you realize the cost of leaving John to follow Me?"
He is still asking the same question today!

They come back with their own question, addressing Him as
"Rabbi," meaning "great one" or "teacher." In verse 38 John, the
writer, translated *"Rabbi"* for his Greek readers. John's disciples ask,
"Where are you staying?" Far more than a street number is involved.
They are asking, "Where is Your dwelling place? Where did You
come from? What is Your purpose? Can we come to know You?"

Jesus meets them where they are, and issues an invitation, *"Come and see,"* that is, "Ask your questions. Let me help you find out who I am." C. S. Lewis had this peculiar evangelistic gift of encouraging people to "come and see." He understood the hopes, longings, and misgivings of sophisticated, thinking people and urged them to check it out all the way. How different our evangelistic style would be if we allowed people to set their own pace while they are seeking for the answers.

These two came and remained until the tenth hour—four o'clock in the afternoon. Here again is the detail in John's Gospel. No one will ever become an authentic follower, a disciple, without remaining. It must have been a long, deep, fruitful time, full of amazing discoveries.

ANDREW BROUGHT HIS BROTHER

40 One of the two who heard John speak, and followed Him, was Andrew, Simon Peter's brother.

41 He first found his own brother Simon, and said to him, "We have found the Messiah" (which is translated, the Christ).

42 And he brought him to Jesus. Now when Jesus looked at him, He said, "You are Simon the son of Jonah. You shall be called Cephas" (which is translated, A Stone).

John 1:40–42

At least one of the two seekers, if not both of them, became an evangelist out of that first encounter. Andrew moved out on a special mission to his brother. And we can be almost certain that the writer, who is beautifully modest, could have told his own story of reaching out to his brother James. He may have been so well known that he did not need to identify himself.

Andrew is referred to as Simon Peter's brother. Andrew never seems to resent taking second place to his brother, even when Peter is included in that intimate group of three so close to Jesus, nor when he becomes the leader of the twelve. Nothing in the later records reflects any jealousy.

Andrew has that wonderful gift of being an introducer. He brings the boy with the loaves and fish to Jesus. "There is a lad here who has five barley loaves and two small fish, but what are they among so many?" (John 6:9). That simple act is used by our Lord to feed a hungry multitude. And when Philip does not seem to know what to do with the Greeks who come to Jesus, he brings them to Andrew who then takes them to Jesus (12:22). It was no small thing to bring non-Jews in those last hours so close to the cross, when Jesus' first mission was to the house of Israel.

Out of that first meeting with Jesus, Andrew does what it is very difficult for most of us to do. He hurries off to find his brother! Where was he? At home? Fishing? Can you imagine Andrew finding Simon in a fish market when he blurts out his first beautiful confession, *"We have found the Messiah"*? Again the writer helps his Greek readers, *"(which is translated, the Christ),"* the anointed One who will fulfill all the longings of Israel.

"And he brought him to Jesus." Isn't this the heart of all our evangelistic endeavor? Jesus looked at Simon—searchingly and penetratingly— and saw what no one else could see. He saw not only what Peter could become, but who he *would* become. This big, blustering, erratic fisherman would become a leader among men, the first among the apostles, and finally, a martyr because of his love for Jesus. Jesus claims him with a new name, Cephas, which signifies what he will become, a stone. "In designating him by his new name, Jesus takes possession of him and consecrates him, with all his natural qualities, to the work which He is going to entrust to him."[3]

Recently I watched Larry Rapp, a thoughtful young attorney, heed the invitation "come and see," then begin to cautiously check it out, and finally decide to follow Him all the way. I remember how intently he listened as I was teaching at a men's Bible luncheon. He had been brought by a deeply concerned friend, Gary Ayers, another attorney in the same law firm who had tipped me off, "I'd really like for you to get together with Larry, this friend of mine. He's got a lot of questions."

That was the start. Then he and his wife came to church and sat so near the front it surprised me. They listened as if their lives depended upon it. She was weeping quietly as I greeted them at the door after the service. Then Larry and I had two or three visits in the office, and Larry aired his questions freely. "What about inconsistencies in the Scriptures?" "How could a loving God allow or even command all that killing in the Old Testament?" "Why was there so much suffering in the world?" "I can't seem to deal with my impure thoughts." But he was willing to take the primary source, the Gospel, the "come and see" accounts of Jesus, seriously. Then there came that sacred moment several weeks later. He said, "Before we get started today I have something I want to say. On the basis of this reading and what I've experienced in this church and in my own struggle to pray, I want to declare that Jesus Christ is my Lord and Savior." Both of us sat there silent for a moment. He was like a witness on the stand in the courtroom. We knelt and Larry surrendered it all to the One who first gave the invitation "come and see," as did his dear wife, Dianne. Eating in their home some weeks later with their dear friends Gary and Charleen, who had brought their brother and sister, was a holy, hilarious celebration. Since then, Larry has begun a quiet work of evangelism among his fellows in the law office.

PASSING IT ON

43 The following day Jesus wanted to go to Galilee, and He found Philip and said to him, "Follow Me."

44 Now Philip was from Bethsaida, the city of Andrew and Peter.

45 Philip found Nathanael and said to him, "We have found Him of whom Moses in the law, and also the prophets, wrote—Jesus of Nazareth, the son of Joseph."

46 And Nathanael said to him, "Can anything good come out of Nazareth?" Philip said to him, "Come and see."

47 Jesus saw Nathanael coming toward Him, and said of him, "Behold, an Israelite indeed, in whom is no guile!"

48 Nathanael said to Him, "How do You know me?" Jesus answered and said to him, "Before Philip called you, when you were under the fig tree, I saw you."

49 Nathanael answered and said to Him, "Rabbi, You are the Son of God! You are the King of Israel!"

John 1:43–49

The next day Jesus sought out Philip who came from the same city as Andrew and Peter. The Greek name *Philip* was not uncommon among Jewish families. It is interesting that there should be a cluster of followers from the same community, but eager disciples always have their own contagion. As Jesus' ministry unfolds much of it seems to have been centered in this city.

The other disciples had either come to or were brought to Jesus, but Jesus found Philip, who may have lacked initiative to come on his own. Philip seems to have been an ordinary kind of man, at times actually in over his head. When Jesus asked him about feeding the five thousand, his answer was that there was very little money on hand, not even enough to buy a small amount for each one (John 6:5–7). He saw only how little there was. And later when the Greeks came seeking Jesus, they first came to Philip, perhaps because of his name. But he seems to be caught off guard, hardly knowing what to do, so he brings them to Thomas (John 12:21). And after following Jesus through all the experiences of His ministry, he still asks near the end, " 'Lord, show us the Father, and it is sufficient for us' " (John 14:8–9).

Yet Jesus singles Philip out and goes after him, an ordinary man like so many of us. Jesus invites him, *"Follow Me,"* which means not just to start out, but to keep on following Him. How encouraging for those of us who are shy, feeling we have so little to offer. Perhaps we are the ones He seeks out most eagerly.

It almost seems Philip is waiting for this invitation. He accepted on the spot and immediately found Nathanael. Godet has put it beautifully: "One lighted torch serves to light another."[4] Every study of evangelistic outreach reveals that 85 percent or more of all converts, new disciples, are brought to Christ by someone they trust—a member of the family, a neighbor, a close friend, or a business associate. And further, they show that the most spontaneous, authentic witnessing takes place in the first two years of Christian experience. Philip is certainly a case in point; Nathanael trusted him and his joyful, unabashed witness, *" 'We have found Him of whom Moses in the law, and also the prophets, wrote—Jesus of Nazareth, the son of Joseph.' "*

Apparently Philip is already a part of a small company of new disciples when he shares the good news with his friend Nathanael, saying, *"We have found Him."* We know very little of Nathanael, a name that means "God has given." John is the only Gospel in which his name appears. However, some surmise that he could have also been known by the name Bartholomew. In each of the synoptic Gospels, the name Bartholomew is coupled with Philip in the listings of the disciples (Matt. 10:3, Luke 6:14, Mark 3:18). Bartholomew means "Son of Tolmai," which makes it likely that he would also have a proper name, possibly Nathanael.

Surely Philip and Nathanael had frequently discussed the witness of Moses and the prophets concerning the coming of the Messiah. It is out of this kind of common talk and wondering that Philip identifies for Nathanael the One to whom he has given his allegiance: *"Jesus of Nazareth, the son of Joseph."* Certainly up to this point there had been little opportunity for anyone to become aware of His miraculous birth, and it was common to identify a person by the head of the house.

The mention of Nazareth brings a skeptical response out of Nathanael. How can the promised One come out of a little, nondescript village like Nazareth? It is almost like that small South Dakota town, Beresford, which has produced a governor or two, but has also been the butt of innumerable Norwegian ethnic jokes. Furthermore, there seems to have been a competitive spirit between Nathanael's hometown, Bethsaida, and Nazareth. Certainly the Messiah deserved to be from better than Nazareth.

But Philip is not to be put off, and he issues the familiar invitation we have heard before, *"Come and see."* What amazing doors that kind of investigation can open. Thus are the circumstances when Jesus identifies Nathanael, not only as a fellow countryman, an Israelite, but his deeper character, his hidden self. Only Jesus can do that. Here he sees a man in whom there are no hidden motives, no deceit. Nathanael is transparent.

No wonder Nathanael is surprised. When Nathanael asks Jesus, *"How do You know me?"* he was referring to that intimate, discerning way that Jesus understood his deepest self. Then Jesus speaks of Nathanael's being under the fig tree, often a place of meditation and thought. Here Jesus has seen again with that penetrating insight with which he had earlier "seen" Simon who is now called Peter. Let it never be forgotten this is how He sees us.

Nathanael's response is a cry of allegiance. He claims Jesus as his *"Rabbi,"* a title of respect which only a disciple would use. He has submitted to Jesus as his teacher. But he also addresses Him as *"the Son of God."* Certainly Nathanael does not understand the full implication of that title, but he senses that Jesus stands in an unusual relation to God. He calls Him the King of Israel, an unusual title, but since

Jesus has earlier referred to him as an Israelite, Nathanael is surrendering to Jesus as his own king.

"HEREAFTER YOU SHALL SEE HEAVEN OPEN"

50 Jesus answered and said to him, "Because I said to you, 'I saw you under the fig tree,' do you believe? You will see greater things than these."

51 And He said to him, "Most assuredly, I say to you, hereafter you shall see heaven open, and the angels of God ascending and descending upon the Son of Man."

John 1:50–51

So Jesus marks Nathanael as the first one to believe in Him when He asks, *"Do you believe?"* But Jesus says Nathanael will be given far deeper grounds for belief than Jesus' perception of who he is. For as Jesus' ministry unfolds, he will see mighty works, great and wondrous surprises, revealing the glory of God.

Seeing these *"greater things"* with the physical eye will open the door to eternal realities through Jesus. The language here is reminiscent of Jacob's dream of a ladder that reached from earth to heaven with angels *"ascending and descending."* And the Lord was standing "above it" affirming again that He is the God of his forefathers and that He will fulfill all the promises made to them. Jacob called this an "awesome place," the "house of God," and the "gate of heaven." Here Jacob consecrated a stone and renewed his vow (Gen. 28:10–22).

Now the time has come when grace is fulfilled. Jesus truly is the "House of God," the place of meeting with the Father, not only for Nathanael and Philip and those first disciples, but for all who believe. To them He has become the very "gate of heaven," for through the life and ministry of the Word made flesh, all the resources of heaven are available to all believers. Angels are ascending and descending upon *"the Son of Man."* Here Jesus identifies Himself for the first time—*"the Son of Man"*—a rich, suggestive, yet simple title.

John the Gospel writer has given us a vast and varied understanding of who Jesus is in these opening verses. "The Word," "life and light," "all things made by Him," "the Word made flesh," "the One by whom grace and truth have come," "the only begotten of the Father," "the Lamb of God," "a man," "the One on whom the Spirit descends," "the Son of God," "Jesus Christ," "Rabbi," "the Messiah," "Jesus of Nazareth," "the King of Israel." What a rich meaning there is in these titles. And the Gospel narrative defines and gives substance to these names.

But Jesus calls Himself simply, "the Son of Man," His most common way of identifying Himself. The title is not associated with any particular messianic expectation, nor is there a nationalistic emphasis in its use. There is a freshness, an openness about "Son of Man." Listeners can give this title whatever content they wish.

But surely, in this first reference to Himself, Jesus is making His humanity evident. He is one of us. This is where love has brought Him. Here He will live, share Himself, and finally suffer and die. Only thus can the door to heaven be opened for all of us. There is a wondrous glory in Jesus' costly offering of Himself for our salvation that runs all through this Gospel.

Jesus is not only "Son of Man," but "*the* Son of Man." He is our Pattern. In Him we see what God intended for each of us in creation. And even though we have fallen, squandered our destiny in angry disobedience, God has not given up on us. Jesus brings the possibility of a new creation. We see in "the Son of Man" what we can become. Here is the "finished product." Here is what it means to be truly human.

When Jesus speaks of Himself as "the Son of Man" throughout the Gospel, it is sometimes veiled with eschatological meanings. But here at the outset Jesus says simply, "As the Son of Man I stand on your side. I am with you."

NOTES

1. Sir Edwyn Hoskyns, *The Fourth Gospel*, p. 173.
2. Wm. Temple, *Readings in St. John's Gospel* (London: Macmillan & Co., Ltd., 1949), p. 26.
3. Frederic Louis Godet, *Commentary on John's Gospel* (Grand Rapids: Kregel Publications, 1978), p. 329.
4. Ibid., p. 332.

CHAPTER THREE

Bringing in New Wine and Driving Out the Old

John 2:1–25

Out of the vast amount of material available to the Evangelist John, he has carefully chosen his material as an eyewitness of all Jesus did and said. In his writing he has a clear, guiding purpose, "these are written that you may believe that Jesus is the Christ, the Son of God, and that believing you may have life in His name" (John 20:31). Then which earthly, daily incidents will best reveal who Jesus is and quicken a living faith among His readers?

At the outset John presents two contrasting events which make known both the rich fullness and the cleansing power of the new life that has come. One is a wedding—intimate and domestic, a joyful celebration in a small town. The other is a decisive, courageous act of cleansing at the center of a major national festival. Here we catch the sweep and intensity, as well as the personal, human concern of Jesus' ministry. That ministry is total, all encompassing, touching all of life, both private and public.

Neither of these incidents is recorded in the synoptic Gospels. As a matter of fact, hardly any of the material shared in the first five chapters of this Gospel is included in the synoptics. Much of what John tells us about Jesus took place in and around Jerusalem, while the synoptics present Jesus' Galilean ministry, particularly centered in Capernaum. It is false to say these accounts are inconsistent or incompatible, assuming that the synoptics are giving us history while John is not too concerned about whether the stories he tells really happened. It has been held that John is concerned more with the "truth" that might be contained in these stories, not in their historical accuracy. John's emphasis is different. These stories are like husks which can be stripped away leaving the kernel of truth.

To say this is to once again proclaim a docetic Gospel, which boasts a non-fleshly Jesus, leading to a historical agnosticism in the end. This is a denial of the basic premise, the cutting edge of John's whole Gospel, "the Word became flesh and dwelt among us"—at a wedding in Cana; at Jacob's well, thirsty and weary; at the tomb of Lazarus, weeping—a particular Man of flesh and blood doing specific things at specific times and places.

No, John's Gospel is through and through a historical account, the careful writing of an eyewitness. Those personal, specific details, which are included so naturally in every recorded event, could not have been ingeniously fabricated. John is too honest, too conscientious for that.

However, he uses particular, unique experiences which make the identity of Jesus stand out sharp and clear. This is his central purpose! When men know who He is they must decide. The house always becomes divided between belief and rejection, light and darkness, life and death, whenever Jesus makes Himself known.

And it is in Jerusalem where His identity and authority are most savagely challenged, and it is there, finally, that His whole ministry is bitterly rejected. John makes these issues clear by focusing on the "Jerusalem story" rather than the Galilean ministry.

WATER INTO WINE

1 On the third day there was a wedding in Cana of Galilee, and the mother of Jesus was there.

2 Now both Jesus and His disciples were invited to the wedding.

3 And when they ran out of wine, the mother of Jesus said to Him, "They have no wine."

4 Jesus said to her, "Woman, what does your concern have to do with Me? My hour has not yet come."

5 His mother said to the servants, "Whatever He says to you, do it."

6 Now there were set there six waterpots of stone, according to the manner of purification of the Jews, containing twenty or thirty gallons apiece.

7 Jesus said to them, "Fill the waterpots with water." And they filled them up to the brim.

8 And He said to them, "Draw some out now, and take it to the master of the feast." And they took it.

9 When the master of the feast had tasted the water that was made wine, and did not know where it came from (but the servants who drew the water knew), the master of the feast called the bridegroom.

10 And he said to him, "Every man at the beginning sets out the good wine, and when the guests have well drunk, then that which is inferior; but you have kept the good wine until now."

11 This beginning of signs Jesus did in Cana of Galilee, and manifested His glory; and His disciples believed in Him.

12 After this He went down to Capernaum, He, His mother, His brothers, and His disciples; and they did not stay there many days.

John 2:1–12

The Wedding at Cana (vv. 1–2). The wedding took place not far from Nazareth in the small village where Nathanael lived, Cana of Galilee. Notice again the specifics. It must have been something of a family affair. The mother of Jesus, whose name is not given, but who is very specifically identified, seems to be at the center of arranging things. And *"Jesus and His disciples"* are invited. This is the first time Jesus is identified in an intimate way with His disciples, and they would surely not have been invited as a group had they been total strangers.

A wedding in those days was a great celebration, no little twenty-minute affair. The ceremony usually took place late in the evening—Wednesday if the girl was a virgin and Thursday if she was a widow—after a feast. Then there was a procession to the home of the groom, a joyous, noisy parade, with an open house and entertainment that went on for at least a week.

Surely the rich, deep meaning of marriage in Jewish religious life was in John's mind as he shared the account of this simple, shining event in Cana. That intimate relation between Yahweh and Israel is portrayed over and over again through the image of the marriage covenant (Hos. 2:7). The fullness of the messianic age was prophesied in Isaiah and spoken of so beautifully through the symbol of marriage (Isa. 62:5), and the vision of the consummation of all history will be celebrated in the marriage of the "Lamb and His wife" when glory is given the Lord God Omnipotent (Rev. 19:7). How highly suggestive then that Jesus' first miracle, inaugurating the messianic age, should be the sign given at a wedding.

And if the Word has truly become flesh, so that heaven and earth, salvation and creation, are joined in Him, then all human experiences—however lowly or lofty—become occasions when His glory can break forth. The possibilities are unlimited! While Jesus was a Man of sorrows and acquainted with grief, He was also a Man who went to parties and enjoyed hearty conversation, laughter, and good food. His showing up at Cana is an invitation for the rest of us to join Him at His party and to enter into His joy.

Rapid City, South Dakota, may not be Cana of Galilee, but Ruth and I have just come home from a glorious wedding in that Black Hills city. Our oldest son, Randy, now thirty-six, having had at least a dozen fairly serious girl friends, and now full of gratitude and joy that the right one had come along, was being married to Elaine, a lovely, gifted, outgoing young woman. It was worth the wait!

The rehearsal dinner was a steak cookout, entirely in keeping with the western country. It was complete with all kinds of warm greetings and friendly banter—two families and close friends getting to know one another.

And then the wedding the next day! A chuckle ran through the congregation when the friendly host pastor of First United Methodist Church welcomed us all and said this might be a longer service because there had been "an invasion of the Baptists." What a joy as we shared in the hymn, "Be Thou My Vision"—native Americans, ranchers, church people, politicians, and families all singing together. It was a time of holy worship—the intermingling of beautiful music and prayer, the hushed sharing of the great old promises, of tears and soft laughter! The One who had visited Cana had come to this wedding, and that made it a celebration.

Freedom from His Mother: His Time (vv. 3–5). But in the midst of this joyous affair at Cana comes the possibility of great embarrassment. *"They have no wine."* What a shocking thing for the bridegroom and his family, for it was their sacred duty to provide ample refreshments for all the guests. They might even be liable to a lawsuit if the wine failed. *"No wine."* Here is the impoverishment of the Old Covenant, the cry of spiritual need, the yearning for the messianic wine, the bankruptcy of all our ingenious human ways and resources.

It is the mother of Jesus who calls this failure to His attention. Surely He can help out. Deep within she carries the mystery of His birth and is aware of His unique identity, although she cannot fully grasp all of its meaning. One can almost sense the subtle parental pressure in her announcement of the wine giving out.

But Jesus is no longer under her roof. The time of her authority has passed, so her concern has no final claim on Him. Jesus has moved out in obedience to His Father, and all His times are set by the higher Authority. He must await the hour fixed by His Father.

How often we parents have smothered and pressured our children, even in college years and beyond, and tried to live our lives through them. We have failed to let them go! We have crippled them because we have been afraid to set them free for a larger purpose than our little plans, never understanding there is Another who has a far greater will for them. And we can trust Him!

When Jesus addresses His mother, *"Woman,"* He is not being aloof or distant, but is speaking with tenderness and respect. It is the same way in which He lovingly commits her to John's care from the cross. "Woman, behold your son!" (John 19:26). *"My hour has not yet come,"* He says to her. This is a phrase He will utter over and over again until He finally comes to the cross. Then, and only then, has His hour come. His time is always in His Father's hands.

And His mother now seems to submit to the mystery of that timing. There seems to be a quiet release, a letting go, in her statement to the servants. *"Whatever He says to you, do it."*

The Best at the End: Grace after Law (vv. 6–10). Now Jesus in His own time turns to six great stone pots that were used for purification. Whenever guests arrived, the water from these pots was poured over their hands in a ritual of cleansing. To eat with unwashed hands was an act of defilement. This purification rite was an external act that did not make anything new or bring any fresh power. These waterpots represent the whole ritual of Jewish law, the Old Covenant, which really has become meaningless in the presence of Jesus who will pour out an abundance of the wine of the new age. The time of Judaism is over. Its major institutions and figures are replaced by Jesus Himself. The old wineskins cannot contain the new wine.

At the command of Jesus the servants obey. The waterpots are filled with water *"up to the brim."* There is a completeness in this simple act with room for nothing else, no cheating or magic. Then out of that provision Jesus asks them to *"draw some out now, and take it to the master of the feast."* It is like taking water from a well, as in the Samaritan woman's discussion later about living water (4:11–15).

The *"master,"* who is the headwaiter or master of ceremonies in charge of seating and other arrangements, has undoubtedly been wondering about the "wine situation."

How quietly it happened. The master tasted *"the water that was made wine."* There is no way we can know when or how the water became wine. Jesus simply moves in His own mysterious way with no fanfare His wonders to perform. He slips in the back door and does His thing—this God of surprises—and it isn't until we have tasted the wine that we know something unusual has taken place. Then, like the master at the wedding feast we ask the bridegroom, what has been the source of this new wine?

The ones in authority, the master and the bridegroom, are ignorant. They do not know *"where it came from."* All through the Gospel there are those who are in darkness, they "do not know"—Nicodemus, the Samaritan woman, the Jews, Pilate. It is the lowly ones, the servants who drew the water, who are like the disciples; they know. Others may be too caught up in their own importance, or their busyness, or even their guilt to understand.

So the wine is poured out, and all those present rejoice at its rich abundance. They have never tasted wine like this before! And the bridegroom wonders why the good wine has been kept back until now. Usually the best wine comes first with the inferior coming at the end when the guests *"have well drunk"* and they cannot tell the difference.

With us humans the best usually comes first. We dress up, put on our best manners, and hope others will not find out how empty and needy we really are. We clean up the front room of the house and hope we can keep the guests from getting into the back bedroom or the basement where we have hurriedly shoved all our messes when we learned the guests were coming.

This is not so with our Lord. With Him the best comes at the end!

The grace we tasted cautiously at the beginning we now drink freely knowing the rich wonder of forgiveness and life in the Spirit; the Jesus we came to know as Savior at the start we now worship as the triumphant, risen Lord of all creation; the Spirit has moved us from the halting phrases of a prayer of requests to the joy of constant communion, an intimate relationship that never ceases where we can say "Abba, Father"; and death at the end will open the door for us to our greatest adventure, unfettered life with the God of glory and all His saints and angels. Surely this will be wine at its best.

However, there is a deeper meaning here. The old wine of the law, without taste or strength, has given out. *"But you have kept the good wine until now."* In God's time, the new creation has come. The age of grace has broken in. There is One among us who now pours out the rich wine of the "end times" and there is enough for everyone!

The Glory Manifested: Believing Disciples (v. 11). This is the first sign. Here we see the authority of Jesus over the physical universe. But the happening points beyond itself. A door to spiritual reality has been opened. Our understanding of who this is that commands the servants to draw some water out is deepened and enlarged. He authenticates Himself by what He does. He is the "Word made flesh," the "Christ who is the Son of God," not simply the teacher of a few disciples who show up at a wedding.

Through this act, Jesus has opened the door to life in His age of Grace. Eternal life, a new quality of existence, is now possible through the One who has come to the wedding. Those present may only see dimly, but the reality is unmistakable! The reign of God has begun! That which is finally to be, the Eschaton, the fullness of the age of the Spirit, has been ushered in at Cana. In the pouring out of this new wine, the glory of Jesus is made known. "They are," says a sensitive Roman Catholic writer, referring to the miracles, "epiphanies of the risen Lord, signs anticipating the ultimate truth about Jesus which will only be fully revealed when His hour has been achieved."[1] And the faith of those who have begun to follow is deepened. They are "buying in" more deeply all the time. The underlying reason for all of Jesus' mighty works is clearly stated in verse 11, *"and manifested His glory; and His disciples believed in Him."*

Interlude (v. 12). Jesus does not minimize or despise His human family ties, even though He has moved out from His mother's authority. He affirms His earthly family by joining them for a "gathering" and in so doing underlines the importance of every family.

CLEANSING THE TEMPLE: THE OLD AND THE NEW

13 Now the Passover of the Jews was at hand, and Jesus went up to Jerusalem.

14 And He found in the temple those who sold oxen and sheep and doves, and the moneychangers doing business.

15 When He had made a whip of cords, He drove them all out of the temple, with the sheep and the oxen, and poured out the changers' money and overturned the tables.

16 And He said to those who sold doves, "Take these things away! Do not make My Father's house a house of merchandise!"

17 Then His disciples remembered that it was written, *"Zeal for Your house has eaten Me up."*

18 Then the Jews answered and said to Him, "What sign do You show to us, since You do these things?"

19 Jesus answered and said to them, "Destroy this temple, and in three days I will raise it up."

20 Then the Jews said, "It has taken forty-six years to build this temple, and will You raise it up in three days?"

21 But He was speaking of the temple of His body.

22 Therefore, when He had risen from the dead, His disciples remembered that He had said this to them; and they believed the Scripture and the word which Jesus had said.

23 Now when He was in Jerusalem at the Passover, during the feast, many believed in His name when they saw the signs which He did.

24 But Jesus did not commit Himself to them, because He knew all men,

25 and had no need that anyone should testify of man, for He knew what was in man.

John 2:13–25

Jesus now moves into the center of Israel's greatest festival. The Passover was anything but a quiet family wedding in a small town. It was a national gathering of God's people in the sacred city to celebrate their deliverance from Egypt and their birth as a nation. No wonder it was a huge, noisy affair. Yet at the heart of it was the sacrifice, the spilling of blood and the offering of life, as God had commanded through Moses long before. Every adult male within a fifteen-mile radius of Jerusalem was required by law to come, and thousands of Jews scattered through the Roman empire made the sacred pilgrimage at great personal cost.

In the middle of this holy festival was a rigged business operation that was enmeshed in the whole ecclesiastical apparatus and controlled by the high priest. Every Jew over nineteen years of age had to pay his yearly temple tax of a half-shekel, the equivalent of two days' wages. The Gentile coins from Rome, Greece, Egypt, and even Palestine were too unclean for this "sacred" tax, so they had to be exchanged for a half-shekel. The hidden cost of this exchange equaled another day's wages. Then there was also the cost of purchasing a sheep, ox, or dove for the sacrifice, which must be without blemish. These came from the temple herds or flocks and were outrageously overpriced. Little wonder the temple coffers were full and overflowing. Barclay has pointed out that when Crassus captured Jerusalem and raided the temple treasury in 54 B.C. he made off with almost ten million dollars without anywhere near exhausting the treasury.[2]

This loud, raucous, competitive marketing had been brought into the outer court of the temple, the place of Gentile worship—another example of religious exclusiveness. How could anyone worship in this carnival-like setting?

Yet the temple was considered sacred, the heir of the tabernacle. "It was the house of God, an earthly counterpart of the heavenly sanctuary" (Exod. 25:40).[3] Here the Ark of the Covenant, containing the tablets of the law, was housed. The temple was the place where God dwelt in the midst of His people. It was so sacred that its physical presence consecrated the city. Yet, as Westcott has pointed out, this "house" had become a market place, "no longer deriving its character from Him to whom it was dedicated, but from the business carried on in its courts."[4]

The New: A Whip (vv. 15–17). Jesus did not come on this scene as an outsider. These were "His own" to use John's earlier phrase. The whole glorious meaning of the Passover was deeply imbedded in His life. He had also been spiritually nurtured by the prophets. He understood the passion and fire of Jeremiah and Isaiah, of Malachi and Zechariah, and understood their cry for righteousness as they waited for the day of the Lord.

Jesus had come to this place to worship, and what He found was *"moneychangers doing business,"* this incredibly selfish, cynical money-making at the expense of the poor. One senses the shame and anger and sorrow welling up in Him as He strikes out at the whole wretched business—all of it—animals, tables, money, and men! *"Do not make My Father's house a house of merchandise!"* One can feel the intimate, eternal passion between the Son and the Father.

The whip is a sign of both authority and force. Entrenched unrighteousness is not dealt with passively. The whole house must be cleansed if true worship is to be restored. The words in the passage are strong: He *"drove them all out,"* and *"poured out the changers' money and overturned the tables."* Here is the fulfillment of the prophecy of Malachi 3:2–3:

> "But who can endure the day of His coming?
> And who can stand when He appears?
> For He is like a refiner's fire
> And like fuller's soap.
> He will sit as a refiner and a purifier of silver;
> He will purify the sons of Levi,
> And purge them as gold and silver,
> That they may offer to the Lord
> An offering in righteousness."

But this act of cleansing, which occurs at the center of the place so laden with sacred meaning, is far more than the reform of a decadent system of worship. Jesus is bringing to an end a way of life and thought. Israel's institutions are to be replaced. The normal business of sacrifice will be unnecessary now that He has come. Jesus is breaking open and deepening the whole reality of worship. *He* is the new "place," the "house" in which the glory of God will break forth. With Jesus' coming there is no earthly building where God lives that we can hang on to. Only Jesus! The new day has come.

When the disciples saw this dramatic event, they remembered Psalm 69:9 which speaks of righteous suffering, also quoted in Acts 1:30 and Romans 15:3: *"Zeal for Your house has eaten me up."* Jesus' holy jealousy for the sanctity of His Father's house, His costly singleness of mind, brought Him finally to His death; and in that final redemptive act, He opened for us the way to the Father's heart.

Destroy and I Will Raise It Up (vv. 18–22). The Jews now demand a sign. The cleansing has really been a messianic act! But there have been many false prophets, imposters claiming to be the Messiah. How is this One different? Can He give them some sign that will further authenticate the fact that He may be the Messiah? It is somewhat surprising that the Jews do not attack Jesus or drive Him out in the face of His bold, decisive act. Many of them may have felt there was a great need for a cleansing of the sacred precincts.

Jesus responds with an answer that is hidden. He clothes the ultimate sign, His own death and resurrection, in the imagery of the temple. In the phrase, *"Destroy this temple,"* the word for "destroy" in the Greek means "loose" or "untie" or "dissolve that which holds things together." The Greek word here for temple is *naos,* meaning "shrine" or "dwelling place of deity," referring to Jesus' own body, which is the home of God in a very unique way. The Greek word *Hieron,* used earlier for temple, means "the sacred enclosure of buildings used for worship." *"And in three days I will raise it up."* None of us can plumb the mystery of what took place when the power of God called forth Jesus from the dead, any more than we understand His changing water into wine. *"I will raise it up,"* says Jesus. How does the Spirit of the Living Father touch the Son so that His response is resurrected life? We bow before the mystery of His sovereign grace.

In this act of destruction and raising we have a converging of meanings. His death is the one sacrifice that will expiate sin so that the physical temple will no longer be necessary for the offering of sacrifice. He is the One who will open the way so we can enter the presence of God knowing the constant grace of forgiveness. The resurrected, glorified Christ then becomes the new temple in whom God can dwell among His people. All of life can now become an act of worship, a living sacrifice.

These nonbelieving, questioning antagonists are baffled by this answer. So they can only mock Jesus. How can He, of all people, rebuild a temple which has been under construction forty-six years, begun in 20 B.C. by Herod the Great, who had a lust for putting up great buildings, and completed in A.D. 64? Apparently, it was now at a finished state in one phase of its construction. The Jews are so imprisoned in fleshly existence and understanding they cannot grasp the deeper spiritual reality. It is impossible for them to see beyond a magnificent complex of physical buildings. What a tragedy to assume they are in the light because they know every jot and tittle of the law, when actually they are bound in the darkness of ignorance.

The disciples later remembered and understood *"when He had risen from the dead."* Then what had been hidden became clear. The word of Scripture then illuminated the word of Jesus. And the word of Jesus then opened up the Scripture. During His ministry, Jesus had spoken of His resurrection over and over again, both directly and in hidden ways. But His disciples had not understood. Then, when Jesus rose from the dead, they believed both the word of Scripture and the word which Jesus had spoken. Really one and the same word! Here is the real authority of Scripture, the Living Christ speaking to us through the words in the book.

Just last Sunday after the morning worship, Larry Rapp, a young attorney and new believer whom I have spoken of earlier, paused for a moment or two at the door. He had been blessed by the teaching that morning and made some very discerning comments to me concerning the Scripture of the day. "How beautiful it is that the Lord is giving you fresh insights into His Word," was all I could say. Gentle tears welled up as he responded, "Ever since Christ came into my life I have had a growing love for the Word of God, and at times it's almost overwhelming." Both of us quietly thanked God. When we meet and surrender to the Lord who is risen from the dead, He opens for us the wonder of the Scripture, and our belief is strengthened.

Belief Because of Signs (vv. 23–25). There is a life-and-death difference between believing in His name *"when they saw the signs which He did,"* and believing in Him *because of who He is.* Seeing signs arouses excitement all right, but it also creates a belief that is sometimes superficial. The dramatic cleansing of the temple is no small matter, nor are the signs which followed as Jesus moved about Jerusalem during the seven feast days after the Passover. Here is a wonder-working Messiah who seems to fit their shallow expectations. How prone we all are to put our trust in whatever will get us what we want.

We are surrounded by subtle pressures to settle for "our kind of Messiah." This religious star system calls for agents and contracts and an amazing variety of advance publicity. This narcissistic gospel promises to solve all my hangups and problems; it's almost like a cocaine fix. Spectacular religious TV specials make all our local church affairs seem drab by contrast. And the show must get bigger and more dazzling all the time. "Show me a sign," we continue to cry, "and we will believe."

Let us confess it. Many of us who belong to the evangelical community and believe we are born again know little of costly discipleship or the calling to be servants. This comes only when we submit to Jesus as Lord on His terms. Often we would rather settle for "cheap grace" than to follow Him and die as Dietrich Bonhoeffer did in his life.

It is only when we accept Jesus on His terms that He will commit Himself to us. *"But Jesus did not commit Himself to them."* He knows, without anyone telling Him, what is in all of us. That kind of knowing is spoken of by the prophet in Jeremiah 17:9–10:

> "The heart is deceitful above all things,
> And desperately wicked;
> Who can know it?
> I, the Lord, search the heart,
> I test the mind,
> Even to give every man according to his ways,
> And according to the fruit of his doings."

NOTES

1. John Huckle and Paul Visokay, *The Gospel According to St. John,* Vol. I of *New Testament for Spiritual Reading,* ed. John L. McKenzie, 25 vols. (New York: The Crossroad Publishing Company, 1981), p. 22.

2. William Barclay, *The Gospel of John,* p. 109.

3. John Huckle and Paul Visokay, *The Gospel According to St. John,* p. 30.

4. W. B. Westcott, *The Gospel According to John,* p. 41.

CHAPTER FOUR

An Encounter and an Affirmation

John 3:1–36

The central issue that has been raised in public settings—at a small-town wedding and a national celebration—is stated clearly and convincingly in a probing personal encounter. If one is to enter the "New Age," the Kingdom of God, he must be cleansed as was the temple at Jerusalem and empowered from above as new wine was made at Cana. He must be "born again."

NICODEMUS: YOU MUST BE BORN AGAIN

1 There was a man of the Pharisees named Nicodemus, a ruler of the Jews.

2 This man came to Jesus by night and said to Him, "Rabbi, we know that You are a teacher come from God; for no one can do these signs that You do unless God is with him."

3 Jesus answered and said to him, "Most assuredly, I say to you, unless one is born again, he cannot see the kingdom of God."

4 Nicodemus said to Him, "How can a man be born when he is old? Can he enter a second time into his mother's womb and be born?"

5 Jesus answered, "Most assuredly, I say to you, unless one is born of water and the Spirit, he cannot enter the kingdom of God.

6 "That which is born of the flesh is flesh, and that which is born of the Spirit is spirit.

7 "Do not marvel that I said to you, 'You must be born again.'

8 "The wind blows where it wishes, and you hear the sound of it, but cannot tell where it comes from and where it goes. So is everyone who is born of the Spirit."

9 Nicodemus answered and said to Him, "How can these things be?"

10 Jesus answered and said to him, "Are you the teacher of Israel, and do not know these things?

11 "Most assuredly, I say to you, We speak what We know and testify what We have seen, and you do not receive Our witness.

12 "If I have told you earthly things and you do not believe, how will you believe if I tell you heavenly things?

13 "No one has ascended to heaven but He who came down from heaven, that is, the Son of Man who is in heaven.

14 "And as Moses lifted up the serpent in the wilderness, even so must the Son of Man be lifted up,

15 "that whoever believes in Him should not perish but have eternal life.

16 "For God so loved the world that He gave His only begotten Son, that whoever believes in Him should not perish but have everlasting life.

17 "For God did not send His Son into the world to condemn the world, but that the world through Him might be saved.

18 "He who believes in Him is not condemned; but he who does not believe is condemned already, because he has not believed in the name of the only begotten Son of God.

19 "And this is the condemnation, that the light has come into the world, and men loved darkness rather than light, because their deeds were evil.

20 "For everyone practicing evil hates the light and does not come to the light, lest his deeds should be exposed.

21 "But he who does the truth comes to the light, that his deeds may be clearly seen, that they have been done in God."

John 3:1–21

The Man at Night (vv. 1–2). How fascinating that a member of the "Who's Who of Jerusalem" should seek out Jesus, a rustic itinerant preacher. Could He have anything in common with Nicodemus, a man with impeccable credentials? John describes Nicodemus as *"a man of the Pharisees,"* which meant he was one of the separated ones, an elite lay theologian dedicated to studying and living out every jot and tittle of the law and *"a ruler of the Jews,"* meaning he was a member of the Sanhedrin, that exclusive council which controlled the religious life of Israel.

Nicodemus had come because of all that had been going on. He said, *"No one can do these things that You do unless God is with him."* The dramatic cleansing of the temple and the works that followed had created quite a stir. Surely these happenings had become common gossip on the streets of Jerusalem. There is a humility in the way he comes. He addresses Jesus as *"Rabbi,"* a title of respect he would use only because he believed he could learn something from this new teacher.

He came *"by night."* Was he ashamed or fearful to be seen with Jesus by day? Or were there too many people clamoring for Jesus' attention by day? Perhaps if there were to be any chance for an honest, uninterrupted conversation it would have to be at night. But the night is also a time of darkness. And is this not where Nicodemus was living? In darkness. Even though he affirms that God must be with Jesus, he is ignorant.

Nicodemus says, *"we know."* He seems to be speaking for more than himself. Nicodemus may have come to voice some of the questions being raised by a group within the Sanhedrin. By what authority was Jesus doing these things? What was His purpose? Did He have some new truth to reveal? Nicodemus is speaking for men who were not falsely complimentary about what Jesus had been doing.

Earthly Birth and New Birth (vv. 3–7). Jesus responds to Nicodemus's friendly statement by coming directly to the heart of the matter. He does not waste time on peripheral issues. His statement, *"Most assuredly,"* at the outset calls for careful, singleminded attention. Nicodemus's destiny will hang on how he hears and answers what Jesus will now say. *"I say to you, unless one is born again, he cannot see the kingdom of God."* Only Jesus has the authority to make this categorical, uncompromising statement! Once again Jesus has used a basic earthly category—human birth—to illuminate a profound spiritual reality.

"Born again"! The phrase is arresting and fresh, alive with meaning.

Another chance, starting over, new life! Is it possible? That is exactly what Jesus is saying.

In our age, which has vulgarized so many great realities, we have tossed these words about as if they were simply another fad, a chic "in" phrase to be bandied about at some cocktail party. "You say he was born again. How delightful!" Even in church circles, sad to say, the words have become shopworn and jaded, part of our professional jargon, sapped of their original radical meaning.

But this was not the case with Nicodemus. He is brought up short, baffled and confused. This is not what he expected. *"How can a man be born when he is old? Can he enter a second time into his mother's womb and be born?"* How else can he respond? In spite of all his religious knowledge and living by the levitical code, he is locked in flesh. He can only understand from an earthly perspective. Nicodemus can "move only within a world of categories and interests circumscribed by itself. Flesh builds its own prison and trivializes its own mysteries."[1] Thus, hemmed in, Nicodemus can only phrase his wondering response in fleshly terms.

His response makes earthly sense. How can anyone who is physically mature start over again within his mother's womb? Surely one cannot undo forty or fifty years of physical growth. And if this is true physically, then how much more difficult it is to start over in the moral and spiritual realm. Is not each one of us the sum total of all his experiences, good and bad, at any stage of life? Surely we cannot wipe that all out and say that now we will start over. Have all these years of study and zealous obedience to the law been in vain for Nicodemus?

Ah, but this new birth is not an intensified continuation of old ways, a deepened interpretation of the law, or a more urgent effort to obey the levitical code. The jars of purification at Cana and the temple worship in Jerusalem have had their day.

No, this is a "new beginning," a starting over again. This is new life given by God Himself, a breaking in of His grace, a supernatural act bringing forth a new creation. Just as a human birth is a mystery, but a very specific reality, so there is a deeper mystery and reality about spiritual birth. Physical life is born through the intimacy of human love shared by male and female in which there is the union of egg and sperm. But there is also a spiritual act of divine grace in which God gives Himself to a particular person, who, in receiving Him, is born anew. It is in the union of the divine and the human, the supernatural and the natural, the heavenly and the earthly, that new life comes.

This newborn person now understands a new order of being, the kingdom of God. He has been given new eyes and a new heart to apprehend what it means to be a member of a new family, a child of God living in joyful obedience to the Father's will. Nicodemus had never grasped that reality, even though he carefully studied the meaning of the law of Moses with the other Pharisees. The reign of God, His gracious rule over all life, can never be outwardly known, for an order that is essentially spiritual cannot be understood with natural powers.

Well over a hundred Southeast Asians have come to be a part of our church family, and what joy they have brought into our congregational life. One in particular is Mr. Nou, a gifted man with many leadership qualities. What a beautiful experience it was a few weeks ago to hear him share the meaning of the new life God had given him. In his "old life" he had frequently beaten his wife and children, often neglecting them while he was "partying with other women" as he put it. His weekends were often drunken orgies. Coming to the United States as a refugee from Laos did not change his situation. In fact, it worsened it!

He finally gave in to one of his persistent friends who almost angered him by constantly urging him to come with him to church. At first, it was all a joke for Mr. Nou. But then, in God's mysterious way, he met the One to whom Nicodemus came at night. It was a radical, life-changing encounter, and Mr. Nou was "born again." He emptied the whiskey bottles in his home and began to treat his wife and children with new love and respect. Then he discovered new friends among the believers and began to eagerly study the Scriptures at 5:00 each morning. What a joy to hear him speak about all the spiritual truths he has already discovered in the Word of God. His wife said, "I don't have a different husband. I have a new one."

As he shared that day with our congregation, there was a radiant joy about him. No wonder Mr. Nou has become a contagious evangelist among his own people, going to their homes, sharing the good news of what has happened to him, and inviting them to church. When I spoke to him commending him for this he seemed surprised. "Isn't that what all of us are supposed to be doing? How could anyone hold back such a good thing?"

So the new birth is not some experience added to our old way of thinking or acting. We have had far too much of this in our churches—people living the old life, ignorant like Nicodemus. They may go through the motions of religion, but there is no reality in it. We have asked people to repeat the "right words," and we have been running in circles, doing things, taking on more projects, and desperately trying to behave "right." But at the center of existence, in their deepest selves, people have been untouched and unchanged. Then we have covered up the old, unconverted self with churchly language. We say, "Of course, he was baptized." "Yes, she's been a member here for over twenty years." "You know what a great job she's done handling that committee." "They are about the best givers we have." And all the time, many of these people are empty and needy, spiritually bankrupt. Little wonder much of what we do in the church is unredeemed and ego-centered.

Nicodemus can now only ask wonderingly, *"How can a man be born when he is old?"* And again Jesus responds, *"Most assuredly."* Nicodemus is still pushing in, and Jesus will give him all he can handle. The new birth is by water. Just as John's baptism was a plunging under, a cleansing, so it is if Nicodemus really wants to enter the kingdom. Unless he dares to let go of his morality and learning and will pass through the humiliation and helplessness of repentance, he cannot be born from above. Neither can we.

But there is more than water. The new birth is also by *"the Spirit."* The Hebrew word for the *Spirit* is *ruach,* translated "the intimate breath of God," and the Greek is *pneuma,* "the wind of His Spirit." The One by whose creative breath every person becomes a living soul also shares His life-changing Spirit with all who will receive. Here is the power from above that liberates and makes all things new.

After being born of water and of the Spirit, we *"enter the kingdom,"* we come into a new dimension of existence. This birth is not an individualistic affair, but a corporate, bodily, family event. We are now under the Father's authority and protection. It is as when the children of Israel crossed over the Jordan River on dry land, by an act of God, to enter the land of promise. Or it is like becoming the citizens of a new country joining a new people and swearing allegiance to a new flag. We *"enter"* a new land.

In verse 7, Jesus confronts Nicodemus directly and personally: *"You must be born again."* Not someone else, but you, Nicodemus, who are so studiously seeking to learn and obey the law. The birth from above is not a general spiritual doctrine to be endlessly discussed, but a specific imperative that addresses this particular man in the depth of his being. So it is with us! The claim of Jesus comes to each of us this way—personally and directly—to the very center of our existence.

A Mystery: As Wind Blows (v. 8). Birth from above cannot be manipulated or programmed. It is a gift given in God's own way and time, an act of sovereign grace. It is a birth as mysterious as the wind, which comes and goes as it wills. Unseen, yet real! Again, Jesus has used a common, earthy reality to illuminate spiritual truth. He has spoken of birth, then water, and now wind. This breath of God brings life, not capriciously, but according to His gracious purpose.

There is a mystery about God's working which we can only anticipate and prepare for. He is the One who moves when He wills! I have learned much about this from sailing. There are times of fresh, stiff winds when it is exhilarating to move out and the boat heels up. Sometimes gentle breezes suddenly give way to unexpected gusts, which can challenge the best sailor. And other times there is a deadly calm when all one can do is wait. So it is in the life of the Spirit. Upon Him, who is the source of the Breath, we are utterly dependent for life and movement.

"How can these things be?" (vv. 9–13). There must have been a long, wondering pause before Nicodemus asked Jesus the question in verse 9. A conversation of this depth cannot be hurried. One can almost hear the gentle sounds of the wind blowing in the still of the night. Once again, Nicodemus can only ask *"How?"* Even though he is a *"teacher of Israel,"* he is imprisoned in fleshly existence. The flesh does not understand the "things of the Spirit." Have you ever heard a religious leader, a theological professor, or a pastor quoting and interpreting Bible verses as an expert, but speaking of them as a stranger, an outsider, alien to their inner meaning?

There is a note of sadness in Jesus' response in verse 10. How can Nicodemus be a teacher of Israel and yet not know these things? Nicodemus's being a religious leader is like the blind leading the blind. What Jesus has shared with him is not sophisticated doctrine. These are the ABCs, and if Nicodemus cannot grasp these truths taught through simple, earthly symbols, there is no way he can ever understand and accept the deeper realities. It is only as we pass through the narrow door of the new birth that our eyes are opened to apprehend deeper spiritual realities.

However, these beginning truths of the kingdom are not out of reach. They have been understood and accepted by others, with far less theological training than Nicodemus. The *"We"* in verse 11 indicates that the testimony of Jesus has been authenticated. The identity of Jesus and His message has been grasped and entered into by others—John the Baptist who "knew" at Jesus' baptism, the first disciples who had "come and seen" and followed. Among them is John, the writer of this Gospel. They had become witnesses.

No one can climb up and take these heavenly truths by force, either by learning or feverish obedience to the law. It is only Jesus who can reveal the secrets of the kingdom of heaven to any eager seeker, because He shares about His "home." Even while He is the Son of man in flesh on earth, He is in heaven. It is when we accept Him, are born into His kingdom, that the realities in which He lives are shared with us. Heavenly things are made clear then. Otherwise we stumble in fleshly darkness.

Descent to Be Lifted Up (vv. 14–15). Now to further clarify His own identity and the meaning of His coming down from heaven, Jesus refers to a peculiar incident in the life of Moses. Near the end of the years of wandering in the wilderness and shortly before they entered the promised land, the children of Israel once again murmured in their unbelief. So the Lord sent fiery serpents among them that brought disease and death. Then the people repented and cried out, "We have sinned." Again Moses interceded for them as he had so many times. The Lord then offered salvation through a strange provision. He commanded Moses to make a fiery serpent of bronze and to hang it on a pole. The people who had been bitten and were sick unto death could be healed only by lifting up their eyes and looking at that serpent. They would be saved by an act of faith (Num. 21:4–9). Then God spared them!

So the Son of Man has come to be lifted up on a pole. This One who sits with Nicodemus has made His descent into flesh and in obedience will die. This amazing and costly sacrifice calls forth the response of faith. Whoever will behold with eyes of faith will be given everlasting life and will not languish and die in the wilderness. This is God's amazing provision for our salvation.

The Decision: Belief or Condemnation (vv. 16–21). We can see in these verses that the lifting up of the Son of Man is an act of love. The act is not an afterthought or a last-minute emergency plan. Love is central to the very nature of God, reaching out to all who are unlovely and sick, like those dying Israelites, like Nicodemus, and like us sinners. That love is not selective or discriminating. It is universal, with no limitations. God comes to the whole world in love.

Love is never passive. It is the very nature of love to give the best and not hold back. And the gift is unique, *"the only begotten."* The greater the object of love, the more costly the gift. "Any old thing" is not good enough. That would not be love.

The invitation is as wide as God's heart— *"whoever believes."* He will not cheapen the terms, or He would not be true to Himself. We can only accept the invitation by trust, faith, submission. It has been that way with God since the beginning.

The gift is everlasting: "a life consistent with the age to come. This life is not an endless duration of being in time, but being of which time is not a measure."[2] This is life with God that is limitless; it is quality, not quantity. Our final destiny is life, not death. But the word *"perish"* is here because those who do not look or believe are condemned. They refuse to accept God's great gift and so must go on without the gift. The judgment then is to remain in their present state.

Here is the great paradox, the two-edged meaning of Jesus' coming. He came in love to save, to heal, and to offer spiritual birth. He did not come to condemn or judge. But His coming sharpens the issue. Now we must decide! There is both wondrous possibility and great peril in Nicodemus's coming to Jesus. If he chooses to lay aside all his preconceived ideas and learning and accepts Jesus as the One who has come down from heaven, he will be born again! But if he chooses to turn aside, to leave, to work out his own salvation by his own stubborn efforts, however noble, he stands under condemnation and will perish.

Here is the mystery of evil, that darkness which keeps each of us from accepting the great gift, that rebellious pride which will not allow us to go through the water of repentance and receive the empowering of the Spirit. There is an egocentricity in each of us that constantly insists I can work out my own salvation. It is the cross, the lifting up of the Son of Man, that finally unmasks this ego and thus becomes the agent of discrimination and judgment (1 Cor. 1:18).

In our deeds, our rejection is revealed most clearly. When the light comes into the world, we love darkness rather than light because our deeds are evil. John does not mince words. He says that men hate the light because they do not want their deeds exposed.

On the other hand, the one who accepts and believes, reveals the fact by obeying (v. 21). He does the truth. His discipleship cannot be divided into words and deeds, for they are one. (Here again we see the Word, the life of Jesus, made flesh through the obedience of the disciples.) It is through their obedience that they come to the light. Jesus is lifted up through the transparence of their lives. This can only be done *"in God,"* because the disciples have been born again.

The deepest experiences of renewal I have witnessed in the life of the church have come when people have opened up and revealed the dark, hidden places in their lives to one another. This always is a costly, cleansing experience in which the light is seen. Doing the truth!

I participated in such an experience this last year at a strong evangelical seminary. A student stood up in a time of sharing and in a trembling, emotion-laden voice spoke of his anger and frustration with one of the professors and then asked for his forgiveness. The professor, who was present, moved toward the student. They met and embraced. There was forgiveness and prayer. This opened up the meeting, which turned out to be a time of confession and healing, a true renewal in the Spirit. It was the light exposing the darkness of bad attitudes and fouled up relationships.

This is the opposite of rejection, an acceptance, a "believing in His name."

JOHN THE BAPTIST: THE FRIEND OF THE BRIDEGROOM

22 After these things Jesus and His disciples came into the land of Judea, and there He remained with them and baptized.

23 Now John also was baptizing in Aenon near Salim, because there was much water there. And they came and were baptized.

24 For John had not yet been thrown into prison.

25 Then there arose a dispute between some of John's disciples and the Jews about purification.

26 And they came to John and said to him, "Rabbi, He who was with you beyond the Jordan, to whom you have testified—behold, He is baptizing, and all are coming to Him!"

27 John answered and said, "A man can receive

nothing unless it has been given to him from heaven.

28 "You yourselves bear me witness, that I said, 'I am not the Christ,' but, 'I have been sent before Him.'

29 "He who has the bride is the bridegroom; but the friend of the bridegroom, who stands and hears him, rejoices greatly because of the bridegroom's voice. Therefore this joy of mine is fulfilled.

30 "He must increase, but I must decrease.

31 "He who comes from above is above all; he who is of the earth is earthly and speaks of the earth. He who comes from heaven is above all.

32 "And what He has seen and heard, that He testifies; and no one receives His testimony.

33 "He who has received His testimony has certified that God is true.

34 "For He whom God has sent speaks the words of God, for God does not give the Spirit by measure.

35 "The Father loves the Son, and has given all things into His hand.

36 "He who believes in the Son has everlasting life; and he who does not believe the Son shall not see life, but the wrath of God abides on him."

John 3:22–36

"He is baptizing and all are coming to Him!" (vv. 22–28). This is an interesting, and in some ways peculiar, passage. At first it seems almost unrelated to the general context. Why is John the Baptist brought into the narrative at this point? But then one becomes aware that it highlights the consistent faithfulness of John the Baptist's witness to Jesus. He does not deviate or falter in his mission even though some of his disciples have now left him to follow Jesus. What is happening to John's ministry now that Jesus is becoming more popular?

This is the only place we read of Jesus baptizing. However, Jesus was probably not doing the baptizing, but His disciples (John 4:2). Apparently, this was also a baptism of repentance like John's, a preparation for the coming of the kingdom, not a full-orbed "Christian baptism." Also, it seems Jesus was spending some leisurely time with His disciples, perhaps a period of deepening intimacy. *"He remained with them"* (v. 22).

John is also continuing to baptize nearby at Aenon where there was *"much water."* Here there were seven springs within a quarter of a mile radius. The way the phrase, *"For John had not yet been thrown into prison,"* is included seems to mark that as a critical, well-known event which had widespread repercussions.

The dispute about purification between John's disciples and the Jews had been an ongoing debate. Here it is brought up again. What was the meaning, the spiritual efficacy, of John's baptism? Was it really different from the Jewish cleansing by water? Where had John gotten his authority to baptize?

Out of this discussion, a statement is thrown at the Baptist that surely could have been an opening for a jealous explosion. This must have come from John's own disciples, for they address him as *"Rabbi."* They speak of One who was with John beyond the Jordan to whom he bore witness. Surely, Jesus, whose name is not mentioned here, must have been in the company of the Baptist longer than we assume. Then these disciples report, *"He is baptizing, and all are coming to Him!"* It is almost as if they are saying, "He is getting into our territory, taking over what you, John, were called to do." What an opportunity for John to strike back.

How difficult it is for those of us who are so-called spiritual leaders to handle the success of some other brother and "his church" down the street. Think of how easy it is to be subtly or openly critical of, or envious of some great church and its pastor and try to imitate them. It can be difficult to pray for him and his people and to rejoice in his spiritual victories.

But John is spiritually mature and sensitive, a true man of God. He is profoundly aware that anyone can only be and do what God gives him. He cannot take by force what only heaven can give. Each of us is to be content and faithful with his gifts and his own calling. So John reiterates what he has so emphatically stated before, *"I am not the Christ, but I have been sent before Him"* (v. 28).

"The friend . . . rejoices greatly because of the bridegroom's voice" (vv. 29–35). Then he uses the beautiful picture of marriage, which had a powerful meaning in Jewish life, to illustrate his own place in relation to Jesus. He is not the bridegroom, but the friend of the bridegroom. The relationship between Yahweh and His people is often spoken of as bridegroom and bride in the Old Testament (Hos. 2:19, Ezek. 16, Mal. 2:11). But Jesus has now come as the bridegroom in this new age to claim the new Israel as His bride. It is John the Baptist, *"the friend,"* who has introduced and turned over some of his disciples, the new *"bride,"* to Jesus, the new *"bridegroom."* The friend of the

bridegroom had an important place in Jewish weddings. He was the liaison, the *shoshbeen,* who presented the bride to the bridegroom, then presided at the wedding, and later, after the wedding, guarded the bridal chamber from all false intruders. "The full, clear voice of the bridegroom's love"[3] for his beloved is the only voice the friend would hear. Then the friend would rejoice, for his task was completed.

Thus, John has finished the task he was given to do. He has announced and prepared the way for the Bridegroom who will now take center stage more and more. The glory of God will be revealed through His mighty works. In spite of unbelief and stubborn resistance, He will claim His bride. John is the friend of the Bridegroom, but belongs to the old age that will pass away and die. Jesus is the Bridegroom of the new age, which will grow and flourish until the glory of the marriage fills heaven and earth. So John says, *"He must increase, but I must decrease."* Only a great man can accept his own demise with joy. Little does he realize how tragically that will take place— through imprisonment, suspense, and finally death.

John knows that he is of the earth. He cannot act, then, as if he has come from heaven. (Neither can we.) This would pervert and destroy his mission. But there is One who has come from above. Therefore, He is sovereign *"above all,"* not only over all earth, including John and all that he has done, but above all creation. This is so crucial that it is repeated twice in verse 31. Only this One, who is over all, can speak the truth from heaven because He bears testimony to what He has seen and heard. In verse 32 we see again the tragedy of rejection because so many will not receive His testimony.

But those who accept His message have *"certified that God is true."* Certified! This is the way an official edict or command would have come in that day. The seal of Rome would be on it with all the power of the emperor behind it. Even an illiterate person could understand that stamp. Anyone then who accepts the testimony of this One from heaven is certified! The stamp of God's very nature is on him. He becomes a living testimony to God's truth.

How can the Father hold back anything from the Son whom He loves? Here is one of the central themes of this Gospel. He *"has given all things into His hand."* Love does not hold back anything, nor does it measure out carefully little portions of the Spirit now and then. God has given all things into the hand of the One whom He has sent. So, those who believe in the Son are given all that the Father has shared with Him. First and foremost, this is life everlasting, the very quality of life that is in the Father. And this is not dangled out there in some way as a prize at the end for those who believe, but is given now. It is a present reality—life in the Father now through the Son.

Not Life but the Wrath of God (v. 36). But those who reject this gracious gift, who will not believe, have turned away from life. The alternative to life is death and darkness, *"the wrath of God."* This is not His angry, peevish response, because we refuse to accept Him. Not at all. The wrath of God is awesome. God's holiness cannot belittle or wink at man's turning away from life. Our egos, which insist they do not need God's gift of life, choose darkness, which is God's wrath.

We moderns have tended to sentimentalize and to tone down "the settled and active opposition of God's holy nature to everything that is evil."[4] This is not a momentary, fleeting experience, but a permanent state of existence. *"The wrath of God abides on him"* (v. 36).

NOTES

1. John Huckle and Paul Visokay, *The Gospel According to St. John,* p. 36.
2. W. B. Westcott, *The Gospel According to John,* p. 215.
3. Ibid., p. 60.
4. Leon Morris, *The Gospel According to John,* p. 249.

CHAPTER FIVE

Living Water and Ripened Harvest

John 4:1–42

How vividly we see that God loves the whole world as Jesus moves
from the nighttime visit with Nicodemus, one of the religious "in
crowd," to an encounter with a woman whose name is never given,
an outsider coming with her burden of loneliness and guilt. And
Jesus touches the spiritual nerve of each. He unmasks the spiritual
emptiness of the one who seems righteously self-sufficient and opens
up the alienation of the second, caught in a maze of tangled relationships. He has no canned, packaged approach in dealing with either.
To one He speaks of being "born again," and to the other He offers
"living water."

THE WOMAN AT THE WELL: LIVING WATER

1 Therefore, when the Lord knew that the
Pharisees had heard that Jesus made and baptized more
disciples than John
2 (though Jesus Himself did not baptize, but His
disciples),
3 He left Judea and departed again to Galilee.
4 But He needed to go through Samaria.
5 So He came to a city of Samaria which is called
Sychar, near the plot of ground that Jacob gave to
his son Joseph.
6 Now Jacob's well was there. Jesus therefore,
being wearied from His journey, sat thus by the well.
It was about the sixth hour.
7 A woman of Samaria came to draw water. Jesus
said to her, "Give Me a drink."

8 For His disciples had gone away into the city to buy food.

9 Then the woman of Samaria said to Him, "How is it that You, being a Jew, ask a drink from me, a Samaritan woman?" For Jews have no dealings with Samaritans.

10 Jesus answered and said to her, "If you knew the gift of God, and who it is who says to you, 'Give Me a drink,' you would have asked Him, and He would have given you living water."

11 The woman said to Him, "Sir, You have nothing to draw with, and the well is deep. Where then do You get that living water?

12 "Are You greater than our father Jacob, who gave us the well, and drank from it himself, as well as his sons and his livestock?"

13 Jesus answered and said to her, "Whoever drinks of this water will thirst again,

14 "but whoever drinks of the water that I shall give him will never thirst. But the water that I shall give him will become in him a well of water springing up into everlasting life."

15 The woman said to Him, "Sir, give me this water, that I may not thirst, nor come here to draw."

16 Jesus said to her, "Go, call your husband, and come here."

17 The woman answered and said, "I have no husband." Jesus said to her, "You have well said, 'I have no husband,'

18 "for you have had five husbands, and the one whom you now have is not your husband; in that you spoke truly."

19 The woman said to Him, "Sir, I perceive that You are a prophet.

20 "Our fathers worshiped on this mountain, and you Jews say that in Jerusalem is the place where one ought to worship."

21 Jesus said to her, "Woman, believe Me, the hour is coming when you will neither on this mountain, nor in Jerusalem, worship the Father.

22 "You worship what you do not know; we know what we worship, for salvation is of the Jews.

23 "But the hour is coming, and now is, when the

true worshipers will worship the Father in spirit and
truth; for the Father is seeking such to worship Him.

24 "God is Spirit, and those who worship Him must
worship in spirit and truth."

25 The woman said to Him, "I know that Messiah
is coming" (who is called Christ). "When He comes,
He will tell us all things."

26 Jesus said to her, "I who speak to you am He."

John 4:1–26

"Give Me a drink": Breaking Down Old Barriers (vv. 1–8). Why does
Jesus leave Judea and move northward to Galilee? Particularly if He
is becoming increasingly popular and the word is out that He is baptizing more disciples than John, although the writer is careful to note
that it was the disciples who did the baptizing. That "success" is
both a blessing and a problem. People are hearing and responding,
but getting the attention of the Pharisees can only mean harassment
and opposition. This is not the time for confrontation with the Pharisees, who become more and more His bitter opponents. That will
come later. So it is better to move to another "front."

Jesus is also a courteous gentleman. He has not come to take over
John's territory, to win a numbers game. He is profoundly grateful
for John's crucial work of preparation, which is now coming to a
close. Jesus has a deeper ministry; He not only calls men to repentance,
but to an acceptance of God's reign. So Jesus and His band of disciples
move to the north—they *"left Judea"* (v. 3). The meaning of this phrase
is somewhat unusual. It is like "abandoning," leaving Judea to itself,
to its own wishes and fate. Jesus will never go back to that ministry
of preparation He at first shared with John.

"But He needed to go through Samaria" (v. 4). What a world of meaning
there is in that phrase. He did not need to save the three days He
could gain by passing through this ill-regarded province rather than
crossing the river and going up the eastern desert route. There did
not seem to be urgent needs in Galilee that would cause Him to
shorten the journey.

No, there is a deeper reason, an inner constraint of love and obedience. He knew the ignorance and spiritual hunger of the Samaritan
people, and the Father had sent Him into the whole world—not just
part of it. He could not avoid these people in spite of the long history
of resentment and antagonism between Jews and Samaritans.

Any Jew could give perfectly valid reasons for this anger and separation. After all, the Samaritans were descendants of those who had not been deported or killed in the fall of the Northern Kingdom in 722 B.C. (2 Kings 17:23–40). These survivors had intermarried with the heathen colonists brought in from Babylonia by the Assyrian conquerors. So these people were looked upon as unclean traitors to Jewish blood.

Furthermore, the Samaritans were confused, even heretical in their religious beliefs. Even though their earlier polytheistic worship, caused by strangers bringing in their own gods, had given way to the worship of Jehovah, they accepted only the five books of Moses as their Scriptures and cut themselves off from the riches of the rest of the Old Testament.

The Samaritans also had hostile feelings toward the Jews. Their offer to help rebuild the temple in Jerusalem after the Jews returned from Babylonian exile had been refused, and this had caused great bitterness (Ezra 4:2). So the Samaritans refused to worship in Jerusalem, preferring their own temple on Mount Gerizim, which had been built about 400 B.C. When this place of worship had been burned by the Jews in about 128 B.C., the relation between these two peoples deteriorated even further. Samaritans on occasion would even detain Jews traveling through their territory. Little wonder then that a Jew would attempt to avoid any contact with these unclean dogs. But not Jesus! *"He needed to go through Samaria."*

It was in broad daylight, at noontime, in this alien atmosphere, that Jesus came to Jacob's well at the fork in the road near the town of Sychar. This was a place rich in the history of His people. For here, centuries earlier, Jacob had dug a well for his family and beasts. And on his deathbed, Jacob had given this land to his son Joseph (Gen. 28:21–22), and eventually Joseph's body had been carried back from Egypt and buried here (Josh. 24:32).

What memories must have stirred in Jesus as He sat down at this well *"being wearied from His journey"* (v. 6). John says it so simply and naturally. He has no need to make a case for Jesus' humanity. He had journeyed in His company and felt His weariness. There is a kinship between Jesus and every weary pilgrim who drops tiredly into the nearest chair after an exhausting day at the office or after struggling with the children and the telephone at home. Jesus has joined us in the frailty of our flesh. Otherwise, salvation is unreal.

But can anything noteworthy take place at an old well where a tired Traveler sits wondering if there is some way He can quench His thirst? This is a little bit like assuming in our time that anything really glorious can happen in a supermarket or a laundromat other than a shopper hurrying in to look for bread and milk just before closing time or a tired mother coming to wash the clothes after finally getting the children down for the night. We really do not expect the glory of God to break forth in these kinds of places, do we? But there is no way we can domesticate or control where and when He chooses to reveal Himself.

It was at this time, at noon, not the usual time for women to come to the well, that *"A woman of Samaria came to draw water"* (v. 7). The well was a social institution, a gathering place with its own particular ritual. Here the women of the village came toward evening to exchange small talk and learn the latest village news while they drew water. But this woman sought to avoid all that. Why go through the pain and embarrassment of being avoided and ostracized, the object of village gossip?

A man who came with fear and trembling to my office recently spoke haltingly of his misgivings, the long debate he had with himself before he dared come to a pastor's study. In twenty-six years, he had been in church but one time, and that for his daughter's wedding. He had been in "lots of trouble" over the years and "done time" in a state penitentiary. He remembered with shame the humiliation he had suffered the last time he had been in church for a regular service. The preacher, he said, had lectured him publicly because of his most recent divorce. He had never gone back. Yet he yearned to belong some place. I was amazed he had come to the office. His pain, I am certain, was not unlike that of the woman who came to the well that day.

All the makings of a dramatic confrontation are present as the woman approaches the well. But the wearied Stranger only makes a simple, unexpected request of her. *"Give Me a drink."* In quietly asking her for help, Jesus had cut through centuries of suspicion and animosity. This breakthrough had not been the outcome of a conference on "cross-cultural evangelism," which had developed a theology for "reaching the Samaritans." No, there had been simply the honest expression of a basic human need. And at a deeper level, there had been the loving concern of one reaching out to touch that other solitary, needy person.

The Gift: Living Water (vv. 9–10). The woman can only respond with undisguised amazement, *"How is it that You, being a Jew, ask a drink from me, a Samaritan woman?"* Jesus has disarmed her. She does not throw up a wall of defensiveness, but rather invites some kind of explanation. With the phrase, *"For Jews have no dealings with Samaritans,"* John seeks to help his Greek reader understand what a wide, deep chasm Jesus has come to bridge, "not only with a sinful daughter of men, but between the Son of God and the whole people of Samaria."[1]

So a dialogue is opened in which there comes an amazing reversal of roles. It is not long before the one who has been asked for water is addressing the thirsty Traveler as *"Sir,"* and asking Him for the water He offers. The One who asks for water is Himself the Giver of the everlasting water of life. And the one who is asked is in desperate need of the water that the Stranger alone can give. How strange and beautiful that the Giver of living water has come in weakness to share God's gift. He is our strength and only hope for this life and the next. What would happen if we Christians let this Stranger teach us about reaching out in our neighborhoods and in our places of work? Becoming transparent and open, being less imperialistic and arrogant and more humble and real in our approach to people.

Next this tired Jewish Traveler makes an unexpected offer. He moves to the central issue quickly. There is *"living water"* that is the *"gift of God"* and it can be this woman's for the asking. Gift! What a beautiful word of generosity and grace. Out of His rich bounty God shares all that He has. And how incredible that His greatest gift is the dusty Stranger at the well.

But the Gift cannot be received without the Giver. *"If you knew the gift of God, and who it is who says to you, 'Give Me a drink,' you would have asked Him"* (v. 10). Jesus seeks to penetrate the woman's spiritual darkness. Unless she comes to know and accept the One who speaks to her, His gift can never be hers. For the Father shares this living water through the Son. It springs forth from an unfailing Source and is not water that seeps into an earthen well, dug by human hands, even Jacob's.

The Thirst: "Where do You get that living water?" (vv. 11–15). How absurd the offer of any kind of water seems coming from this nondescript Traveler. He has nothing with which to draw and the well is close to a hundred feet deep. She can only grasp physical matters, for she is locked in fleshly categories as was Nicodemus. She is ignorant, but curious. There is a wondering respect in her response, for she addresses him now as *"Sir,"* a form of "Lord."

Now she raises the crucial question of identity, *"Are You greater than our father Jacob?"* One catches a sense of possessive pride in her inquiry, for she belonged to a people who claimed Jacob as their greatest ancestor, descendants of Joseph's sons Ephraim and Manasseh. Surely this Stranger cannot be greater than their "father." She has brought the conversation nearer to the heart of the matter. The question has become, "Who is this Stranger?" "By what right can He make any offer of water?"

Jesus does not argue about the place of Jacob in Samaritan history. But He makes it clear that water from this well can satisfy thirst only for a brief time. She will have to return to the well again and again. No "water from below" can quench the parched longing this woman brings to this well. Neither the teaching of Moses nor the institution of the law can bring her life and newness.

God's age of grace has come. The One at the well offers "water from above" that can quench this woman's deepest thirst, not for a day, but forever! Water that is not tame and tepid, but full and abundant, *"springing up"* within her into everlasting life.

All through the Scriptures water has a rich and varied spiritual meaning, but always of life. It seems that the precious physical water, coming from well or river, bringing life and beauty to the barren land of Jesus, had become a symbol of that everlasting water which could quench and revive the parched, dying human spirit. So the Psalmist cries out, "As the deer pants for the water brooks, so pants my soul for You, O God" (Ps. 42:1). And the prophets speak repeatedly of its rich spiritual meaning: "living water shall flow from Jerusalem" (Zech. 14:8); "with joy you will draw water from the wells of salvation" (Isa. 12:3); and there is the promise of the day when "waters shall burst forth in the wilderness, and streams in the desert" (Isa. 35:6).

So the teaching of Jesus, His words of wisdom and truth, is life, water for man dying of thirst. There is no inner newness without receiving God's wondrous gift, the Holy Spirit, promised and offered by the Son. Nicodemus in that earlier conversation had heard Jesus say he could only be born again "by water and the Spirit." And on the last day of the feast (John 7:37–39), Jesus flings out that urgent invitation, " 'If anyone thirsts, let him come to Me and drink. He who believes in Me, as the Scripture has said, out of his heart will flow rivers of living water.' But this He spoke concerning the Spirit." It is this invitation the woman at the well is now hearing.

She responds by asking, *"Sir, give me this water."* But the request is still at the fleshly level. Is it possible that her physical thirst can be so quenched by this Stranger that she will not need to make constant trips to this well? But is there a deeper stirring, a wondering if there is something more here than the physical water which has never quenched her deepest thirst?

The Sin Issue: "Go, call your husband" (vv. 16–19). An opening has come. Everything that has taken place between Jesus and this woman has been a preparation for this delicate moment. Now with an incisive, deft stroke of His spiritual scalpel Jesus lays bare the woman's deepest self. With one simple sentence, *"Go, call your husband,"* the One who is Light has exposed her evil deeds, the disorder of her domestic life. If she cannot face herself and admit that her tangled, sick relationships are sin, she can never drink of living water. The gift is free, but it cannot be received without repentance.

One catches a note of sad regret in the woman's terse reply, *"I have no husband."* Jesus commends her for telling the truth. All of us need to be aware of the flashes of beauty and goodness we see in every sinner. And then He opens up her whole confused situation. She has lived with a passing parade of men, five of them technically husbands, and the latest a live-in affair. None of them are lasting, meaningful relationships. "She belongs to no man, but has been the property of five."[2]

What a symbol she is of our own age—lonely and restless, desperately casting about for some kind of deep belonging, going from one manipulative arrangement to another, always hoping that this "roommate" will work out better than the last one. Ours is an age which supposes itself to be sophisticated in all sexual matters, which is noted for office affairs and wife-swapping, in which all kinds of live-in arrangements, orgies, and perversion are more and more the order of the day. Yet it is an age that is tragically ignorant of what it means to be truly human and has neither pondered nor grasped the mystery of human sexuality.

The woman shows deepening respect, addressing the Stranger, *"Sir,"* again, convinced now that He must be some kind of prophet. It is the least she can say. After all, a prophet is one who has the gift of discernment and boldly speaks God's truth about a given situation. Surely this man knows her condition.

True Worship: "In spirit and truth" (vv. 20–24). But she falls back on the old antagonism, the competition between Jerusalem and Gerizim. This woman had good reason to be proud of Mount Gerizim because Abraham and Jacob had both built altars there (Gen. 12:7; 33:30), and this Mount was to be blessed and Mount Ebal was to be cursed after the people had crossed the Jordan and come into the promised land (Deut. 11:29). According to tradition, it was on this mountain that Abraham had come to sacrifice his son Isaac. This woman was also well aware of the stubborn loyalty every Jew had for the Jerusalem, the "Holy City." She said, *"You Jews say that in Jerusalem is the place where one ought to worship."*

At a deeper level, one wonders if the woman is not seeking for the "right" altar. At which place can she find forgiveness—Jerusalem or Gerizim? Now that this "prophet" has exposed her sin, she desperately needs a priest who can assure her of cleansing and new life. Where can she be set free from her burden of guilt?

Jesus again moves beyond the old resentments to deal with the reality of worship. His coming has ushered in God's new age. The old institutions and places of worship are passing away. Earlier in the cleansing of the temple Jesus made it clear that He will be the "place" of worship, that He is the temple of God (John 3:19). So it is no longer a question of Jerusalem or Gerizim, but of being rightly related to the One we worship.

So truth and spirit are at the center of living worship. Knowing *who* it is we worship is of utmost importance. Worship in ignorance, regardless of what name we give it, is a sham and an empty form. This had become the situation among the Samaritans who had removed themselves from so much of the prophecies and teaching of the Old Testament. Sadly, they worshiped what they did not know.

On the other hand, salvation came from the Jews. After centuries of faithfulness to the law and prophets, now the Messiah, the Chosen One, has come among them. The One at the well has not only come to reveal the truth, but is Himself the Truth. The Living God can only be known and worshiped through Him.

But it is not only Whom we worship, in truth, but in *what way,* by what spirit, we worship Him. God, whose essence is Spirit, as well as light (1 John 1:5) and love (1 John 4:8), will share His Holy Spirit, through the Son, at the completion of His work. Thus He will touch, heal, and recreate the deepest self of any who hear and receive. That water which the Stranger offers the woman will spring up into everlasting life, freeing her from her attachment to Mount Gerizim and bringing her into authentic worship of the Living God.

There is a divine dialectic in worship. The Spirit and the truth are always interacting, the one leading to the other, then back again. The Spirit brings us into truth, and the truth draws us into the Spirit. In Jesus, we live in Spirit and truth, and He brings us to the Father whom we worship and adore.

His Identity: "I who speak to you am He" (vv. 25–26). The woman has heard unexpected teaching from this "prophet," truth that is heavy with messianic allusions. The hour that is coming signals crisis and decision, a time of judgment and opportunity. According to her tradition, she knows the Messiah is coming, a teacher and lawgiver in the tradition of Moses. He will announce God's final and absolute truth. The "He" used here is emphatic and can only refer to all that the Messiah is (v. 26).

The woman has come far enough to hear the secret. The dusty Traveler, this Jew whom she has called "prophet," now reveals His identity. He is the Messiah, the eternal "I Am" translated from the Greek *ego eimi.* It is an arresting phrase, reminiscent of the divine name revealed to Moses in the wilderness, "I AM WHO I AM" (Exod. 3:14). This is the only place in the Gospel where Jesus speaks of Himself as the Messiah prior to His trial. And He does so to a Samaritan. In this declaration, Jesus has issued an invitation, a challenge to respond. Glory has broken forth at the well!

THE RIPENED HARVEST

27 And at this point His disciples came, and they marveled that He talked with a woman; yet no one said, "What do You seek?" or, "Why are You talking with her?"

28 The woman then left her waterpot, went her way into the city, and said to the men,

29 "Come, see a Man who told me all things that I ever did. Could this be the Christ?"

30 Then they went out of the city and came to Him.

31 In the meantime His disciples urged Him, saying, "Rabbi, eat."

32 But He said to them, "I have food to eat of which you do not know."

33 Therefore the disciples said to one another, "Has anyone brought Him anything to eat?"

34 Jesus said to them, "My food is to do the will of Him who sent Me, and to finish His work.

35 "Do you not say, 'There are still four months and then comes the harvest'? Behold, I say to you, lift up your eyes and look at the fields, for they are already white for harvest!

36 "And he who reaps receives wages, and gathers fruit for eternal life, that both he who sows and he who reaps may rejoice together.

37 "For in this the saying is true: 'One sows and another reaps.'

38 "I sent you to reap that for which you have not labored; others have labored, and you have entered into their labors."

39 And many of the Samaritans of that city believed in Him because of the word of the woman who testified, "He told me all that I ever did."

40 So when the Samaritans had come to Him, they urged Him to stay with them; and He stayed there two days.

41 And many more believed because of His own word.

42 And they said to the woman, "Now we believe, not because of what you said, for we have heard for ourselves and know that this is indeed the Christ, the Savior of the world."

John 4:27–42

The Witness of the Woman (vv. 27–30). It is at this dramatic juncture in the dialogue that the disciples return. They are somewhat taken aback that He is conversing with a woman, but interestingly, no reference is made to her being a Samaritan. There were meticulous rules governing the relations of men and women in public, even husbands and wives. One of the sayings of the Rabbis ran: "A man shall not be alone with a woman in an inn, not even with his sister or his daughter, on account of what men may think. A man shall not talk with a woman in the street, not even with his own wife, and especially not with another woman, on account of what men may say."[3] In view of this, the disciples showed unusual reticence by not voicing any of their questions. It seems that John noted this detail because he is proud of them. Perhaps the disciples were beginning to understand Jesus' loving, unorthodox style of ministry.

There is an urgency, an air of authority, about the woman as she hurries back into the city. She *"left her waterpot"* (v. 28). Why slow herself down with a pot when she is compelled to share her awakening faith? Living water springing up into eternal life cannot be contained in earthen pots. The woman has tasted the water of God's grace and knows that the old age of Jacob's well is passing.

She may not have a message of fullblown Christian theology to share, but she has met a Man who knows all about her. This she blurts out, inviting everyone to come out and see Him. *"Could this be the Christ?"* (v. 29). The account of what has happened to her is so electrifying that it arouses her whole village.

How often I have been brought up short by the unrehearsed witness of someone who has just gotten started, just become a believer. It is like the first cry of life from a newborn baby. So often the language is fresh and earthy, and there is life and power in what is said. We "domesticated Christians" wonder wistfully, "Was I like that once? What has happened to me along the way?"

This account reminds me so much of Janet, our new friend. My first contact with her was Monday of Holy Week in 1979. As I walked into the office that day, my secretary said I had a long distance call. Janet was calling from New Haven, Connecticut, and it was obvious she was weeping. She had been up most of the night reading a first-hand testimony I had written of God at work in a well-established, middle-class, suburban church that I had served as pastor for sixteen years. It is a story of how God sent some "losers" to us and how they helped us "respectable church members" discover that we were losers too—that all of us only have a chance by the grace of God. The publishers had insisted we call it *God Loves the Dandelions,* which was a quote from a lovely woman who had met the Lord. And it was *the Dandelions* standing out in the title of the book on a library shelf that had intrigued Janet.

She poured out her story in nervous gulps. She hesitatingly identified herself as having been a call girl for seven and a half years. She later reported she could not believe there was no change in the tone of my voice when she identified herself. That could only be by the grace of God. Janet had finally come to the end of her rope when in despair she had failed even in trying to end her own life. She had come to New Haven to "get her head screwed on right."

I assured her I wanted to be her friend and encouraged her to write me. In a few days a five- or six-page letter written on yellow legal paper arrived, which I tried to answer as best I could. My experience with ex-call girls is a bit limited. She quickly answered and again I tried to respond. Later she said she could hardly believe I would answer her and that she carried those first two letters with her like lucky charms. Then there were phone calls and more correspondence—eventually a thick file folder full. All this communication was a mixture of newsy daily items and a desperate cry for friendship. My wife, Ruth, became very much a part of this also.

Then about a year later, Janet visited us—a fascinating and educational four-day stay in our home. Ruth and I have chuckled many times about how she walked off the plane carrying a gallon of Vermont maple syrup in one hand and two live lobsters in a plastic container in the other. Then a year later, we visited her in New Haven on a trip to Maine. We were entertained royally in some of the choice eating places of New Haven—Janet is almost recklessly generous—met her two lovely, but troubled, children, and again had long rambling visits. All through this the conversation and correspondence was deepening, moving nearer the Center, focusing more and more on that Stranger at the well. The first simple prayer I heard Janet utter publicly was an unforgettable experience.

Then in 1982—almost three years to the day from her first call—Janet called again. This time to announce she had made her confession of faith and would be baptized on Palm Sunday. The pastor, a dear friend, later reported that the church had never heard a confession quite like Janet's, so open and honest that "ordinary" believers hardly knew how to handle it.

Later that spring when Janet learned that I was to take part in a Billy Graham School of Evangelism in Boston, in typical fashion she volunteered to come up and help in any way she could. So I suggested she might "say a few words" at the close of the seminar I was leading. When I introduced her as a friend who had a word to share about what Christ had done in her life, none of the several hundred pastors and church leaders knew what they were in for—nor did I.

Janet is brutally honest, and there was no point in covering up where she was coming from. So she plunged in. "Seven years ago at this time of the day I would have been in a bar waiting for my 'pimp' to give me the sign that he had a 'john' and a room." One could almost hear a gasp in the hushed silence. From there on it was a story of alienation and fear, of her passage through the dark night of guilt and self-hatred, always hoping for something better.

But then she, too, had met that Friend at the well who gave her a drink of living water. "And now," she concluded, shyly like a little girl with a lovely, new gift, "I can even say there's joy in my life. That's something new." I saw strong men weep with gratitude. They had heard a modern-day woman of Samaria who had left her waterpot to hurry into the village to tell them what had happened.

And in that Samaritan village, this unexpected news coming from such an unlikely source did not fall on unresponsive ears. The people hurried out to see who it was that had opened up this woman. They *"came to Him,"* which literally means they "kept coming out" in the Greek tense John uses. Can you imagine this news being gossiped about and people excitedly leaving whatever they were doing, hurrying out to see who this is that has given life to this woman?

Jesus' Food: "To do the will of Him who sent Me" (vv. 31–34). The disciples are eager that Jesus eat the lunch they have brought from the neighboring village. After all, they had left Him hungry and weary, and their journey has not been a short one. But He ignores their offer for He has *"food to eat of which you do not know"* (v. 32). What does this mean, they wonder? Has this woman or someone from the village come along and shared food with Him? The disciples are ignorant like Nicodemus and the woman. They do not understand that which is from above, the hidden spiritual food of which He partakes. They, too, are earthbound, caught in the limitations of fleshly existence.

Jesus' ultimate Source of nourishment is that divine, eternal relationship He shares with the One who has sent Him. It is in obeying Him and doing His will that He finds fulfillment, His most satisfying food. And He will see that work through to the end (v. 34). It will be finished in His death on the cross. This will be His final, earthly banquet! Is it not true that any one of us who has been caught up in God's mighty work, however small it may have seemed, discovers food in an entirely different dimension than any physical lunch?

"The fields are white" (vv. 35–38). It is this obedience to His Father's will which has brought Jesus to a great harvest. The response of this one Samaritan woman which has made her an uninhibited witness among her own people, despised and rejected as they are, now brings

them running to hear and believe. In God's age of grace, which Jesus is ushering in, all the neat calculations about harvesting four months after sowing, as the ancient proverb put it, are upset and transcended. We are now dealing with God's timetable. This is *kairos,* Greek for "the proper time," that time of great opportunity, of which the prophet Amos spoke concerning the restoration of Israel, " 'Behold, the days are coming,' says the Lord, 'When the plowman shall overtake the reaper' " (Amos 9:13). The word of Jesus, thrown out at the well, has grown and ripened almost immediately and is now being harvested.

In this age, no one can carefully project who will receive the greatest wages, sower or reaper. Their work is intertwined, interdependent, and the wages are the same for both, the joy of eternal life. This is the time of grace.

The disciples can only reap a harvest because others have faithfully sown. Is not the costly ministry of John the Baptist a part of this? And the woman who is even now eagerly sharing among her own people what she has so recently heard and believed? Is she not sowing? Even the witness to the Messiah found in the Pentateuch, which the Samaritan understood so vaguely, may be part of the preparation for later reaping. So the disciples are entering into the faithful labors of others. Only then can sowing take place.

Many Believed Because of Jesus' Own Word (vv. 39–42). The woman's "word" to her own people is really a report, a testimony, a piece of news. She is faithfully telling what has happened to her. Many *"believed in Him"* because of this woman's witness. It caused them to come to Him, which is the chief purpose of anyone's witness. It has been pointed out by students of evangelism that most of the spontaneous, real witnessing is done by new believers within two years after their conversion. As they are drawn into more and more church activities, they become domesticated, begin to worry about what people will think, and lose that early, joyous abandon. What a tragedy!

These Samaritans are spiritually thirsty, longing for living water. All prejudices are brushed aside as they urge the Jewish Traveler, who has had such a profound effect on this needy woman, *"to stay with them."* This is no surface invitation, but an urgent cry, "Come and live with us." The Word made flesh now tabernacles among these estranged and needy people. And while it was only two days— notice again John's detail—what a rich, full time it became. A few hours with eternal consequences, a time of celebration.

How vividly I recall visiting our fellow believers in Burma in 1967 on a twenty-four-hour visa enroute from Bangkok to Hong Kong. It was a time of heavy military restrictions in that country. I was in Rangoon for exactly twenty-one hours. But what an unforgettable time of sharing, singing, praying, and rejoicing it was! Of course, we could not waste it by sleeping.

During those two days Jesus spent in that village, it was His word the people heard, and they came to believe in the One who shared the Word. Faith is never faith if it is based only on someone else's testimony, however thrilling it may be. No, saving faith comes by hearing the word of the Messiah and trusting Him!

It is these Samaritans, not the Jews, who first know that Jesus is the *"Savior of the world."* He has performed no physical miracle among them, only made Himself known. They have been outsiders and now they know they are included. He has come for them as well.

NOTES

1. Sir Edwyn Hoskyns, *The Fourth Gospel,* p. 236.
2. Ibid.
3. Leon Morris, *The Gospel According to John,* p. 274.

CHAPTER SIX

Mighty Works and Rejection

John 4:43—5:47

REJECTION AND ACCEPTANCE

43 Now after the two days He departed from there
and went to Galilee.
44 For Jesus Himself testified that a prophet has
no honor in his own country.
45 So when He came to Galilee, the Galileans
received Him, having seen all the things He did in
Jerusalem at the feast; for they also had gone to the
feast.

John 4:43–45

Jesus now moves on to Galilee where He is *"received."* These people
have witnessed *"all the things He did in Jerusalem at the feast."* At least
they accept Him because of these works. While faith can never finally
rest on mighty works, they can be a point of beginning. How gracious
that He starts with any one of us where we are, often with our
gawking curiosity asking for more wonders, but He knows that our
only hope will be to finally believe in Him.

It was the rejection by Jerusalem, the center and symbol of all
that was His *"own country,"* that caused Him to journey northward
to Galilee. And in doing this, He refers to an ancient proverb that
"a prophet has no honor in his own country." Here is that somber theme
that John has introduced at the very outset of his Gospel, "He came
to His own, and His own did not receive Him" (1:11).

108

HEALING BEYOND SIGNS AND WONDERS

46 So Jesus came again to Cana of Galilee where
He had made the water wine. And there was a certain
nobleman whose son was sick at Capernaum.

47 When he heard that Jesus had come out of Judea
into Galilee, he went to Him and implored Him to
come down and heal his son, for he was at the point
of death.

48 Then Jesus said to him, "Unless you people see
signs and wonders, you will by no means believe."

49 The nobleman said to Him, "Sir, come down
before my child dies!"

50 Jesus said to him, "Go your way; your son lives."
So the man believed the word that Jesus spoke to him,
and he went his way.

John 4:46–50

So Jesus returns to Cana, the place of His first sign. Here a royal
official from the court of Herod Antipas, seeks Him out. How ironic
that while the religious leaders of Jerusalem reject Jesus, the servant
of a worldly prince should come to believe in Him "with his whole
household" (v. 53). The mission of this official is urgent. His son is
ill, near death. No wonder he *"went to Him and implored Him"* to heal
his son.

Jesus seems to almost brush this official aside because He perceives
that he is expecting him to continue doing the signs and wonders
he has seen in Jerusalem. There is far more at stake here than saving
the physical life of a child, crucial as that is. And that is the spiritual
birth, the total healing of this official and his household. This can
only happen if one has authentic faith in the One who is the Healer.
So Jesus will allow this man to come to that lonely, helpless place
where all his false defenses and supports are surrendered and he
will obey any command that is given.

Now the official is insistent. The child whom he loves is desperately
ill and there is no one other than this Man who can help. His cry
for help is now rooted in Jesus, not in signs and wonders. He says,
"Sir," which is a term of beautiful respect placing himself under the
authority of Jesus, *"come down before my child dies!"*

And in response to this cry of faith Jesus speaks the word, *"Go your way; your son lives."* And the man took Jesus at His word and made off for home, a bold act of faith! He asked no questions and needed no further proof. Jesus' word was enough. *"Your son lives."* Three times in this brief narrative these words ring out like the joyous refrain of a resurrection hymn!

He Himself Believed and His Whole Household

51 And as he was now going down, his servants met him and told him, saying, "Your son lives!"

52 Then he inquired of them the hour when he got better. And they said to him, "Yesterday at the seventh hour the fever left him."

53 So the father knew that it was at the same hour in which Jesus said to him, "Your son lives." And he himself believed, and his whole household.

54 This again is the second sign that Jesus did when He had come out of Judea into Galilee.

John 4:51–54

There is the confirmation that life has come when the servants of the official meet their master on the road to share the good news! *"Your son lives!"* It is like the Samaritan woman hurrying back to her village to let her neighbors know what has happened. And while some commentators discuss at what hour by human calculation the healing took place, the point is that when Jesus spoke the word, the fever left the boy, and he was healed. As a dear friend, Howard Rees, who has struggled for years with illness and pain, but always with the radiance and joy of God's grace, said years ago, "God's trains always run on time."

And in the coming of physical health to this home, spiritual life is born. *"He himself believed, and his whole household."* There is a contagion about the new life. It always reproduces itself. It is corporate, communal. Again John, the evangelist, gives us a significant detail—this is the second sign of Jesus in Galilee *"when He had come out of Judea."* The unbelief and hostility of Judea opens the door for this healing ministry in Galilee where there is still a climate of acceptance. Judea's loss is Galilee's gain.

A CRIPPLE WALKING HOME: "DO YOU WANT TO BE MADE WELL?"

> 1 After this there was a feast of the Jews, and Jesus went up to Jerusalem.
>
> 2 Now there is in Jerusalem by the Sheep Gate a pool, which is called in Hebrew, Bethesda, having five porches.
>
> 3 In these lay a great multitude of sick people, blind, lame, paralyzed, waiting for the moving of the water.
>
> 4 For an angel went down at a certain time into the pool and stirred up the water; then whoever stepped in first, after the stirring of the water, was made well of whatever disease he had.
>
> 5 Now a certain man was there who had an infirmity thirty-eight years.
>
> 6 When Jesus saw him lying there, and knew that he already had been in that condition a long time, He said to him, "Do you want to be made well?"
>
> 7 The sick man answered Him, "Sir, I have no man to put me into the pool when the water is stirred up; but while I am coming, another steps down before me."
>
> 8 Jesus said to him, "Rise, take up your bed and walk."
>
> *John 5:1-8*

Chapter 5 begins with *"After this."* There is a sequence in the events, movement from one sign to the next, each deepening in intensity and meaning. John's Gospel makes it clear that Jesus delighted in the feast days of His people that celebrated the saving acts of God. So He journeyed again to Jerusalem. Which feast it was in this case is incidental to the main point. The fact that He deliberately healed a needy, lonely man on the Sabbath (see v. 9) becomes the crucial issue of this visit. This act of mercy caused suspicion and anger among the Jews and a determination that this blasphemer must be killed.

Again we have the "feel" of an actual happening. The details of this encounter, which are included so naturally, can only come from one who was an eyewitness. The Sheep Gate was in the northeast area of the temple, so called because here the animals were brought for the sacrifices. The pool was called *Bethesda* in the native Hebrew tongue. There is now evidence from the copper scroll found at Qumran that the name of this area or pool seems to have been "Bell 'Esda" meaning "house of the flowing."[1] "The pool was trapezoidal in form, 165 to 220 feet wide by 315 feet long, divided by a central partition. There were colonnades on the four sides and on the partition—thus John's 'five porticos.' "[2]

Apparently there were underground springs, and it was believed the waters had curative powers whenever they bubbled or moved. Here lay a *"great multitude"* of the crippled, blind, and paralyzed waiting for some movement. Imagine the shuffling sounds of those needy, hurting people struggling to get into the water as it began to gurgle and move a bit. I have haunting memories of seeing a vast throng of people bathing in the supposedly sacred, but filthy, water of the Ganges River in Calcutta, even though a mile or two up the river sewage was being dumped into the water.

Here lay *"a certain man,"* one single, solitary human being in the midst of this vast throng (v. 5). And *"Jesus saw him."* This is the Gospel! Jesus sees and cares for the one person—whether it is Nicodemus, the woman at the well, this needy man, or any one of us. Jesus was never falsely impressed by a crowd, whatever its size, and never let it get in the way of the one who desperately needed Him. This man had been sick for thirty-eight years. His situation is hopeless. He has given in to his illness, become a prisoner of his own despair. What chance is there he will ever get into the pool?

So Jesus' question, *"Do you want to be made well?"* seems quite unnecessary. But how can Jesus cut through the excuses and defenses that have grown with the years like layers of fat and get through to who the man really is? Is there some deep, untouched shred of hope within the man, a longing to just get up and go home, to take on again the frustrating, challenging responsibilities of everyday life? Will he hear and obey?

So often people succumb to their illness, "bedding down" with their alcoholism or heart trouble or partial paralysis, or whatever. They become psychological and spiritual invalids, retreating within themselves, avoiding responsibilities, becoming more and more self-centered as they demand sympathy from others. Every now and then in dealing with this kind of defeated person in the office or at a hospital bed or in a luncheon appointment I have asked that question, "Do you want to be made well?" Otherwise we will go on visiting, skirting the issue. Sometimes the response is puzzlement. "What do you mean?" Sometimes it has been anger, and every now and then an urgent, "Yes, come on, let's go!"

Something in this crippled man clicked. Deep within there was a small opening. Perhaps this friendly Stranger could do something for him. He addressed Jesus with a respectful *"Sir."* He put himself under the authority of Jesus. But even then, there is a note of self-pity in his answer, *"I have no man to put me into the pool . . . another steps down before me."* He has waited in vain so long one gets the feeling he has become a permanent loser, a complainer who is avoided by the others.

The Controversy: "Who Is the Man?"

9 And immediately the man was made well, took up his bed, and walked. And that day was the Sabbath.

10 The Jews therefore said to him who was cured, "It is the Sabbath; it is not lawful for you to carry your bed."

11 He answered them, "He who made me well said to me, 'Take up your bed and walk.' "

12 Then they asked him, "Who is the Man who said to you, 'Take up your bed and walk'?"

13 But the one who was healed did not know who it was, for Jesus had withdrawn, a multitude being in that place.

14 Afterward Jesus found him in the temple, and said to him, "See, you have been made well. Sin no more, lest a worse thing come upon you."

15 The man departed and told the Jews that it was Jesus who had made him well.

John 5:9–15

Jesus sees that small glimmer of hope and cuts through all the cripple's hopelessness. Jesus gives a simple command, "Rise, take up your bed and walk." And the quiet, creative power of God begins to flow through his crippled limbs and spirit, and once again he knows the warmth of life. *"And immediately . . . made well . . . took up his bed*

. . . *walked."* These strong words describing the action signify that life has broken in. The man is on his way home.

Then John adds a simple phrase, almost an afterthought it seems, *"And that day was the Sabbath"* (v. 9). They are words that are laden with potential controversy. It is almost as if Jesus has done this work of mercy on the Sabbath to get an explosive issue into the open. By this act He has declared His authority and mission at a place and time which will cause confrontation.

The Sabbath originally was set as a day of rest and worship, but also of celebration, to rejoice before God who was in the midst of His creation. But it had become a dreary institution hedged in by all kinds of scribal regulations as if the holiness of God could be protected by legalisms. For example, "carrying things from one domain to another" on the Sabbath was one of the works forbidden and "carrying empty beds" was implicitly forbidden, as were "works of healing."[3] So when the healed man comes carrying his bed, he is immediately confronted by the Jews who remind him of the rules.

His defense is to blame the Man who commanded him to take up his bed and walk. And when he is then asked, *"Who is the Man?"* he can only confess ignorance. He has accepted the gracious gift of healing without discovering who has dealt with him so kindly. The Healer has slipped away in the crowd. But once again Jesus' identity has become the crucial issue!

Jesus is eager that this man should know who it is that has healed him. So He seeks him out in the temple—does He not seek us all out?—and reminds this man who is so uncertain in his witness that he has been made totally whole. There is no halfway healing with this Physician. But He also warns him not to sin again lest a *"worse thing come upon [him]."* This is not a characteristic teaching of Jesus, who was never too interested in speculating about the causes for illness, but was passionately concerned that any healing be to the glory of God. So we cannot help but wonder if some lustful, fleshly sin had caused this man's illness.

In this temple encounter, the healed one discovers the identity of his Healer. One wonders at what point and in what way that happened. For each person the coming of that awareness is a unique and personal mystery. The man then *"departs"*—almost too quickly—to give the Jews this choice bit of news. He is obviously too eager to please the Jews to take his stand with Jesus.

THE ISSUE: THE RELATION OF FATHER AND SON

16 For this reason the Jews persecuted Jesus, and
sought to kill Him, because He had done these things
on the Sabbath.

17 But Jesus answered them, "My Father has been
working until now, and I have been working."

18 Therefore the Jews sought all the more to kill
Him, because He not only broke the Sabbath, but also
said that God was His Father, making Himself equal
with God.

19 Then Jesus answered and said to them, "Most
assuredly, I say to you, the Son can do nothing of
Himself, but what He sees the Father do; for whatever
He does, the Son also does in like manner.

20 "For the Father loves the Son, and shows Him
all things that He Himself does; and He will show
Him greater works than these, that you may marvel.

John 5:16–20

Now the issue is in the open, and Jesus' enemies react quickly
and violently. They *"persecuted Jesus, and sought to kill Him, because He
had done these things on the Sabbath."* In response to their anger, Jesus
declares His relationship to His Father. He is not off on His own
defying tradition as a lone star faith healer. He has healed this man
on the Sabbath because He is doing the work of His Father.

And God does His unique work even on the Sabbath. Even with
their intense desire to regulate and control the Sabbath, Jewish theologians knew that all created things would cease to exist, that all birth
and growth and life would come to an end, if God did not continue
His work on even this holy day. So, in this work of mercy, the
healing of this man, Jesus has done the work of His Father.

The crux of the matter is Jesus' relation to God, whom He calls
"My Father." For this itinerant, free-wheeling, unorthodox wonder-worker to dare call God *"My Father"* is the ultimate blasphemy. He
has made Himself equal with God! And for these rigid, angry monotheists, this is the sin which deserves only death!

But Jesus is not seeking to make Himself equal with God. That
charge is a perversion of the truth! This fleshly Man, Jesus, who
stands before these angry Jews, has been sent by God. He has come
in loving obedience to do the works of Him who sent Him. The

works of the Son and the Father are the same, for the Son and the Father are One! That eternal, intimate relationship is the source of His authority and mission. The initiative is God's, not man's!

So He is utterly dependent upon the Father. He can do nothing without Him! He does only what He sees the Father doing. It is because the Father loves the Son that He has revealed everything to Him. The Son will continue to do even greater works throughout His earthly ministry which will culminate in the raising of Lazarus from the dead!

One wonders what would happen in the life of our churches if the works we seek to do were the work of the Father, rather than our own, if they grew out of our intimate, loving relationship with the Father instead of coming out of our brainstorming sessions and program packets. There is little power or life in any work we do, even though we call it Christian, where the source is our own ingenuity and effort!

LIFE AND JUDGMENT ARE IN THE SON

21 "For as the Father raises the dead and gives life to them, even so the Son gives life to whom He will.

22 "For the Father judges no one, but has committed all judgment to the Son,

23 "that all should honor the Son just as they honor the Father. He who does not honor the Son does not honor the Father who sent Him.

24 "Most assuredly, I say to you, he who hears My word and believes in Him who sent Me has everlasting life, and shall not come into judgment, but has passed from death into life.

25 "Most assuredly, I say to you, the hour is coming, and now is, when the dead will hear the voice of the Son of God; and those who hear will live.

26 "For as the Father has life in Himself, so He has granted the Son to have life in Himself,

27 "and has given Him authority to execute judgment also, because He is the Son of Man.

28 "Do not marvel at this; for the hour is coming in which all who are in the graves will hear His voice

29 "and come forth—those who have done good,

to the resurrection of life, and those who have done
evil, to the resurrection of condemnation.

30 "I can of Myself do nothing. As I hear, I judge;
and My judgment is righteous, because I do not seek
My own will but the will of the Father who sent Me.

John 5:21–30

The Father has given His power of life to the Son. The work of
the Father is revealed in the works of the Son as He freely shares
life with whomever He chooses. Every devout Jew knew that God
was the Source of all life—not only in the act of creation, but even
in raising the dead. They accepted the accounts of life being given
to the dead in the Old Testament records, but for this itinerant
preacher to claim that gift of life was an affront to their rigid ortho-
doxy. Yet, specific proof that the life of God was in Him was before
them in the one who had been healed.

With that power came the authority of judgment. This, too, the
Father had committed to the Son. In His coming, *"the ruler of this
world is judged"* (John 16:11). Those who reject the gift of life come
under that judgment. These very Jews who refused to hear and accept
this One who stood before them are even now experiencing judgment!
All through the Gospel there is a "division of the house" wherever
Jesus goes. His words and deeds either bring men to acceptance or
rejection, to life or death. There is no neutral ground. Since life and
judgment have been given to the Son, He is to be honored as is
the Father; and if the Son is dishonored, the Father will be dishonored.

There is both life and judgment in the challenging invitation Jesus
issues to the very antagonists He faces. If they hear His Word—
His whole message—and through that Word come to believe in the
One who sent Him, they have eternal life at this moment. But there
is judgment for those who refuse to hear. They remain in death.
This invitation and challenge comes to each of us. It is addressed
to me! At His bidding I can either take up my bed and walk or
linger in death among the lame and blind.

For the third time in this discourse Jesus says, *"Most assuredly"* (v.
25). These are life and death words, for the destiny of those who
listen hangs on how they hear and respond. There is an *"hour coming
. . . when the dead will hear the voice of the Son"* and come forth to face
judgment. The Father has given Him the authority to speak that
final word. But that time of crisis and judgment is also now! In Jesus,

the present moment of decision and the final hour of judgment are brought together. The word of life and death that He will speak at the end is heard now. And the response given in this moment of faith or rejection will be clearly known at the end. So all of us live in an eschatological tension between this time of decision and the final revelation of all things.

But the place and time for making that decision is now, in this fleshly situation. The One who faces these men does not call for some kind of mystical, unearthly vision or activity, but for a concrete, specific decision in the midst of life. They are invited to hear and believe and follow in their rabbinic robes or at their fish nets or carpenter benches. Here is where we all know either life or judgment.

The man Jesus, who issues this invitation, calls Himself the *"Son of Man,"* in this context the One spoken of in Daniel 7:13, 14.

"And behold, One like the Son of Man,
Coming with the clouds of heaven! . . .
Then to Him was given dominion and glory and a kingdom, . . .
That all peoples, nations, and languages should serve Him. . . .
And His kingdom the one
Which shall not be destroyed."

This mighty Man of God, now clothed in flesh, confronts these men. This is the "place of decision."

That authority to call forth the dead to life or condemnation is not His own. It has been given Him by His Father. Since Jesus lives only to do the will of His Father, His judgments are righteous.

THE WITNESSES WHO SURROUND HIM

31 "If I bear witness of Myself, My witness is not true.

32 "There is another who bears witness of Me, and I know that the witness which He witnesses of Me is true.

33 "You sent to John, and he bore witness to the truth.

34 "Yet I do not receive testimony from man, but I say these things that you may be saved.

35 "He was the burning and shining lamp, and you were willing for a time to rejoice in his light.

36 "But I have a greater witness than John's; for the works which the Father has given Me to finish—the very works that I do—bear witness of Me, that the Father has sent Me.

37 "And the Father Himself, who sent Me, has testified of Me. You have neither heard His voice at any time, nor seen His form.

38 "But you do not have His word abiding in you, because whom He sent, Him you do not believe.

39 "You search the Scriptures, for in them you think you have eternal life; and these are they which testify of Me.

John 5:31–39

Day after day all kinds of needy people come to our church doors asking for some kind of help—a few dollars for gas to get up the road a bit, some morsels of food for hungry stomachs, or some rent money so they will not be evicted. And so often they will pull out some dog-eared papers which are supposed to prove their identity and need. And so many of us are trying to do the same thing, trying to prove who or what we are to people around us. "Let me tell you who I am." "Look at me; I'm really doing some things that are important."

But Jesus had no need to prove who He was or why He had come. If He had constantly pointed to Himself, His own witness would have eventually become a lie. He had come to glorify His Father, not Himself. He was a Man of transparent integrity surrounded by witnesses who eagerly validated His mission.

His Father gave these differing witnesses their authority, and was constantly placing His stamp of approval on Jesus and His work!

At the outset of Jesus' ministry there was one witness who prepared the way for His coming. For some, John the Baptist had been a passing fad or another interesting prophet. Yet the power of his influence lived on. In faithfully pointing to "the Lamb of God who takes away the sin of the world," John had been a "burning and shining lamp," a witness to the Truth.

And the works which Jesus was doing could not be divorced from who He was! Nor could they be divorced from the One who had sent Him! They, too, were a witness. So while many were dazzled and intrigued and even made shallow commitments because of His signs and wonders, there were others who knew they could only be the work of God. What they saw Jesus doing revealed the glory of the Father.

I have just asked a man I hardly know to "scalp" our lawn, which he has agreed to do for ninety dollars. And the reason I have hired him is because a dear neighbor whose word I trust said, "Oh yes, Tony does great work. He really took care of my lawn." It is the same with Jesus! He could be trusted because of His works!

Nothing would have happened—no work of mercy, no teaching with authority, no sharing of life—if the Father's approval had not rested on the Son. He could do nothing of Himself! All that Jesus was and said and did witnessed to the intimate, eternal, loving relationship He shared with the Father!

And finally, the Scriptures bear witness to Him. On every page there is some promise, some claim, some echo which speaks of His living presence. The Scriptures, rightly understood, are centered in Him and lead us to Him!

THE TRAGIC REJECTION

40 "But you are not willing to come to Me that you may have life.

41 "I do not receive honor from men.

42 "But I know you, that you do not have the love of God in you.

43 "I have come in My Father's name, and you do not receive Me; if another comes in his own name, him you will receive.

44 "How can you believe, who receive honor from one another, and do not seek the honor that comes from the only God?

45 "Do not think that I shall accuse you to the Father; there is one who accuses you—Moses, in whom you trust.

46 "For if you believed Moses, you would believe Me; for he wrote about Me.

47 "But if you do not believe his writings, how will
you believe My words?"

John 5:40–47

What an awesome tragedy, then, that the very ones who searched the Scriptures, who prided themselves on being experts as they worked over every jot and tittle, thinking in all this they had eternal life, were not willing to come to the One of whom the Scriptures spoke. They rejected Him! Here He was standing before them, bold and clear, inviting them and challenging them, and they turned on Him in anger—all the time believing they were being faithful to the Scriptures. So they did not hear the voice of the Father, nor could they perceive His form, and in the end, the words they studied did not abide in them.

Because they would not come to Him, they did not have the love of God in them. They had rejected the love of God, and in their rejection, they would not allow the One who came in love to bridge the chasm. So they ended up honoring one another, which almost sounds like what goes on at some ministers' conventions. They became spiritually blind, accepting anyone who came along as an authority, rather than the One who had come in the Father's name!

I have seen much power and life released in a great variety of Bible study groups. As a matter of fact, I have helped initiate and encourage the formation of many of these groups since my first encounter with Faith at Work years ago. But I am also aware that these groups can become self-righteous ghettos filled with criticism and pride, spiritual dead ends, where the members strain over commentaries, as well as one another's opinions and interpretations, but where there is no love or obedience. The Scriptures then do not lead to life, but to death. The participants may honor one another, but in so doing have neither heard the voice nor seen the form of the Lord of the Scriptures. It is better then to deal with unlettered, fresh, and at times almost vulgar, new believers who are eager to devour the Word because here they have found life—hot and powerful!

The great irony in all this is that the very one these Jewish leaders felt they knew and trusted, Moses, ended up being their accuser. For if they really understood and believed what Moses had written, they would have accepted Jesus, the One to whom he bore witness. But they misread and misinterpreted because they came to the Scrip-

121

ture with hard, unbelieving hearts. So they missed His message and consequently missed life. They were condemned, having rejected the One of whom he spoke!

NOTES

1. Raymond E. Brown, *The Gospel According to John I–XII,* pp. 206–07.
2. Ibid., p. 207.
3. Ibid., p. 208.

CHAPTER SEVEN

A Costly Meal

John 6:1–71

Jesus Spreads a Feast

1 After these things Jesus went over the Sea of
Galilee, which is the Sea of Tiberias.

2 Then a great multitude followed Him, because
they saw His signs which He performed on those who
were diseased.

3 And Jesus went up on a mountain, and there
He sat with His disciples.

4 Now the Passover, a feast of the Jews, was near.

5 Then Jesus lifted up His eyes, and seeing a great
multitude coming toward Him, He said to Philip,
"Where shall we buy bread, that these may eat?"

6 But this He said to test him, for He Himself knew
what He would do.

7 Philip answered Him, "Two hundred denarii
worth of bread is not sufficient for them, that every
one of them may have a little."

8 One of His disciples, Andrew, Simon Peter's
brother, said to Him,

9 "There is a lad here who has five barley loaves
and two small fish, but what are they among so many?"

10 Then Jesus said, "Make the people sit down."
Now there was much grass in the place. So the men
sat down, in number about five thousand.

11 And Jesus took the loaves, and when He had
given thanks He distributed them to the disciples, and
the disciples to those sitting down; and likewise of
the fish, as much as they wanted.

12 So when they were filled, He said to His

disciples, "Gather up the fragments that remain, so that nothing is lost."

13 Therefore they gathered them up, and filled twelve baskets with the fragments of the five barley loaves which were left over by those who had eaten.

14 Then those men, when they had seen the sign that Jesus did, said, "This is truly the Prophet who is to come into the world."

15 Therefore when Jesus perceived that they were about to come and take Him by force to make Him king, He departed again to a mountain by Himself alone.

John 6:1–15

The phrase, *"After these things,"* probably covers several weeks of eventful ministry, a time during which John the Baptist had come to his gruesome end at the hand of the nervous, fearful Herod. And Jesus had withdrawn! The synoptic Gospels have given this account in some detail (Matt. 4:12–13, Mark 6:14–32, Luke 9:7–10). Surely grief and a poignant sense of loneliness must have engulfed Jesus as He poured out His heart to His Father. John's faithfulness and flaming courage had cost him his life. Surely Jesus could not help pondering the agony of His own approaching death.

But even here the crowd followed Him, because *"they saw His signs which He performed on those who were diseased."* They found Him on a *"mountain,"* probably a hill, with His disciples, eager to spend all the time He could with these men. Undoubtedly they were on the east side of the Sea of Galilee, also identified here as Tiberias because of the nearby city built in about A.D. 20 by Herod Antipas to honor the emperor. John never forgets his Greek and Roman readers.

His comment about this being near the time of the Passover highlights the deeper meaning of this occasion. *"A feast of the Jews,"* he calls it, once again to help his Gentile audience (v. 4). Jesus could not deal with this great throng of hungry people without being deeply conscious of the time and setting. The sanctity of the Paschal supper had been a part of His life since early boyhood. He was well aware that the most perfect animal available must be slain that its blood might be poured out on the horns of the altar and its flesh become the food His family would eat together. There was a solemn mystery about this celebration which commemorated a past event but which also gave hope for present deliverance. The memory of the Baptist's ringing cry by the river, "Behold! The Lamb of God who takes away the sin of the World!" (John 1:29), identifying Jesus as the ultimate sacrifice must have surged through Him as He dealt with this crowd.

So Jesus seems eager to welcome this host of people like a Father gathering His family for the Paschal meal as they keep *"coming toward Him."* He knows how He will provide for their needs, even though His disciples only point out how meager their resources are. It is fitting that Jesus should ask Philip where they could buy bread since he was from nearby Bethsaida. He answers that all the money they can gather up, the equivalent of two hundred days' wages at fifteen cents a day, would hardly provide even a small scrap for each person. This sounds much like scores of discussions I have heard over the years at church finance committee meetings.

Then Andrew, who earlier had brought his brother Simon, now brings a lad, who has but five barley loaves and two fish. This was bread eaten by the very poor, and the fish were little more than large dried minnows. No wonder Andrew questions *"But what are they among so many?"*

Now Jesus takes over! He commands the people to sit down like a great family invited to a sumptuous banquet. There is no white table cloth, but *"much grass"* for all to recline on (v. 10).

As He accepts the boy's gift He gives thanks. And in the mystery of that blessing, the small becomes great. They all received *"as much as they wanted."* With Jesus there is always enough and more! What a lesson in God's sovereign, gracious provision for these timid, hesitant disciples who were now given the honor of bringing this meal out to group after group spread out on the hillside. Then Jesus commands them to gather up what had not been eaten that nothing be lost. The Creator does not squander His creation.

Jesus gives sacred meaning to the daily bread which graces our tables. Without Him we merely selfishly satisfy our appetites as we thoughtlessly gulp down whatever we can pick up at some fast food place. We often carelessly toss out whatever remains uneaten, filling countless garbage cans with our leftovers while two-thirds of the people of the world fiercely struggle for enough scraps to stay alive.

This meal on the hillside was a sign foreshadowing that later eating and drinking which was to become a memorial of His sacrificial death.

That "last supper" was to be a covenant that the offering of His flesh and blood, which seemed so shamefully insignificant to those non-believing bystanders, was God's saving provision for the world's salvation. Again what seemed so little became so vastly much.

And the feeding on the hillside could never have come to pass without the *"thanks"* He gave. This word "thanks" is translated from the Greek word *eucharisteo*. And His thanks are at the heart of His covenant with His chosen ones in His last supper. Little wonder then that centuries later we celebrate the eucharist, a meal of thanks for His sacrifice.

The crowd responds to this *"sign"* by insisting that He must truly be *"the Prophet who is to come into the world,"* the return of Elijah or one greater (v. 14). Would not this new Prophet give them permanent physical security, full bellies and instant healing, and supply all their fleshly needs? So they will make Him their king! What an irony that they believe they can pressure the One who is already King into being a king on their terms.

But Jesus has dealt with the temptation to use His spiritual power for self-centered earthly ends before when Satan asked Jesus to prove himself by turning stones into bread or calling down a legion of angels, which would draw a huge following quickly (Matt. 4:3–7). He will have none of this! So He simply walks away from the crowd to be alone again. He has come to call men to a radical, costly disciple-ship, not to a kingdom of bread. He will be King only of those who enter by the narrow door of spiritual surrender.

THE ASSURANCE OF HIS PRESENCE

16 And when evening came, His disciples went down to the sea,

17 got into the boat, and went over the sea toward Capernaum. And it was now dark, and Jesus had not come to them.

18 Then the sea arose because a great wind was blowing.

19 So when they had rowed about three or four miles, they saw Jesus walking on the sea and drawing near the boat; and they were afraid.

20 But He said to them, "It is I; do not be afraid."

21 Then they willingly received Him into the boat,

and immediately the boat was at the land where they
were going.

John 6:16–21

The disciples must have been baffled by this turn of events. Why
would He walk away from a great opportunity to enlist a whole
army of disciples if He were really serious about His new kingdom
movement? But they let Him go off alone and apparently agree to
meet Him later in or near Capernaum.

So, these disciples push out to cross the sea, but shortly find themselves in dire straits. For now darkness and a violent wind and a
heavy sea are suddenly about to overwhelm them. And Jesus is not
with them. What a picture of our contemporary existence—terrifying
problems that defy any human solution, the breakdown of our primary human relationships, violence and anger becoming more and
more the disorder of the day, while a sense of hopelessness and despair
seem to paralyze the human spirit. Everything seems out of control.
It is a dark, stormy night at sea. And there does not seem to be
anyone in the boat who can save us.

But in the midst of this violent Galilean storm, a barely visible
figure can be seen walking on the water toward their boat. How
strange! John writes, *"and they were afraid"* (v. 19). They were probably
thinking how much better off they would have been if they had
stayed back there on the shore with the crowd. But then they hear
that strong, familiar voice, *"It is I; do not be afraid"* (v. 20). And they
eagerly receive Him into the boat.

Jesus is giving these men the powerful assurance of His presence.
He will be to them all that *"It is I"* can mean, however dark and
stormy any night may become. So it is because of who He is that
Jesus can give these men the peace that overcomes their fear. When
Jesus is welcomed into the boat, they *"immediately"* come to the land
where they were going. His presence will always bring us to our
destination in His own time and way.

I have vivid memories of a long night of feverish nightmares when,
as a boy of seven or eight, I cried out again and again because, in
my fantasy, my bedroom was being stuffed with huge boxes and I
was suffocating. Then in the darkness, I felt the strong arm of my
father and his quiet words, "Don't worry, Roger, everything is going
to be all right. I am here!" That changed everything. Surely the intimate, personal coming of Jesus on the water to join His disciples

brought far more peace and comfort than even my father's coming.

The unconditional guarantee of Jesus' presence to the end must have called forth Simon Peter's confession later, "Lord, to whom shall we go? You have the words of eternal life" (6:68).

DIALOGUE AND DECISION

22 On the following day, when the people who were standing on the other side of the sea saw that there was no other boat there, except that one which His disciples had entered, and that Jesus had not entered the boat with His disciples, but His disciples had gone away alone—

23 however, other boats came from Tiberias, near the place where they ate bread after the Lord had given thanks—

24 when the people therefore saw that Jesus was not there, nor His disciples, they also got into boats and came to Capernaum, seeking Jesus.

25 And when they found Him on the other side of the sea, they said to Him, "Rabbi, when did You come here?"

26 Jesus answered them and said, "Most assuredly, I say to you, you seek Me, not because you saw the signs, but because you ate of the loaves and were filled.

27 "Do not labor for the food which perishes, but for the food which endures to everlasting life, which the Son of Man will give you, because God the Father has set His seal on Him."

28 Then they said to Him, "What shall we do, that we may work the works of God?"

29 Jesus answered and said to them, "This is the work of God, that you believe in Him whom He sent."

30 Therefore they said to Him, "What sign will You perform then, that we may see it and believe You? What work will You do?

31 "Our fathers ate the manna in the desert; as it is written, *'He gave them bread from heaven to eat.'"*

32 Then Jesus said to them, "Most assuredly, I say to you, Moses did not give you the bread from heaven,

but My Father gives you the true bread from heaven.

33 "For the bread of God is He who comes down from heaven and gives life to the world."

34 Then they said to Him, "Lord, give us this bread always."

35 And Jesus said to them, "I am the bread of life. He who comes to Me shall never hunger, and he who believes in Me shall never thirst.

36 "But I said to you that you also have seen Me and yet do not believe.

37 "All that the Father gives Me will come to Me, and the one who comes to Me I will by no means cast out.

38 "For I have come down from heaven, not to do My own will, but the will of Him who sent Me.

39 "This is the will of the Father who sent Me, that of all He has given Me I should lose nothing, but should raise it up at the last day.

40 "And this is the will of Him who sent Me, that everyone who sees the Son and believes in Him may have everlasting life; and I will raise him up at the last day."

41 The Jews then murmured against Him, because He said, "I am the bread which came down from heaven."

42 And they said, "Is not this Jesus, the son of Joseph, whose father and mother we know? How is it then that He says, 'I have come down from heaven'?"

43 Jesus therefore answered and said to them, "Do not murmur among yourselves.

44 "No one can come to Me unless the Father who sent Me draws him; and I will raise him up at the last day.

45 "It is written in the prophets, *'And they shall all be taught by God.'* Therefore everyone who has heard and learned from the Father comes to Me.

46 "Not that anyone has seen the Father, except He who is from God; He has seen the Father.

47 "Most assuredly, I say to you, he who believes in Me has everlasting life.

48 "I am the bread of life.

49 "Your fathers ate the manna in the wilderness, and are dead.

50 "This is the bread which comes down from heaven, that a man may eat of it and not die.

51 "I am the living bread which came down from heaven. If anyone eats of this bread, he will live forever; and the bread that I shall give is My flesh, which I shall give for the life of the world."

52 The Jews therefore quarreled among themselves, saying, "How can this Man give us His flesh to eat?"

53 Then Jesus said to them, "Most assuredly, I say to you, unless you eat the flesh of the Son of Man and drink His blood, you have no life in you.

54 "Whoever eats My flesh and drinks My blood has eternal life, and I will raise him up at the last day.

55 "For My flesh is food indeed, and My blood is drink indeed.

56 "He who eats My flesh and drinks My blood abides in Me, and I in him.

57 "As the living Father sent Me, and I live because of the Father, so he who feeds on Me will live because of Me.

58 "This is the bread which came down from heaven, not as your fathers ate the manna, and are dead. He who eats this bread will live forever."

59 These things He said in the synagogue as He taught in Capernaum.

John 6:22–59

Exposing False Motives (vv. 22–26). The following day a crowd gathers, almost greedily, to satisfy both their curiosity and their bellies. Some even come in boats from Tiberias, *"near the place where they ate bread after the Lord had given thanks"* (v. 23). John speaks of the event so modestly. The deeper meaning of what has taken place seems to be conveyed by his referring to Jesus as *"Lord,"* the sacred name for the living God of Israel.

There appears to be some confused wondering among those gathering. They seem to know that the disciples have left in a boat, but without Jesus. He is the One they want, but where has He gone?

So they strike out for Capernaum *"seeking Jesus,"* apparently aware that this was where He centered much of His ministry.

When they find Him, they address Him as *"Rabbi"* (v. 25), perhaps expecting that He will teach them some new thing. But their question, *"When did You come here?"* is almost a petulant "Why did you leave us?" Food for their bellies is really more important than anything He can teach them. How true this is of much introverted, narcissistic modern-day religion, even that which calls itself "evangelical." "What can I get out of this?" "Will it save my skin?" Listen to the invitation being given, "Why don't you come to Jesus right now? He will take care of all your needs."

But as with Nicodemus, Jesus brushes that question aside and unmasks their real motive. They have come seeking Him, not because the gift of food has been a sign through which they have glimpsed the glory of God, but because they ate and *"were filled."* Here Jesus uses a very earthy term, literally meaning they were "satisfied with food as animals with fodder."[1]

Belief, the Work of God (vv. 27–29). As tasty and nourishing as the loaves and fish may have been, this is food which perishes. The whole digestive process, so necessary to sustain physical life, is part of an order that passes away. Death is its inevitable end. How foolish then to make this food the end of all labor. Jesus does not despise the fleshly needs of human existence. If so, He would never have come in the flesh, nor fed these people. But He is speaking of an earthly system that will pass away.

However, there is a food which *"endures to everlasting life"* (v. 27). It feeds the deepest center of human existence, the spiritual self, and continues to satisfy. This food is not a reward that can be earned, but is given by the Son of Man, whose origin is in heaven, but who is identified with all men. He is the authentic Source of this everlasting bread because the Father approves what He does. He bears the seal of the Father's ownership.

Still these people do not understand who it is that has fed them, nor the meaning of this gift. They only seem to hear the phrase *"labor for the food"* and assume there is more work they must do. What can they do to please God? They are caught in the old legalisms, slaves of the flesh. But the food that Jesus shares is given by the Father. It is a work of grace, food that cannot be earned, only received.

So it is the response of faith, believing in the One whom the Father has sent, receiving what He has to give; that is the *"work of God."*

The Greek word John uses for *"believe"* is *pisteuo*, an active verb, not the form *pistis*, a passive noun.

Living Bread, but by What Sign? (vv. 30–33). Neither the feeding nor the teaching can satisfy these people. They clamor for an even greater sign. The flesh always cries out for some final visible proof, a last climactic argument, which will wrap it all up and make belief inevitable. They are insisting that they be taken care of permanently, even quoting Scripture, as if Jesus needed to be reminded that their fathers had been fed manna in the wilderness for forty years. They are not shy in demanding a sign even greater than that. Then they will see and believe. But hardened, carnal eyes and hearts can never understand and accept what can only be grasped by the Spirit.

Now Jesus uses again those crucial words, *"most assuredly."* If they do not hear what He says now, they will continue in darkness and death. Even the physical bread given in the wilderness, to which they refer, was not Moses' doing, but God's. And that gift which sustained physical life was a sign, a promise, of the *"true bread"* that the Father is now giving.

The *"true bread"* is the bread of God—bread that comes directly from Him, not even by the hand of Moses. This bread is personal, *"He who comes down"* (v. 33), not an impersonal law. It comes continuously, not sporadically. And the life that is in the Father, which He shares with the Son, is given to the whole world, not a particular race or chosen few. This is a sweeping statement of Jesus' mission made to people who have a parochial expectation of the Messiah's coming.

Are we not like that crowd, often particularizing and cutting down the vast ministry of Jesus to our comfortable "in" group? Church becomes a social, institutional world, subtly or deliberately eliminating the "out" group, the poor, the alcoholic, the aged, the divorced, or the rich.

"I am the bread of life" (vv. 34–36). Now this crowd, so enslaved to the flesh, continues to make its demand, still not understanding what Jesus is saying. How glibly they call Him *"Lord,"* without submitting to His authority, but expecting to gain a favor. They are hungry to have this "bread from heaven," which they still assume will be a continuous supply of physical bread. They have neither heard nor grasped that the One standing before them is the source of that life.

So Jesus openly declares His identity. He is the "I AM," who faced and called Moses at the burning bush, the One, as John has earlier affirmed, by whom "all things were made." He is "the food which endures." Sooner or later any serious dialogue with Jesus will bring us to the place where we must deal with who He is.

The revelation of His identity is also His invitation. As He opens His heart, He invites anyone who hears to come and believe in Him, not to satisfy a physical appetite nor to assume that we can earn this bread. That would be false pride. We can only come as beggars, hungry and needy, if we are to accept the "true bread" which only He, the "I AM," can give. The inclusion of thirst here seems to under-line the total fulfillment of all our needs.

However, no sooner has the invitation been given when Jesus speaks sadly of their unbelief. They have seen Him and what He has done, but only with physical eyes. So they have failed to under-stand even the meaning of His invitation.

The Father Gives: The Son Keeps (vv. 37–40). In this passage, Jesus moves from the misunderstanding and unbelief of this crowd to the mystery of belief. It is only by the sovereign grace of God that we come to believe. It is not our own doing. For coming to accept and believe in the One whom the Father has sent is finally not a human decision based on convincing and reasonable arguments. We cannot talk ourselves into faith. Often in our free church tradition we have overemphasized our human capacity "to come to Jesus" or "to be saved." Salvation then becomes "our business" because we put human choice in the center.

It is true, however, that there is a response that we humans make, a sacred journey often fraught with struggle, from indifference and unbelief to faith and acceptance.

But it is God's sovereign grace that invites us, chooses us, and marks out the way of this pilgrimage into faith. The initiative is His! We respond! As John Calvin has put it, "Faith is not at man's disposal, so that this man or that may believe indiscriminately and by chance, but that God elects those whom He hands over, as it were, to his Son."[2] Here we see the perfect harmony of the Father and the Son. Eight times in this chapter Jesus speaks of His having "come from heaven." The Son is eager to please the Father, for the will of the Father is His will. So whoever the Father draws and gives to the Son, He receives and keeps.

"All" are kept! None is cast out!

The salvation of those who are drawn and believe is assured. In

vv. 39–54 Jesus speaks of keeping these till the end, of "raising these up at the last day" four times. It is not our feeble hold on Christ that is our assurance of salvation, but His sure grip on those who believe.

The Father is patiently working, gathering His whole family of believers, a complete, inclusive community. This calling together of God's people is the deepest key to history. "This gospel of the kingdom will be preached in all the world . . . then the end will come" (Matt. 24:14).

Murmuring Rather than Being Taught (vv. 41–47). It is the *"Jews,"* the term used for those who constantly oppose Jesus, who now murmur against Him. It is the same noise of unbelief their fathers made in the wilderness. This crowd is becoming more and more aware of the staggering implications of what Jesus has been saying. How can this nondescript, ordinary appearing Man make the absurd claim that He is "bread from heaven"? What blasphemy! Why, this is only the *"son of Joseph."* The miracle of Jesus' birth is unknown to the general populace. His *"father and mother"* are small-town laboring folks seen at the religious feast days or at family gatherings. How can this man then make such a ridiculous statement? The vast, incredible humanity of God is here revealed again. Jesus puts Himself at their mercy, even though He is a King hidden in the flesh of a simple peasant.

Jesus meets their anger and unbelief head on. Only those who have been *"taught by God"* are drawn and sent to the Son. The everlasting, patient Teacher is God Himself (Ps. 71:17, Ps. 119:102, Isa. 54:3, Jer. 32:33). It is only the humble, teachable ones who hear and understand what the Father says. His teaching opens and prepares them for the coming of the One whom He has sent. So they believe and obey and discover in Him eternal life.

What an indictment that the very people who assume they know what God has said, because they have pored over the Scriptures, discussing every jot and tittle, have not been taught by God! Their rejection of the One whom He has sent means they have read, but never understood.

But what a joy when someone comes, eager and open though theologically unlearned, to trust and confess Christ with unashamed freshness. One knows immediately they have been taught and brought by the Father to the Son. Such is the case with Bounheng, a new Laotian believer who has come into our "international community," a part of our church family. He has come in recent weeks out of the old life of superstitious Buddhism and drunken partying into a joyful radiance in Christ. He is literally soaking up the Scriptures and his profound, childlike grasp of God's truth is almost breathtaking. Whenever he speaks or shares, his face glows with the light of Christ and he becomes our teacher. He is being taught by God.

My Flesh for the World (vv. 48–51). Again Jesus makes that simple, unequivocal assertion, *"I am the bread of life."* The contrast with all physical bread, particularly the manna given their fathers in the wilderness, is sharply drawn. That bread, Jesus says, they ate and are dead. But Jesus is *"the bread"* which comes down from heaven. His coming is once for all. The Incarnation will not be repeated! Yet He continues to come. Whoever *"eats of this bread"* will not die. He states it negatively at first, contrasting it with the physical bread. Then, as is so often done in this Gospel, it is stated positively, *"He will live forever."*

But how do we eat this bread? For even eating physical bread is a mystery and a gift of grace. On a few rare occasions I have been overwhelmed watching desperately hungry people gulping down a few scraps of bread, far more precious than pieces of gold.

But here is an ever deeper reality, the intimate, personal, trusting act of eating the bread of life. This is, as John Calvin has said, "the effect or work of faith" for "Christ is eaten only by faith."[3] So as Nicodemus was invited to be born again by "water and Spirit" and the woman at the well urged to quench her thirst by drawing and drinking "living water," these people are invited to eat of this *"bread of life."*

In verse 51 Jesus makes an even more offensive claim. The bread these Jews are invited to eat is His flesh, which He shall give for the life of the world. "Flesh" to their ears is a lowly, vulgar word. How can the life of God be given through flesh "which in its appearance is contemptible"?[4] And yet it is precisely here, in this Man of flesh, that God, in His surprising mercy, has set life before us. That which has been despised as the "material of death" God has chosen to make the vehicle of redemption. For Jesus offers both His life of perfect obedience and His death on the cross in the flesh. Here is where we discover and receive life.

And this *"living bread"* is flesh that is *given,* not just for those to whom He speaks, but for the whole world. This is his vast, far-flung mission. The final giving of His flesh will be His sacrifice on the cross where He offers Himself as the Victim. He is the unique

Paschal Lamb, who will be slain that the world might be given life; He is the only true food, which brings life when it is eaten. Here is the new Passover for the entire human race.

But, like the Jews, we are often offended by this fleshly offer. We would rather have a vague, diffused presence or some impersonal abstract deity, not a particular Man who has come from heaven to live among us in the flesh at a very specific time and place. He is too near, too much with us. Our specific sins are now unmasked. We are caught swearing and telling lies, succumbing to our lusts and killing one another. So we struggle to make the flesh of the Son of Man unreal, to keep God Incarnate out of our world. This docetic lie, this denial of Jesus' flesh, is so deep a perversion that John calls it elsewhere "the spirit of the Antichrist" (1 John 4:2–3).

For the Jews, the Final Obscenity (vv. 52–59). Earlier the Jews have murmured, but now they *"quarreled among themselves."* They are confused and angered by what they have heard. This Man has led them to face issues vastly different from anything they had expected. Some in this crowd have heard and begun to move toward belief. They are wondering, "Perhaps we will follow this One who seems to speak the truth, strange as it seems." But they face a hostile majority who refuse to accept anything Jesus has said. And out of their wrangling a question emerges, *"How can this Man give us His flesh to eat?"*, a completely sensible question if one is referring to physical eating alone.

So Jesus comes at them a last time. Their spiritual destiny hangs on how they now hear and respond. He is not presenting some new religious option which can be added to what they already know. But He is laying before them a single, life-and-death spiritual imperative.

Jesus insists, *"Unless you eat the flesh of the Son of Man and drink His blood, you have no life in you."* Then He states it positively in verse 54, *"Whoever eats My flesh and drinks My blood has eternal life, and I will raise him up at the last day."* This feasting must finally be experienced to be understood! Professor Westcott has said it simply, "To 'eat' and to 'drink' is to take to oneself by a voluntary act that which is without, and then to assimilate it and make it part of oneself. It is, as it were, faith regarded in its converse action. Faith throws the believer upon and into its object. This spiritual eating and drinking brings the object of faith into the believer."[5]

This eating and drinking is continuous and ongoing, not simply a meal at the beginning! Those who feast on Him constantly dwell in Him. He becomes their permanent "home." This is also a reciprocal relationship, a "double dwelling." They dwell in Him, and He dwells in them.

Recently our beloved son-in-law, Frank, was sharing some of the joys in bringing his wife and children back to Austria to meet his family. One of the highlights of the whole trip was the visit to his aged grandmother, who had cared for him as a small boy when his father and mother were separated. He spoke tenderly of her caring relationship with him, frequently allowing him to sleep with her even though at times he wet the bed. Now she was in ill health, spending most of her time in bed. Going back to see her he was somewhat concerned. How would nine-year-old Elizabeth and five-year-old Sarah understand and accept his grandmother, and how would she welcome them? After all, they had never met before and had no language in common.

But when the little girls saw her for the first time in her bed, there was immediate rapport. They jumped into the bed as they greeted their great-grandmother with joy. There was instant communication deeper than words. And their father rejoiced. Is this not a simple picture of what it means to continually dwell in our Father and He in us?

This bread that is eaten and the blood that is drunk are separate realities, signs of Jesus' life and death. It was through His flesh that Jesus lived out a life of holy obedience. In eating His flesh we partake of this life of surrender and begin to manifest His life in all those fleshly places into which we are thrown or called—at sales conventions, on used car lots, laundering our clothes, making love and bearing children, watching TV and going to church. It is in our temptations and defeats, our joys and our victories, that we are to bear in our bodies the marks of the Lord Jesus (Gal. 6:17).

But we are also to drink His blood. How abhorrent this was to the Jews who had been forbidden by law to partake of blood. But in this act we appropriate, or take into ourselves, His life sacrificed, His expiation, and His atonement. In accepting His life poured out we are reconciled to God and live in grace as forgiven sinners. The Son of Man, the One who has identified Himself with us, offers us this incredible feast of life. We shall become like Him as we continue to feed on Him.

It is the life of the Father that the Son shares with us. The Son has come in obedience to the Father and has no life apart from Him.

So He who feeds on the Son is given the life of the Father. We then have the same relation to the Son that the Son has to the Father and are as dependent upon Him as the Son is on the Father. What an incredible relationship!

The primary purpose of these verses is to teach us how to feed on the Son of Man, to take Him into our innermost being by faith. But surely an important secondary teaching here is the meaning of the Lord's Supper. Is there not a particular sense in which Christ's presence is made real among His people when we eat the bread and drink the wine?

For too long many of us have stripped this celebration of its deeper meaning, making it a barren exercise. We have spoken of the Eucharist as being "only a memorial" when we partake of the "elements," a term never used in Scripture. It is as if we have allowed our subconscious and unexamined prejudices against the "sacramentarians" to define the meaning of the Lord's Supper.

But it is Jesus' teaching and the giving of Himself that guide and inform us in our understanding of the Supper. He is the Host who gathers us and has us feed on Himself. We are constituted as His people by the very events we celebrate, fed with fleshly, common gifts. And is there not a mystery and reality in the bread and wine which goes beyond a remembrance of Christ and His sacrifice? We cannot redo what Jesus has accomplished for our salvation once for all, nor can we say that Jesus *is* the wine and bread. But surely we are nourished by Him in a unique way when we partake of this physical food. And as that crowd of five thousand became a family when Jesus fed them, so we, in eating and drinking, become a believing community. We do not eat and drink as isolated individuals.

If we are to grow in our understanding of the Lord's Supper, we need humility and openness so that we may learn from one another as the Lord teaches all His people the meaning of the Supper.

THOSE WHO FINALLY REMAIN

60 Therefore many of His disciples, when they heard this, said, "This is a hard saying; who can understand it?"

61 When Jesus knew in Himself that His disciples murmured about this, He said to them, "Does this offend you?

62 "What then if you should see the Son of Man ascend where He was before?

63 "It is the Spirit who gives life; the flesh profits nothing. The words that I speak to you are spirit, and they are life.

64 "But there are some of you who do not believe." For Jesus knew from the beginning who they were who did not believe, and who would betray Him.

65 And He said, "Therefore I said to you that no one can come to Me unless it has been granted to him by My Father."

66 From that time many of His disciples went back and walked with Him no more.

67 Then Jesus said to the twelve, "Do you also want to go away?"

68 Then Simon Peter answered Him, "Lord, to whom shall we go? You have the words of eternal life.

69 "Also we have come to believe and know that You are the Christ, the Son of the living God."

70 Jesus answered them, "Did I not choose you, the twelve, and one of you is a devil?"

71 He spoke of Judas Iscariot, the son of Simon, for it was he who would betray Him, being one of the twelve.

John 6:60–71

Words That Live and Divide (vv. 60–66). In the truth of Jesus' teaching and the depth of His invitation there comes a division of the house. The casual, superficial disciples, those who have not counted the cost, find what He has said to be too hard for them. The truth is always hard for those of us who thought He would settle for less than He demands. It is not that the saying is hard, but that our unbelieving hearts reject what He asks of us. John Calvin said, "The hardness was in their hearts and not in the saying. But the reprobate are wont to gather together stones out of the Word of God to dash themselves against; and when in their hard obstinacy they rush against Christ, they complain that his saying is hard, which really ought to have softened them. For whoever submits humbly to Christ's teaching will find nothing hard or rough in it."[6]

If the acts and teachings of Jesus thus far offend these loosely attached disciples, what will happen when He comes to the climax of His ministry—being lifted up in death and resurrection and *"ascend-[ing] where He was before."* In these final events, the words Jesus has spoken are fulfilled and lived out gloriously in His flesh.

If these words Jesus speaks are simply of the flesh, they have no power. But the Spirit fills His words with the very truth of God, so they are life to those who hear and accept. That Spirit, which was revealed in the act of Jesus feeding the hungry crowd, is manifested also in the words He speaks. Both the deed and the word are given enlivening power by the Spirit. Jesus is really saying, "My words are the incarnation and communication of the Spirit; it is the Spirit who dwells in them and acts through them; and for this reason they communicate life."[7]

This Spirit is also at work in those who are drawn and given to Him by the Father. But Jesus knows that among His listeners are those who have made the initial response, but they have not believed. They have seen and heard and started, but have not been "given by the Father." So there is a separation. *"From that time many of His disciples went back and walked with Him no more"* (v. 66). A sorrowful parting, but it is better to have a handful who will eat His flesh and drink His blood than a crowd who will simply observe curiously from afar.

Commitment and Confession (vv. 67–71). But what of the twelve? Here is the first mention of *"the twelve"* in this Gospel. Is this the time of their being chosen? Are they being given to Jesus by the Father here?

They have seen Him welcome the crowd and feed them, have experienced the guarantee of His eternal presence in the stormy night at sea, have listened to His strong demand that only those who eat His flesh and drink His blood will live, and then have watched the easy starters leave. And they are still with Him.

Now Jesus gives them the chance to leave, *"Do you also want to go away?"* (v. 67). This is the time to decide! It is Peter who speaks for all of them. There is no one else to whom they can go. They know there is eternal life in His words.

Then Simon Peter confesses: We believe and we know! It is in hearing and trusting that certainty comes, that the mind and heart are enlightened and the will is moved to decide. And what do they know? That He is the Chosen One of God, His very Son, the Messiah! It is not factual, conceptual knowledge they have been given, but personal, intimate trust that He is the One. They will cling to Him for the rest of the journey!

But even then, Jesus knows that among them there is one who will betray Him (vv. 70–71). This is the mystery of rejection and unbelief. How can one be so near and yet be a friend of the enemy?

NOTES

1. W. B. Westcott, *The Gospel According to John*, p. 100.
2. John Calvin, *The Gospel According to St. John, Part One, 1–10*, p. 160.
3. Ibid., p. 167.
4. Ibid.
5. W. B. Westcott, *The Gospel According to John*, p. 107.
6. John Calvin, *The Gospel According to St. John, Part One, 1–10*, p. 173.
7. Frederic Louis Godet, *Commentary on John's Gospel*, p. 605.

CHAPTER EIGHT

Conflict at the Feast: Whose Descendants?

John 7:1—8:59

HIS TIME, NOT HIS BROTHERS'

1 After these things Jesus walked in Galilee; for He did not want to walk in Judea, because the Jews sought to kill Him.

2 Now the Jews' Feast of Tabernacles was at hand.

3 His brothers therefore said to Him, "Depart from here and go into Judea, that Your disciples also may see the works that You are doing.

4 "For no one does anything in secret while he himself seeks to be known openly. If You do these things, show Yourself to the world."

5 For even His brothers did not believe in Him.

6 Then Jesus said to them, "My time has not yet come, but your time is always ready.

7 "The world cannot hate you, but it hates Me because I testify of it that its works are evil.

8 "You go up to this feast. I am not yet going up to this feast, for My time has not yet fully come."

9 When He had said these words to them, He remained in Galilee.

John 7:1–9

"After these things." It may now be September or October, about six months after the feeding of the five thousand. Jesus has *"walked in Galilee,"* a beautiful way to describe His ministry.

I have recently taken part in an unforgettable service celebrating the life of my eighty-seven-year-old uncle, Bengt Anderson, a vibrant, pioneering missionary among the Naga hill people of northeast India for twenty-eight years. All through the joyful worship service of singing, sharing, and preaching, I was remembering the incredible journey Ruth and I were able to make some years ago representing Bengt in a four-day anniversary celebration among the Sema-Nagas, one of the tribes among whom he had evangelized and taught. Seventy-five years earlier, the Gospel had come to these people, and fifteen thousand of the twenty-eight thousand believers came to sing and dance, hear the Word, and to remember how they had been set free in Christ.

Here we met Kijung Luba Ao, a trusted, beloved leader among these people, now well into his seventies. He was so eager to share his profound debt to "Papa Anderson," who had introduced him to Christ and baptized him. Kijung told us, "Everything I am I owe to Anderson, who taught me the Bible and the meaning of the Jesus way as we walked from village to village. He showed me how to drive a nail and said that if I agreed to be at a place at 7:00, then I must be there at 7:00." That "walking discipling" between these two men had taken place over fifty years earlier. But how fruitful it was, for Kijung has trained innumerable pastors among the hill people, passing on what he learned from Anderson.

This was Jesus' style of ministry—teaching, sharing, and modeling as He walked from place to place with His small band—the most valid, lasting kind of discipling. His ministry for these months had been in Galilee because in Judea His opposition, the Jews, were determined to kill Him. But now the Feast of the Tabernacles was at hand and Jesus was eager to attend. He rejoiced in all these national celebrations. Dr. Edgar Goodspeed, a New Testament scholar of an earlier generation, has called this feast "the Jewish camping festival," which marked the ingathering of harvest and was a time of thanksgiving for God's mighty works during the years of His people's wandering in the wilderness.

Jesus' brothers put pressure on Him to go to Jerusalem at this time so that the great holiday audience could see His works. If He was to get a movement going, why limit Himself to out-of-the-way places in Galilee? This is a subtle temptation for Jesus, particularly because it comes from His own brothers who are not believers. *"Show Yourself to the world,"* they told Him. It is possible that if He accepted their challenge they might submit to His guidance. This is simply a continuation of the wilderness temptation, "the devil took Him up into the holy city, set Him on the pinnacle of the temple, and said to Him, 'If You are the Son of God, throw Yourself down' " (Matt. 4:5–6). Dazzle them and You will win a following. But we have seen that miracles do not bring belief.

Jesus has another time schedule, a moment of opportunity, which is yet to come. When He says He is not yet *'going up"* to this feast, it is really a play on words, for it will be at the Passover, which will come in a few months, that He will be lifted up. This will be His time!

With His brothers it is different. They do not face the hatred of the Jews as does Jesus. They will not precipitate any special crisis, for they live casually and easily with the fleshly moods and understandings of the world.

GOING UP TO THE FEAST: CONFUSION—A GOOD MAN OR A DECEIVER?

10 But when His brothers had gone up, then He also went up to the feast, not openly, but as it were in secret.

11 Then the Jews sought Him at the feast, and said, "Where is He?"

12 And there was much murmuring among the people concerning Him, for some said, "He is a good Man"; others said, "No, on the contrary, He deceives the people."

13 However, no one spoke openly of Him for fear of the Jews.

John 7:10–13

But then Jesus does go up to the feast. Not with the train of worshipers that traveled together, but alone.

And here there is confusion about this strange wonder-worker. Who is He? This is the central issue. The people murmur and wonder, "Is He a good man or a deceiver?" Theirs is the quiet gossip of the back streets, for they fear their leaders who are intent on destroying Him.

Halfway through this eight-day feast, Jesus walks into the center of everything and begins to teach (v. 14). Here is a free man who takes the initiative, as truth always does. There is no need to hide in the shadows. His words have life and authority. No wonder the

Jews are amazed. To them, Jesus is an uneducated fellow who has never studied under the scholars. His claim to interpret the truth is to them a blasphemous impertinence.

HIS OPEN TEACHING: DOCTRINE FROM GOD

14 Now about the middle of the feast Jesus went up into the temple and taught.

15 And the Jews marveled, saying, "How does this Man know letters, having never studied?"

16 Jesus answered them and said, "My doctrine is not Mine, but His who sent Me.

17 "If anyone wants to do His will, he shall know concerning the doctrine, whether it is from God or whether I speak on My own authority.

18 "He who speaks from himself seeks his own glory; but He who seeks the glory of the One who sent Him is true, and no unrighteousness is in Him.

19 "Did not Moses give you the law, and yet none of you keeps the law? Why do you seek to kill Me?"

20 The people answered and said, "You have a demon. Who is seeking to kill You?"

21 Jesus answered and said to them, "I did one work, and you all marvel.

22 "Moses therefore gave you circumcision (not that it is from Moses, but from the fathers), and you circumcise a man on the Sabbath.

23 "If a man receives circumcision on the Sabbath, so that the law of Moses should not be broken, are you angry with Me because I made a man completely well on the Sabbath?

24 "Do not judge according to appearance, but judge with righteous judgment."

John 7:14–24

The Source of Jesus' teaching cannot be compared with any Rabbi, however wise he may be. And His doctrine does not originate within Himself. It is God Himself, the One who sent Him, whose truth He is opening to them. Therefore, He does not speak for Himself, because He is not seeking His own glory. He speaks this truth out of a life of obedience to His Father's will. His words are righteous,

God's speech lived out among men. So there is an integrity and authenticity about what He says.

But those to whom He speaks are strangers to the truth of the law which they extol and seek to teach. In fact, they are breaking the very law they profess to obey. Their disobedience is revealed in their obsessive desire to kill this One who is Truth incarnate.

When Jesus unmasks their evil intent, the Jews accuse Him of being insane, full of fanciful fears because He has the spirit of a demon.

But Jesus is not imagining things. He is well aware that His *"one work"* (v. 21), the healing of the crippled man on the Sabbath some months before, has aroused their fierce opposition. It was then they first began seeking to kill Him. He had freely done His Father's will on the day they are attempting to fence in, making it so holy they have perverted its meaning.

So Jesus now deals with them on their own ground. Did not the law of Moses, which they claimed to obey so absolutely, allow the act of circumcision to be performed on the Sabbath? And this was only a partial healing, a sign of belonging for God's people. How then could they condemn the total healing of a man on the Sabbath? They cannot understand that a new order has broken in. By this act of healing on the Sabbath Jesus has declared the superiority of His ministry over the law of Moses and the old order. "The covenant between God and Israel is now supplanted with the coming of Jesus."[1]

They can no longer judge in this new age by the old rigid rules. They must have new eyes of faith to see where and how God is at work in all kinds of surprising ways and places. Only then will their judgment become righteous.

SEEKING, BUT NOT FINDING HIM

25 Then some of them from Jerusalem said, "Is this not He whom they seek to kill?

26 "But look! He speaks boldly, and they say nothing to Him. Do the rulers know indeed that this is truly the Christ?

27 "However, we know where this Man is from; but when the Christ comes, no one knows where He is from."

28 Then Jesus cried out, as He taught in the temple,

saying, "You both know Me, and you know where I am from; and I have not come of Myself, but He who sent Me is true, whom you do not know.

29 "But I know Him, for I am from Him, and He sent Me."

30 Then they sought to take Him; but no one laid hands on Him, because His hour had not yet come.

31 And many of the people believed in Him, and said, "When the Christ comes, will He do more signs than these which this Man has done?"

32 The Pharisees heard the crowd murmuring these things concerning Him, and the Pharisees and the chief priests sent officers to take Him.

33 Then Jesus said to them, "I shall be with you a little while longer, and then I go to Him who sent Me.

34 "You will seek Me and not find Me, and where I am you cannot come."

35 Then the Jews said among themselves, "Where does He intend to go that we shall not find Him? Does He intend to go to the Dispersion among the Greeks and teach the Greeks?

36 "What is this thing that He said, 'You will seek Me and not find Me, and where I am you cannot come'?"

John 7:25–36

Jesus' strong declaration in verses 28–29 causes some of the people in Jerusalem to wonder if this might be the Messiah, the Chosen One. They think this not so much because of the content of His teaching, but because the rulers make no effort to restrain Him. On the other hand, they argue among themselves. "We know that this man comes from Nazareth and Galilee, and the Messiah is to have hidden, unknown origins." They assume that takes care of the matter. How easily we rationalize our ignorance and prejudices when we are afraid to face the real issues.

These people know about Jesus' geographic origins, but they cannot grasp the real Source of His mission. They are too blinded and earth-bound. It is His Father who has sent Him. Jesus is not running around "doing His own thing." Here again in verses 28–29 Jesus speaks of His deep, intimate relationship with His Father, whom He knows as His antagonists do not!

Even though His enemies now seek to lay their hands on Him,

they cannot, for His time has not yet come. No group, however violent and strong, can change God's plan, neither His time nor His method. It is the sovereign God who is making the moves, not the enemies of Jesus. It is the same today. Otherwise, none of us could sleep in peace in this mad, confused world.

Yet many of the people did believe in Him (v. 31). What they have seen and heard has convinced them that Jesus is the Messiah. But when the Pharisees hear this underground murmuring about Him, they make their move and join with the chief priests in sending officers to take Him. It seems that evil always organizes and becomes institutionalized.

But it is Jesus who knows His own time and sets the pace. And the time is not now, but in a little while at the Passover in a few months, not at the Feast of the Tabernacles. That will be the time of His sacrifice and His victorious return to the bosom of the Father who sent Him. Then the Pharisees will not be able to come to the place where He is because the door has been closed. "Their terrible seeking comes when the day of grace is past."[2] It is the believing disciples who alone can follow Jesus to the Father.

The attempt of the Jews to work out some kind of explanation of Jesus' going where they cannot come is a caricature. Does this strange man, who so angers them, plan to lose Himself among the Gentiles in their dispersion, spreading His heretical message? Where else could He go and not be found? Of course none of these Jews would contaminate themselves by going among these unclean heathen. But how prophetic is their explanation. Little do they realize that the presence of the resurrected Christ will come to be known and accepted throughout the whole Gentile world.

RIVERS OF LIVING WATER

37 On the last day, that great day of the feast, Jesus stood and cried out, saying, "If anyone thirsts, let him come to Me and drink.

38 "He who believes in Me, as the Scripture has said, out of his heart will flow rivers of living water."

39 But this He spoke concerning the Spirit, whom those believing in Him would receive; for the Holy Spirit was not yet given, because Jesus was not yet glorified.

John 7:37–39

It is on the *"last," "great"* day of celebration that Jesus issues a dramatic invitation. Every morning during the feast there has been a procession to the fountain of Gihon which supplied the water for the pool of Siloam. Here the priest has filled his golden pitcher with water as the choir sang, "With joy you will draw water from the wells of salvation" (Isa. 12:3). Then the crowd has made its way to the temple carrying branches and twigs in the right hand, reminding them of the huts they constructed in the wilderness, and a lemon or citron in the left hand, a sign of harvest. They proceeded to the altar waving the branches singing, "Save now, I pray, O Lord; O Lord, I pray, send now prosperity" (Ps. 118:25). Then the priest went up to the altar at the time of the sacrifice and poured the water into a silver funnel through which it flowed to the ground.

On the seventh day, the crowd circumambulated the altar seven times to celebrate God's gift of water when Moses struck the rock in the wilderness at Meribah. It was at this moment in the midst of the celebration that Jesus stood and cried, *"If anyone thirsts, let him come to Me and drink"* (v. 37). The symbolism of this dramatic invitation ran deeper than the outpoured water at this festival. It was rooted in that moment and place when Moses faced that vast thirsty crowd at Sinai crying out for water, and almost in desperation, he struck the rock "and water came out abundantly, and the congregation and their animals drank" (Num. 20:11).

But the crowd Jesus faces—those curious, wondering seekers as well as those angry ecclesiastics—have far deeper, more urgent needs than their ancestors in the wilderness. For their thirsts are spiritual and eternal. One cannot help but be aware of the restless, parched multitudes all about us. They desperately seek to quench their thirst in a constant round of parties or in one sexual escapade after another or in feverishly struggling to keep up with the crowd, and at the end, always being left more hopeless and disillusioned. And often the church, so busy with its little institutional business, has no living water to share.

Jesus' offer of water to these is strong and clear. Here are two imperatives that are really one— *"come"* and *"drink."* He is the rock from which eternal water flows giving life to all who will step forward.

In speaking of Himself as water, Jesus has used a striking Messianic symbol. As the rock was struck in the wilderness, so He will be struck and broken open and life will flow forth to be shared with all who will come and drink (John 19:34). And *"he who believes"*—a phrase used forty-one times in this Gospel—will himself become a rock out of whose deepest self will flow healing, life-giving water. He will be so filled that there will be a spontaneous overflowing, an outgoing sharing of life, with all those nearby.

I have seen this happen beautifully in the life of Jerry Johnson, a husky, tall state highway patrolman in our church. In the days of his old life it must have been a terror to be arrested by him. He was so full of conflict and confusion that the air would become heavy with his "purple language," particularly if the victim were black, because, as Jerry has said, "I used to hate blacks." Then he heard Jesus' strong invitation and came and drank of that *"living water."* And a quiet, but noticeable, change began to come over his life. I heard him say shortly after his baptism, "I can't explain it, but when I had to stop a black man for speeding the other day I actually had a great love for him." That living water, which he had drunk, was now flowing out of his heart. Now he and his gracious wife Becky have literally turned their home into a place of hospitality and healing for needy children and young people. Our congregation is constantly amazed at who the Johnsons have living with them.

It is the gift of the Holy Spirit that releases and sets free that stream of living water. Godet[3] has made the interesting suggestion that the disciples quenched their thirst on Jesus until Pentecost, but after that event, they became a blessing to others in a new style of outgoing life. It was then a tide of living water flowed out of their life together, manifesting itself in a bold witness and wondrous works.

But the Spirit could only be given after Jesus had been lifted up in glory. It was through the suffering and death of the cross that His glory broke forth. It was almost as if when His side was pierced He released the Spirit that was in Him to be shared with those who believed.

REJECTION, BUT A CAUTIOUS DEFENSE

40 Therefore many from the crowd, when they
heard this saying, said, "Truly this is the Prophet."

41 Others said, "This is the Christ," but some said,
"Will the Christ come out of Galilee?

42 "Has not the Scripture said that the Christ comes
from the seed of David and from the town of
Bethlehem, where David was?"

43 So there was a division among the people because
of Him.

44 Now some of them wanted to take Him, but
no one laid hands on Him.

45 Then the officers came to the chief priests and
Pharisees, who said to them, "Why have you not
brought Him?"

46 The officers answered, "No man ever spoke like
this Man!"

47 Then the Pharisees answered them, "Are you also
deceived?

48 "Have any of the rulers or the Pharisees believed
in Him?

49 "But this crowd that does not know the law is
accursed."

50 Nicodemus (he who came to Jesus by night, being
one of them) said to them,

51 "Does our law judge a man before it hears him
and knows what he is doing?"

52 They answered and said to him, "Are you also
from Galilee? Search and look, for no prophet has
arisen out of Galilee."

John 7:40–52

Again the crowd struggles with Jesus' identity. On the basis of
Jesus' tremendous claims some are convinced He is a prophet, like
Elijah. Others say He is the Christ, the Chosen One. But others say,
"This cannot be the Messiah because He is to come from David's
city, Bethlehem, and this man has come from Galilee." So there is
a divided house as there always is when Christ comes.

But in their ignorance about the origin of Jesus, these wondering
people unknowingly speak the truth. John is a master of so arranging
his material that mistakes or ignorance become a subtle means of
underlining the truth. It is ironic that these people, who are so tena-
cious about tracking Jesus down, are not even familiar with His place
of birth.

When the temple police who have been sent by the Sanhedrin to
take Jesus return empty-handed, they are accused of being duped
by His clever talk. These religious leaders are in effect saying, "Look
at us. This man is not leading us astray with His wild claims. But
this crowd is so ignorant of the law that it is damned." What a
paradox that these interpreters of the law, who are so certain of

their own wisdom and expertise, are the ones who have misled the people.

It is here that Nicodemus, quietly and unexpectedly, speaks a word of cautious defense. He is raising the question of justice and legality by simply asking, "Are we living up to the law which we profess to believe? Do we judge a man before he has had a chance to defend himself?" How suggestive that John identifies Nicodemus both as the one who came to Jesus by night and also as one of the Pharisees. One senses the tension within Nicodemus as he tries to live in both these worlds with some integrity. He is entering into new life with Jesus while at the same time trying to be faithful within the system of which he has been a part since early manhood. We cannot criticize Nicodemus too easily because his defense was not stronger. He has at least spoken up in the face of the disdain and arrogance of his colleagues.

The Merciful Judge

53 And everyone went to his own house.

8:1 But Jesus went to the Mount of Olives.

2 But early in the morning He came again into the temple, and all the people came to Him; and He sat down and taught them.

3 And the scribes and Pharisees brought to Him a woman caught in adultery. And when they had set her in the midst,

4 they said to Him, "Teacher, this woman was caught in adultery, in the very act.

5 "Now Moses, in the law, commanded us that such should be stoned. But what do You say?"

6 This they said, testing Him, that they might have something of which to accuse Him. But Jesus stooped down and wrote on the ground with His finger, as though He did not hear.

7 So when they continued asking Him, He raised Himself up and said to them, "He who is without sin among you, let him throw a stone at her first."

8 And again He stooped down and wrote on the ground.

9 And those who heard it, being convicted by their

conscience, went out one by one, beginning with the oldest even to the last. And Jesus was left alone, and the woman standing in the midst.

10 When Jesus had raised Himself up and saw no one but the woman, He said to her, "Woman, where are those accusers of yours? Has no one condemned you?"

11 She said, "No one, Lord." And Jesus said to her, "Neither do I condemn you; go and sin no more."

John 7:53—8:11

Here is an incident which seems out of place in the flow of the intense tabernacle dialogue, an account that is abruptly inserted with somewhat artificial transitional language. It is almost certain that this account was not written by the Apostle John. For neither the language nor the style of writing are his. Yet this account has shown up in the inspired record in a variety of places, most recently and permanently in this Gospel, and it is a lovely witness to Jesus' caring love for one lonely, frightened sinner. The details in the story are so unusual that it is highly unlikely it could have been fabricated, as some have claimed. Professor Westcott says, "It is beyond doubt an authentic fragment of apostolic tradition."[4]

Then why include it, particularly at this point? Because, I believe, the incident makes visible the meaning of judgment. All through the verbal encounter at the feast Jesus is being judged by His antagonists. They say that He has never studied (John 7:15), or He has a demon (7:20), or He comes from the wrong place to be the Messiah (7:27). They claim His witness is not true (8:13), that He is a Samaritan (8:48), and repeatedly seek to take Him (7:30).

But paradoxically Jesus becomes their judge, not because He came to judge them, but because of who He is, "the true witness," the "One who has come from above." So as light reveals darkness, Jesus unmasks His enemies' angry motives.

So, in the incident, they test Him *"that they might have something of which to accuse Him."* A woman, whose name we do not know, has been caught in the very act of adulterous sex. According to the law, this could mean her death (Lev. 20:10; Deut. 22:20–24). The Pharisees push Jesus to pronounce the final word of judgment, a clever trap, for they surely know of Jesus' compassion for the weak and sinful. So if He said, "Let her go," they could accuse Him of breaking Moses' law. But if He gave them permission to stone her, He would break the Roman law which did not allow death for anyone without their approval.

In the face of this pressure, Jesus deliberately *"stooped"* and *"wrote on the ground with His finger."* He disregards them, for He is a free man. He has His own thoughts and no one can tell Him what to do. We can only wonder about what He wrote. Did He list the sins of those seeking to trap Him? Or the sins of the woman? Did He write down the probing challenge He would throw out in a moment? In any event, the wind would shortly erase whatever He had written. It is His independent action, the way He sets His own pace, that is important. These enemies could not corner or push Him. He is their judge.

His response to their insistent demand for some verdict is spiritually devastating for these Pharisees. *'He who is without sin among you, let him throw a stone at her first.'* Suddenly what they have attempted to make a legal issue is seen as a deeply personal, moral matter. A group of proud, righteous men now find themselves on the same ground as the woman they are about to stone. Their pious armor has been pierced as each one faces the depths of his own sinful nature. Each has to deal with the inner darkness which is so closely intertwined with self-righteous legalism—the savage delight in catching this woman in the act of sinning, the pompous pride in being able to use her as a shameful test case, or the vengeful anger which drives them to get at Jesus. Are not these the ugly passions we all seek to hide?

Then which of these men, or who of us, can stand up to this test and be the first to pick up a stone? None. All they can do is leave, one by one. And it is the one with the most experience, who has lived more of life, who leaves first.

There is a royal dignity about Jesus as He quietly stoops to write again on the ground. He has no need to speak a further word. The truth has judged them. And now He seems to ignore them as they leave. A sad scene, for in their departure they walk away from any word of cleansing or hope.

Now Jesus raises Himself and sees no one but the woman. Augustine has written, "Two persons were left, the unhappy woman and Compassion Incarnate!" What a trembling, fragile moment. If there was a crowd present, because she was still *"standing in the midst,"* the two are oblivious of that, only aware of each other. It is always that way when Jesus deals with us.

Jesus lets her tell Him, when words are finally spoken, that her accusers have left without condemning her. She is now facing this merciful Judge, who is not her enemy. But He neither minimizes nor covers up her sin. She is to rid herself of it, cut it out like she would a cancer. Otherwise it will destroy her. Jesus will always judge our sin.

But Jesus also shows her mercy. The door of grace has been opened and she has been given an opportunity for a new beginning. He will not condemn her. Guilt is not the last word, but hope. This besmirched woman has faced "a tribunal more searching, and yet more tender, than the tribunals of men."[5]

Is this woman not like the vacillating crowd that we see and hear through the tabernacle dialogue, seeking and needy, longing to come out in the open and claim Jesus as their Messiah, but constantly not wanting to displease their religious leaders? They are so hopeful, but so uncertain! They too stand at the door of grace but are fearful to enter.

Any word of judgment, healing, or cleansing the church seeks to speak that is not spoken in the name of Jesus Christ is a false, empty word. It has no authority. It is only by His name and by His authority that we can say, *"Go and sin no more."*

THE OPEN WITNESS

12 Then Jesus spoke to them again, saying, "I am the light of the world. He who follows Me shall not walk in darkness, but have the light of life."

13 The Pharisees therefore said to Him, "You bear witness of Yourself; Your witness is not true."

14 Jesus answered and said to them, "Even if I bear witness of Myself, My witness is true, for I know where I came from and where I am going; but you do not know where I come from and where I am going.

15 "You judge according to the flesh; I judge no one.

16 "And yet if I do judge, My judgment is true; for I am not alone, but I am with the Father who sent Me.

17 "It is also written in your law that the testimony of two men is true.

155

18 "I am One who bears witness of Myself, and
the Father who sent Me bears witness of Me."

19 Then they said to Him, "Where is Your Father?"
Jesus answered, "You know neither Me nor My Father.
If you had known Me, you would have known My
Father also."

20 These words Jesus spoke in the treasury, as He
taught in the temple; and no one laid hands on Him,
for His hour had not yet come.

John 8:12–20

The temple dialogue is now resumed. Jesus boldly faces the Pharisees and claims that He is the light of the world. He does so against
the background of four great candelabra in the court of the women
that had been lighted on the first day of the feast, a reminder that
the children of Israel had been guided at night by a pillar of fire in
their wilderness pilgrimage.

But now a greater living Light has come, not simply to guide a
particular people who sit in darkness, but for the whole world. This
went beyond all orthodox messianic expectations of the day. These
scholarly Pharisees had not grasped the mighty vision of the prophets
that the Messiah would come as a light to the Gentiles as well as
to their own people (Isa. 43:6, 49:6; Mal. 4:2).

And all those who followed Him, including the first disciples who
had "come to see" and now walked with Him, would know the
very character and glory of God. They would no longer be in darkness
for they would have the gift of life. "In Him was life, and the life
was the light of men" (John 1:4).

Jesus' bold witness about Himself—who He is and why He has
come—is crucial! And this is where the Pharisees attack Him. They
say His *"witness"* is a lie, and His claim to be light is a grandiose
illusion! However, there remains an integrity in Jesus' claim about
His being. He knows the Source of His nature and mission.

Jesus takes these accusers a step further in establishing the truth
of His witness. According to their law, He points out, *"the testimony
of two men is true"* (v. 17). Each authenticates the word of the other.
This is precisely the relationship of Father and Son. The Son seeks
only to be a faithful witness to the Father, who has sent Him. And
the Father bears witness to the Son by approving and blessing His
mission. This is the calling of the believing community and the disci-

ples—to bear witness to the One who has sent them. Only then will their witness be authenticated by the Father.

The question the Pharisees finally ask, *"Where is Your Father?"* cannot be answered. Some questions only reveal the distance between two differing parties. It is really impossible for Jesus to communicate with them, for they are not at the place of healing or understanding.

Jesus is fearlessly speaking these truths in an open place between the court of the women and the inner court. He is light and has nothing to hide. And no one can take Him until His hour comes.

THE INFINITE CHASM

21 Then Jesus said to them again, "I am going away, and you will seek Me, and will die in your sin. Where I go you cannot come."

22 Then the Jews said, "Will He kill Himself, because He says, 'Where I go you cannot come'?"

23 And He said to them, "You are from beneath; I am from above. You are of this world; I am not of the world.

24 "Therefore I said to you that you will die in your sins; for if you do not believe that I am He, you will die in your sins."

25 Then they said to Him, "Who are You?" And Jesus said to them, "Just what I have been saying to you from the beginning.

26 "I have many things to say and to judge concerning you, but He who sent Me is true; and I speak to the world those things which I heard from Him."

27 They did not understand that He spoke to them of the Father.

28 Then Jesus said to them, "When you lift up the Son of Man, then you will know that I am He, and that I do nothing of Myself; but as My Father taught Me, I speak these things.

29 "And He who sent Me is with Me. The Father has not left Me alone, for I always do those things that please Him."

John 8:21-29

He is going away! Leaving this world beneath, returning to the Father by way of the cross and the resurrection. It is an infinite journey that cannot be measured by any earthly standards. These hostile listeners will seek for Him after He has gone, but it will be a search of despair, for they cannot come where He is.

All through His ministry Jesus has sought to penetrate their darkened, unbelieving world, longing to kindle faith that He might bring them where He is. Here He speaks of Himself for the first time as *"I am He"* (v. 24). But they have stubbornly refused to believe, rejecting His every overture. This is the nature of sin. All their acts of sinning are the expression of their rebellious unbelief as boils on the body are evidence of poison in the blood. Now they can only die in their sin. When Jesus leaves, the Source of their life is gone. The opportunity has passed. This is the final sorrow of His going.

The separation between these two realms, His and theirs, becomes final, an infinite chasm fixed between the world above and the world beneath. An abyss that cannot be crossed.

As I have meditated on the awful finality of this passage my mind has turned again and again to a dark abyss which haunted our lives in our earlier ministry. We lived in a lovely suburban section of the city with neatly trimmed lawns and well-kept homes. And these neighbors were such bright, gifted people. No one would have guessed it, but they lived in a world of isolated alcoholism, frequently withdrawing from all of us, pulling down the shades, waiting for the cab to come every few days with another supply of booze. It was a world we could not penetrate, even though on a couple of occasions we called in the law to get them into an alcoholic treatment program at the state mental hospital. But this only deepened their suspicion and hostility toward those of us who wanted to help. As they moved further and further into a hazy, twilight world of semiconsciousness they finally died tragically and hopelessly! Here was a chasm, an abyss, which we non-alcoholics simply could not cross!

The response of Jesus' opponents to His telling them He was going where they could not come only reveals again the darkness of their unbelief. They can only assume that Jesus proposes to kill Himself. And according to the Pharisee's teaching, anyone who committed self-murder would be condemned to the deepest region of Gehenna, a place of unrelieved darkness and judgment, which is translated *hell* in the New Testament. Unbelief can lead to the strangest attempts to rationalize.

Only through this obedience will the disciple know the truth. The deepest knowing comes only through doing, a constant theme in this Gospel. This means far more than learning and memorizing concepts which can then be verbalized. The discovery of truth comes in encountering and yielding to the One who is living truth.

The disciple will be set free *from* the bondage of sin and set free *to* live out the will of the Teacher. This becomes the very purpose of his existence. The disciple has entered an eternal, liberating relationship eager to do the will of His Lord. He is no longer shackled by the endless demands of legalisms which have always bred self-righteousness, for he has been set free. In the words of George Matheson's great hymn, "Make me a captive, Lord, and then I shall be free."

I have discovered a joyful freedom in a faithful covenant I made with Ruth, my beloved wife, more than thirty-nine years ago. This is a liberation which comes only because I have given myself to another and accepted the commitment of that relationship. I would never have known this freedom if I had gone from one affair to another as a swinging bachelor or been unfaithful in marriage.

But Jesus' antagonists attempt with some arrogance to brush aside this talk of freedom. Are they not the children of Abraham? In their thinking, that means they have never been in bondage to anyone. They are living in an illusion because even at this time the Jews are the political pawns of Rome, and in the past they have been captives of both Egypt and Babylon. Jesus is trying to communicate that the issue of freedom runs far deeper than any external, biological ties. It is a personal inner spiritual matter. If these people continue to sin, they are the slaves, regardless of who their ancestors are.

So their condition is very precarious. The slave can be put out of the house at any moment. It is not so with the children, who live in the Father's house easily and comfortably. It is their home because they have been set free by the Son who now welcomes them as part of the family.

In this passage of John, Jesus clears up the misconceptions the Jews had about their ancestry. The Jews obsessively cling to the illusion that they are the *spiritual* children of Abraham because he is their *physical* father. Is not this an old trick which all of us constantly use to establish spiritual credentials? We are either Baptist or Catholic or middle-class or black or our forebears came over on the Mayflower or we were here when the church was founded.

These Jews are doing the same thing by seeking to prove their ancestry by insisting they have never committed spiritual adultery with other gods. They say they have always worshiped the one true God. (In using this language they may be implying by innuendo that Jesus has been born under suspicious circumstances.)

In verse 39 Jesus asks why they are not doing the works of Abraham if they are his children. This is the crucial test. They will not even listen to Jesus' words. He tells them the truth, but His word has no place in them. In fact, the darkness in them is so perverse that because Jesus tells them the truth they will not believe. If they were the children of God they would hear Jesus' words because His words come from God. They would then love Jesus because He has come from the very bosom of God; He *"proceeded"* from Him. We catch something of the meaning of the Incarnation again in this truth.

Because they will not accept Jesus' word they seek to kill Him. Since this is not the work of Abraham, then surely they are not the children of God. Then who is their father?

None but the devil! He is the father of lies. He can only deceive and spread darkness out of the abyss of his own nothingness. His children are liars, perverters of the truth. These *"Jews"* have not only stubbornly resisted the truth Jesus has spoken, but have made their lies seem as truth. This has revealed who their father is. Untruth becomes division, spreads disorder, pits brother against brother, and finally kills both by word and deed, as Cain killed his brother Abel. The devil is the father of all murder, and as these religious leaders plot to kill Jesus they are doing his works.

Is not the work of this deceiver and murderer all around us? In a million homes where lies and violence tear people apart and the courts are left to decide what will "happen to the children"? Or in scores of church business meetings where ugly words are spoken and people divide up into sides insisting they must have their own way, often in the name of God? Or in the massive, overwhelming build-up of weapons for war which continues to rob the poor and the dispossessed of the resources of life while the "great powers" throw propaganda lies at one another calling it diplomacy? Who is really in charge here and whose children are we?

One senses in this passage the intensity of the spiritual warfare between Jesus and Satan. Jesus unmasks him, calls his bluff, and identifies him as the real enemy. As Jesus nears the cross, this battle with the evil one becomes more deadly and more open. Even His most intimate friends are used by the devil in the struggle in their moments of weakness and confusion.

This Gospel is written not only to highlight the nature and mission of Jesus for seekers, but also to strengthen and encourage the early Christian believers, many of whom were Jews now facing intense pressure and persecution from those with whom they had previously worshiped. In the intense conflict between Jesus and His Jewish antagonists the issues are clarified: we see repeatedly the intimate relationship of Jesus to His Father from whom He has come; the true meaning of Abraham as a spiritual ancestor but also the bankruptcy of the Jews claiming spiritual credentials because of their blood ties with him; and the diabolical role of Satan in seeking to destroy the Christian community through the ridicule of Jewish non-believers.

HIS MAJESTIC IDENTITY

48 Then the Jews answered and said to Him, "Do we not say rightly that You are a Samaritan and have a demon?"

49 Jesus answered, "I do not have a demon; but I honor My Father, and you dishonor Me.

50 "And I do not seek My own glory; there is One who seeks and judges.

51 "Most assuredly, I say to you, if anyone keeps My word he shall never see death."

52 Then the Jews said to Him, "Now we know that You have a demon! Abraham is dead, and the prophets; and You say, 'If anyone keeps My word he shall never taste death.'

53 "Are You greater than our father Abraham, who is dead? And the prophets are dead. Whom do You make Yourself out to be?"

54 Jesus answered, "If I honor Myself, My honor is nothing. It is My Father who honors Me, of whom you say that He is your God.

55 "Yet you have not known Him, but I know Him. And if I say, 'I do not know Him,' I shall be a liar like you; but I do know Him and keep His word.

56 "Your father Abraham rejoiced to see My day, and he saw it and was glad."

57 Then the Jews said to Him, "You are not yet fifty years old, and have You seen Abraham?"

58 Jesus said to them, "Most assuredly, I say to you, before Abraham was, I AM."

59 Then they took up stones to throw at Him; but Jesus hid Himself and went out of the temple, going through the midst of them, and so passed by.

John 8:48–59

Jesus could not call His antagonists the children of the devil without having them strike back. So they not only accuse Him of being an outcast, a Samaritan, but a crazy one with a demon. In verse 48 John quotes what is apparently their common judgment, *"Do we not say rightly?"* How often we struggle to belittle the one who confronts us when we hear the truth that unmasks and shames us. But their attempt to degrade Jesus only focuses the issue of His identity more sharply. Jesus can have no demon for He seeks only to honor His Father, which is the central thrust of His whole ministry (v. 49). So in attempting to belittle Jesus, these Jews actually dishonor His Father.

In verse 51 there is a crucial turn of thought. Jesus declares there is the power of life in the very word He speaks. Anyone who *"keeps"* His whole teaching, or in other words obeys it and does not let His words slip away, will never *"see"* death; he will not face the dreaded abyss of eternal spiritual separation. Jesus can only make this claim because He is the Source of life. "In Him was life" (John 1:4).

His enemies are now utterly convinced Jesus is demon-possessed. Why, even Abraham, their greatest hero, as well as all the mighty prophets, is dead! None of them could make the unbelievable claim they could avoid or prevent death. Does this strange fellow think He is greater than they? Who is He making Himself out to be?

But the question is not who is He making Himself out to be, but who He is! Jesus knows the Father intimately and eternally. He has come only to do His bidding. If He does not confess this truth about Himself, He will be a liar like these enemies who claim to know God, but are in spiritual darkness, deceiving themselves.

We cannot help but wonder about the smug certainty of so many in evangelical circles who claim to know God on a "buddy-buddy basis." It is all so glib and easy, but knowing a few Bible verses or moving with the "in" Christian group does not guarantee that deep, burning relationship of which Jesus speaks in verse 55. That knowing comes only in honoring the Son in word and deed.

In verses 56–58 Jesus relates His own mission to the status of Abraham, who saw what his descendants now refuse to accept. By referring to Abraham as *"your father,"* Jesus is, wisely and subtly, underlining the physical ties of these Jews, but making their spiritual rejection obvious. For in his obedience and sensitivity, Abraham was allowed to see the fulfillment of all that God had promised him. Jesus called it *"My day"*—His coming, His whole earthly ministry, and finally His saving death and resurrection. Abraham had rejoiced in what was to take place.

The Jews are baffled, and again can only apply worldly standards of measurement. Jesus does not even seem to be fifty years of age, the time of mature manhood, and Abraham had lived and died centuries earlier. Then how can Jesus make the absurd statement that Abraham had seen Him?

The moment has come for Jesus' triumphant proclamation, *"Before Abraham was, I AM."* He makes clear the towering meaning of His claim by contrasting His own eternal existence with that of Abraham, who, though he was the father of his nation, was a fragile human being. Jesus is not saying, "I was," but *"I AM."* Abraham died, but Jesus is the Giver of life; the one is created, the Other is uncreated.

"I AM" is that sacred name for deity Moses heard at the burning bush. "Thus you shall say to the children of Israel, 'I AM has sent me to you'" (Exod. 3:14). Raymond Brown, a careful Catholic scholar, has written "no clearer implication of divinity is found in gospel tradition."[6] And Leon Morris, a renowned evangelical writer, says that Jesus' dramatic statement brings out the meaning of His preexistence in a "more striking fashion" than anywhere else in the Gospel.[7] We can only fall down in awe before the majesty of His Being.

Now there is no way that these Jews can miss the startling meaning of Jesus' claim. He has spoken blasphemy, openly and brazenly. According to the law there is only one thing they must now do, stone Him to death (Lev. 24:16). And this they hurry to do, but Jesus hides and slips away *"and so passed by"* (v. 59). What a suggestive phrase. He had come to the feast, quietly and alone, and so He leaves!

NOTES

1. John Huckle and Paul Visokay, *The Gospel According to St. John,* p. 101.
2. Leon Morris, *The Gospel According to John,* p. 417, quoting R. C. H. Lenski.
3. Frederic Louis Godet, *Commentary on John's Gospel,* pp. 638–39.
4. W. B. Westcott, *The Gospel According to John,* p. 125.
5. Ibid.
6. Raymond E. Brown, *The Gospel According to John I–XII,* p. 367.
7. Leon Morris, *The Gospel According to John,* p. 473.

CHAPTER NINE

New Eyes for Old

John 9:1–38

THE HEALING

1 Now as Jesus passed by, He saw a man who was blind from birth.

2 And His disciples asked Him, saying, "Rabbi, who sinned, this man or his parents, that he was born blind?"

3 Jesus answered, "Neither this man nor his parents sinned, but that the works of God should be revealed in him.

4 "I must work the works of Him who sent Me while it is day; the night is coming when no one can work.

5 "As long as I am in the world, I am the light of the world."

6 When He had said these things, He spat on the ground and made clay with the saliva; and He anointed the eyes of the blind man with the clay.

7 And He said to him, "Go, wash in the pool of Siloam" (which is translated, Sent). So he went and washed, and came back seeing.

John 9:1–7

Here is one solitary human being who has never seen the face of his parents or his friends nor known the beauty of a sunrise or a lily. *"Blind from birth"* says the record, as each of us is born spiritually blind. And Jesus sees him, as He *"passed by."* And He stops! For Him, no one is ever lost in the crowd. He knows each of us, where we are, and what our need is. This is our hope.

The disciples cannot help raising the inevitable theological question, Whose sin has caused this man's blindness? They are the children of orthodox Jewish thought which assumed that any physical illness or calamity was caused by someone's wrongdoing. But in calling Him *"Rabbi"* they seem open to deeper truth.

Do we not all seek for the hidden cause that brings on tragedy—cancer, a car accident, or the mongoloid child? Who is responsible? We feel we must identify the culprit.

I recall an earnest, hardworking deacon in the first congregation I served having a nervous breakdown when his life savings were washed away in a few terrifying moments when the Marais de Cynes River flooded unexpectedly. The water came in like a deadly, silent wall. Wesley had been down the street helping a friend move the furniture in his store to a safer place, and there was no way he could get back in time to save all the precious watches, rings, china, and silver in his own well-stocked jewelry store. Some days later, after the water had subsided, fellow businessmen saw him trying desperately to find some of those costly items in the mud with no success. He had been wiped out. As his pastor I could not convince this dear, conscientious man that God had not punished him for some hidden, unknown sin he had committed in bygone years. I do not believe he ever really recovered.

But we humans persist in wanting to know who to blame. We discuss the matter endlessly, sometimes earnestly, but often foolishly. However, Jesus brushes this question aside. He does not focus on the past, nor is He interested in answering theological speculation, for He sets the needs of this man in the context of what God can do. He knows that the work of God will be done in this situation even though men call it impossible.

And this must be done while it is still day. Night is coming. The powers of darkness are closing in, for Jesus' death is not far off. Then it will be too late for any earthly act of compassion. But is this not the lot of all of us? The opportunities we have this day to do God's work will pass.

Jesus will do His work here as the *"light of the world."* He is the only One who can penetrate the darkness of this man's life. His blindness represents dramatically the ignorance and slavery of every man. Jesus now moves decisively in a surprising, almost strange, way to drive out the darkness. An intimate part of Himself is given as

He mingles His own saliva with some soil, that lowly, earthy stuff out of which we have all come. It is almost as if He reenacts that first trembling moment of creation when the Lord breathed His life into the man He had formed from the soil. When Jesus anoints the man's eyes with the clay, we are made aware again how the intimacy of caring touch is at the heart of all healing—physical, spiritual, and psychological.

He then commands this man to go to the Pool of Siloam, which means "he who has been sent," and wash. Jesus' own mission is identified with the meaning of this pool from which water came for the libations at the Feast of the Tabernacles. Here there is life, "for the water of Siloam disappeared in the living water of Christ."[1] How simply the writer notes the obedience of this needy man. He *"went and washed, and came back seeing"* (v. 7). The ways of Jesus in healing are rich and varied. But He always calls for obedience, the active response of faith.

Can any of us imagine the wonder of those first incredible moments of sight for this man? I will never forget the spontaneous comment of Jerold Hayes at a recent Sunday evening communion service. We had invited people to come to the table to serve one another the bread and the cup as fellow priests in God's family. When I returned to my seat next to Jerold he leaned over and whispered enthusiastically, "Boy, I understand things about this now I didn't even know when I first came here."

That had been two years before when he came to us out of the work release program for ex-prisoners. He had done twenty-two years in half a dozen state penitentiaries, most of his trouble caused by mixing booze with his destructive hatred. Then Jerold showed up in church and made an unexpected commitment to Christ, insisting that he be baptized. But it was a short, emotional trip, for in a few weeks he dropped out of sight back into his old ways. A year and a half later he showed up again, repentant and scared, but much more honest. I will never forget that gray, gaunt look about him as he moved forward from the back of the church to make a public declaration of a new beginning. It was obvious he had "been to hell and back again" since we had last seen him.

Now it was as if Jesus had again formed clay by mingling the saliva of His own Word with the earthiness of our congregation's shared experiences to anoint the darkened eyes of Jerold's heart. As he washed in the cleansing pool of Christ's forgiveness, Jerold was given new eyes, a divine illumination. And he has been a blessing and a challenge to all of us ever since.

THE WITNESS

8 Therefore the neighbors and those who previously had seen that he was blind said, "Is not this he who sat and begged?"

9 Some said, "This is he." Others said, "He is like him." He said, "I am he."

10 Therefore they said to him, "How were your eyes opened?"

11 He answered and said, "A Man called Jesus made clay and anointed my eyes and said to me, 'Go to the pool of Siloam and wash.' So I went and washed, and I received sight."

12 Then they said to him, "Where is He?" He said, "I do not know."

John 9:8–12

Now the neighbors, who have watched this man come and go, struggling to eke out an existence, are confused. Can this new vibrant, seeing man be the one who used to sit and beg? The contrast is so great. But the healed man makes his identity clear. He alone knows who he is and what has happened to him. So he answers their wondering questions with an unequivocal *"I am he."* Unknowingly he has already begun to bear the name of his Healer, "I AM." But when the neighbors ask how it happened, he tells them what he knows. It was a gift. He heard Jesus' command, obeyed, and now he sees. There is an uncluttered honesty and a directness about this man that is appealing.

HE IS A PROPHET

13 They brought him who formerly was blind to the Pharisees.

14 And it was a Sabbath when Jesus made the clay and opened his eyes.

15 Then the Pharisees also asked him again how
he had received his sight. He said to them, "He put
clay on my eyes, and I washed, and I see."

16 Therefore some of the Pharisees said, "This Man
is not from God, because He does not keep the
Sabbath." Others said, "How can a man who is a sinner
do such miracles?" And there was a division among
them.

17 They said to the blind man again, "What do you
say about Him because He opened your eyes?" He
said, "He is a prophet."

John 9:13-17

When the man who was healed admits he does not know the
whereabouts of this man Jesus, apparently his neighbors are convinced
there needs to be some kind of "investigation," a verification by
the "religious experts." How ironic that they would bring him to
the Pharisees, who, in their spiritual blindness have rejected Jesus
at every turn. That little innocent-appearing phrase, *"it was a Sabbath,"*
referring to the time of the healing, is loaded with legalistic dynamite
for these Pharisees. For both kneading, the making of clay from saliva
and dirt, as well as healing, the opening of the man's eyes, were
absolutely forbidden on the Sabbath.

But it is almost as if Jesus had again deliberately healed on the
Sabbath to declare His sovereign reign over every day and occasion
in this age of grace. He is Lord of the Sabbath. And when the man
is questioned about how he received his sight, he states the simple
facts again with refreshing candor, *"He put clay on my eyes, and I washed,
and I see."* He doesn't change his story for the officials.

Immediately some of the Pharisees dismiss this Healer as a law-
breaker. How can He possibly be from God when He heals on the
Sabbath? But others see the happening with different eyes. How
can a sinner open any man's eyes? Here is the watershed that divides
those who are locked into legalistic prejudices, stubbornly protecting
"sacred cows" regardless of the facts, from those who are struggling
to be open to what God might do in some unexpected way or place.
The life of grace is carrying them beyond the rigidities of the law.

How often the church has been torn asunder by prejudice and
dogmatic assumptions and hardness of heart. If we haven't been angered about the charismatics, it may have been the Roman Catholics

or those who are committed to a nuclear freeze in the arms race or to the Scofield Reference Bible or to putting the new organ on the east side of the church. The list goes on and on.

I recall a leader in our church becoming violently upset when beautiful banners were hung around the balcony on Pentecost Sunday to celebrate the creative gifts of the Holy Spirit. He felt the building was being violated. And in one church where I was to report on a friendship mission in which I had been involved among our courageous Baptist brethren in the Soviet Union, I overheard an usher blurt out, "The only good Russian is a dead one." So we often refuse to deal with the facts. We would rather live by our false assumptions and prejudices even though in the end we miss seeing and live on in blindness.

In verse 17, it is out of their own division that these Pharisees now turn to the healed man and ask, *"What do you say about Him?"* How interesting that the learned interpreters of the law should turn to an unlettered ex-beggar seeking for an answer to their differences. Again he makes a terse, direct response. *"He is a prophet."* On the basis of what he knows, this is the loftiest title he can give his Healer. But these Jews cannot deal with the truth this man speaks. They have now convinced themselves that he was never blind, that there really has been no healing. Attempting to substitute lies for the truth always becomes a complicated, drawn out maneuver.

QUESTIONING HIS PARENTS

18 But the Jews did not believe concerning him, that he had been blind and received his sight, until they called the parents of him who had received his sight.

19 And they asked them, saying, "Is this your son, who you say was born blind? How then does he now see?"

20 His parents answered them and said, "We know that this is our son, and that he was born blind;

21 "but by what means he now sees we do not know, or who opened his eyes we do not know. He is of age; ask him. He will speak for himself."

22 His parents said these things because they feared the Jews, for the Jews had agreed already that if anyone

confessed that He was Christ, he would be put out
of the synagogue.

23 Therefore his parents said, "He is of age; ask
him."

John 9:18–23

These Pharisees take another tack and call in his parents. Perhaps
here they can discover evidence that will discredit the story of their
stubborn son. But these parents can only answer what they know.
Yes, this is their son, and he was blind and now he sees. But they
do not know how this happened. Their son is of age. He can speak
for himself.

How unlike their honest, independent son these parents are. There
is a tentativeness, a hesitating kind of fear, in all they say. After
all, they are facing hostile interrogators who have already decided
that if anyone comes near admitting that this healing may have been
done by the Messiah, he will be *"put out of the synagogue,"* which would
be a humiliating ostracism. They would then be outcasts among the
non-believing Gentiles, cut off from the house of Israel.

THIS MAN MUST BE FROM GOD

24 So they again called the man who was blind,
and said to him, "Give God the glory! We know that
this Man is a sinner."

25 He answered and said, "Whether He is a sinner
or not I do not know. One thing I know: that though
I was blind, now I see."

26 Then they said to him again, "What did He do
to you? How did He open your eyes?"

27 He answered them, "I told you already, and you
did not listen. Why do you want to hear it again?
Do you also want to become His disciples?"

28 Then they reviled him and said, "You are His
disciple, but we are Moses' disciples.

29 "We know that God spoke to Moses; as for this
fellow, we do not know where He is from."

30 The man answered and said to them, "Why, this

is a marvelous thing, that you do not know where
He is from, and yet He has opened my eyes!

31 "Now we know that God does not hear sinners;
but if anyone is a worshiper of God and does His
will, He hears him.

32 "Since the world began it has been unheard of
that anyone opened the eyes of one who was born
blind.

33 "If this Man were not from God, He could do
nothing."

34 They answered and said to him, "You were
completely born in sins, and are you teaching us?"
And they cast him out.

John 9:24–34

Now there is a final confrontation. The Pharisees are into this case
too deeply to leave it hanging. So the healed man is called in again
and put under oath, *"Give God the glory!"*, a solemn charge to tell the
whole truth. And a united attack is pressed against the One he claims
has healed him. *"We know that this Man is a sinner"* (v. 24). This has
become their common judgment. But this simple, lonely man will
not be intimidated. He speaks the truth as he has experienced it.
And since his kind Healer has thus far not revealed His identity to
him, he does not know whether or not He is a sinner. One detects
in his answer a stubborn refusal to capitulate to the charge of the
Pharisees. But one thing he does know, and this he clings to tena-
ciously, *"I was blind, now I see"* (v. 25). No council of Pharisees, however
powerful, can change that.

This man's witness has become more convincing, more appealing,
each time he has been challenged or questioned. He boldly shares
what he knows, no more and no less, under all conditions, regardless
of who his audience is. His clear, lean honesty is a model for all of
us who attempt to say that Jesus has opened our eyes.

But when they ask again how it happened, he seems irritated,
weary of it all. *"You did not listen,"* he says. Do they want to hear
him rehearse again what took place because they also want to become
His disciples? His use of *"also"* in verse 27 is significant. This healed
man has begun to follow Jesus in spite of how little he knows.

It is as if there has been a reversal of roles. The healed man is
not on trial; the Pharisees are. His newly found freedom judges their

darkness. And the defense of the Pharisees is pathetic. They attempt to fall back on what they assume is their superior spiritual position. After all, they are the students of the law and Moses is their teacher. They are certain this man has been led astray by the One he claims as his Healer. The man has foolishly become His disciple, no longer under their control. All they can do now is damn him, literally calling him a bastard.

What a temptation it is for those of us who call ourselves "Christian leaders" to fall back on our credentials—a seminary degree or an ordination certificate, our many years of Bible study or the number of church offices we have held—when we are confronted and even embarrassed by the spontaneous, often naive, witness of a newly born disciple of Jesus.

This unlettered man who now sees, not only physically, but with an inner spiritual illumination, is amazed that these learned doctors do not know from whence *"this fellow,"* as they call Him, has come. But He must be from God, who surely would not listen to his Healer's prayers if He were a sinner. At least He must worship God and do His will. Otherwise how could He open his eyes which have been closed from birth? He has never heard of this happening to anyone before.

His simple spiritual reasoning is too much for these Pharisees. How can someone *"completely born in sins"* become their teacher? So they *"cast him out."* Often we throw out those who threaten us with the truth. But in being thrown out of Judaism, this man is "cast" into new life.

BELIEF AND WORSHIP

35 Jesus heard that they had cast him out; and when He had found him, He said to him, "Do you believe in the Son of God?"

36 He answered and said, "Who is He, Lord, that I may believe in Him?"

37 And Jesus said to him, "You have both seen Him and it is He who is talking with you."

38 And he said, "Lord, I believe!" And he worshiped Him.

John 9:35–38

Jesus does not leave this man to his lonely fate. When He hears he has been cast out, He comes to him. He *"found"* the man. Now His work of healing can be completed.

Here again is the tragic chasm between faith and rejection, between light and darkness. As the man faced his hostile interrogators, he honestly confessed ignorance. Yet his eyes are being opened more and more to understanding who it is that healed him. The Pharisees, who seem to be aware of this, accuse him of being this Healer's disciple. They become "more obdurate in their failure to see the truth."[2] Their rejection of Jesus is climaxed by casting out the one who has already begun to cling to Jesus. As Jesus was later to say, "If the world hates you, you know that it hated Me before it hated you" (John 15:18). Jesus is always seeking out the rejects and the losers, coming as a Friend to include all of us in His family. Chrysostom, the church father, has said it beautifully, "The one whom the Jews had cast out of the temple, the Lord of the temple found."[3]

At the moment of this writing, I have just been called by a physician, a member of our congregation. While ministering to a patient in the terminal stages of lung cancer, he became aware of this man's deeper spiritual need. And almost hesitatingly, fearing he might be getting out of his territory, asked the man about his spiritual condition. The patient responded as if this might have been the real reason he had come to the hospital. In the next few moments this lonely man came to know God's forgiveness and peace. He was healed for eternity by the One who sought him out through words of love and truth spoken by Richard Shoffner, a caring, believing physician.

The man finally discovers who it is that has healed him. The One he first called "Jesus," then a "Prophet," and then "One from God," now reveals Himself as the *"Son of God."* Here is the end of all the blind man's seeking, the fulfillment of all for which he has yearned. He has seen and listened with eyes and ears of faith, not carelessly or critically as the Pharisees. Now an eternal light floods his inmost being and he can only cry out, *"I believe!"* And in trusting wonder he falls to his knees in worship and adoration!

The stubborn, courageous witness of this man was a word of renewing strength for those tiny communities of Jewish Christian believers scattered throughout the Roman empire. John surely had these fellow believers in mind when he wrote. Like this man, they had heard the voice of Jesus and obeyed, and their eyes had been opened! They had come to know Him as the new Moses "full of grace and truth."

But in turning to Him they had been ridiculed and cast out from their people. In the face of continuing hostility these Jewish Christians must have become weary and fearful and even wavered. So this lonely, healed man, so bold in his witness, was a model for the early church. Jesus had welcomed and received him when he was cast out. So these early believers were heartened. They knew Jesus would not leave them. They could continue to know the joy of His presence and worship Him with fresh devotion.

NOTES

1. Sir Edwin Hoskyns, *The Fourth Gospel*, p. 355.
2. Raymond E. Brown, *The Gospel According to John I–XII*, p. 397.
3. Sir Edwyn Hoskyns, *The Fourth Gospel*, p. 359.

CHAPTER TEN

The Shepherd's Last Appeal

John 9:39—10:42

Judgment: "Your Sin Remains"

39 And Jesus said, "For judgment I have come into this world, that those who do not see may see, and that those who see may be made blind."

40 Then some of the Pharisees who were with Him heard these words, and said to Him, "Are we blind also?"

41 Jesus said to them, "If you were blind, you would have no sin; but now you say, 'We see.' Therefore your sin remains."

John 9:39–41

A man healed of physical and spiritual blindness has "been driven from one fold and received into another."[1] And the One who has received him now faces the false spiritual leaders who have cast him out, but who remain in their sin. They stubbornly insist they see, but continue in darkness. Their fierce pride shuts out any hope of healing. This is the judgment: Jesus can only heal those who know they are blind.

Truth Hidden in a Parable

1 "Most assuredly, I say to you, he who does not enter the sheepfold by the door, but climbs up some other way, the same is a thief and a robber.

2 "But he who enters by the door is the shepherd of the sheep.

3 "To him the doorkeeper opens, and the sheep
hear his voice; and he calls his own sheep by name
and leads them out.

4 "And when he brings out his own sheep, he goes
before them; and the sheep follow him, for they know
his voice.

5 "Yet they will by no means follow a stranger,
but will flee from him, for they do not know the voice
of strangers."

6 Jesus used this illustration, but they did not
understand the things which He spoke to them.

John 10:1–6

In this last public discourse Jesus put this whole experience in
the imagery of shepherd and sheep, familiar symbols deeply imbedded
in Hebrew life and history (Ps. 23; Ps. 78:52–53; Ps. 74:1–2; Isa. 40:11;
Jer. 23:1–4). This is not only a tender pastoral teaching, but a stinging
indictment of those who profess to be shepherds but are actually
thieves and robbers, strangers and hirelings.

Those who will not enter the sheepfold by the one door have
not come to care for the sheep, but are thieves and robbers coming
to divide and destroy. They attempt to bypass the doorkeeper, who
would never allow them to enter, by climbing over the fence unno-
ticed. And there are strangers, masquerading as shepherds, disguising
their voices, trying to come between the shepherd and his sheep.
But the sheep flee, frightened by the unfamiliar voice.

How different is the shepherd who enters the sheepfold with authority because he is a familiar figure to the doorkeeper. And the
sheep are at ease with him because they know his voice when he
calls them. There might be several flocks in the same fold, which
was a courtyard adjoining the house. But each flock knew the voice
of his own shepherd.

In the interweaving of these familiar pastoral symbols Jesus is making vividly clear the contrast between the shepherd and those who
came to plunder the sheep, however innocent they might appear:
the differing ways by which they entered the sheepfold—the shepherd
openly through the door, but the others surreptitiously; the contrast
in their voices—the one familiar, and the others strange and unknown;
the utterly differing motives with which they came to the fold—
the shepherd to care and provide pasture, and the others to plunder
and destroy, taking what was not theirs.

This picture Jesus has drawn is not simply a comparison or an allegory. His illustration is a general parable, called a *mashal,* "a mysterious saying full of compressed thought."[2] Those whose eyes have been opened spiritually, such as this new disciple healed of blindness, would see the truth hidden in the figurative language. But the spiritually blind, those who had cast the healed one out, would be baffled and angered. They *"did not understand the things which He spoke to them"* (v. 6).

THE ONLY DOOR

7 Then Jesus said to them again, "Most assuredly, I say to you, I am the door of the sheep.

8 "All who ever came before Me are thieves and robbers, but the sheep did not hear them.

9 "I am the door. If anyone enters by Me, he will be saved, and will go in and out and find pasture.

10 "The thief does not come except to steal, and to kill, and to destroy. I have come that they may have life, and that they may have it more abundantly.

John 10:7–10

Now Jesus becomes very specific and personal in illuminating the meaning of His illustration. There is a singleness, an exclusiveness, about His solemn declaration, *"I am the door of the sheep."* One theologian has called this "the offense of the particular." He is the one entrance by which the sheep can enter the fold and join the flock. There is no other way for them to have access to the full treasure of life.

I vividly recall the brief, intense visit I had backstage with John R. Mott more than thirty years ago. That amazing world Christian, a visionary layman whom God used in the early part of this century to call a whole generation of students to Christ and missionary service, was now well into his eighties. And although he had just finished pouring out his heart to several thousand students in one of his characteristically passionate missionary addresses, he was fresh and eager. His clear, piercing eyes and great mane of white hair reminded me of a shaggy old lion.

When I asked him about his Christian pilgrimage he spoke simply and tenderly of his "capitulation to Christ," as he called it, as an undergraduate student at Cornell University and of his continuous growth in the Spirit ever since. It had all been a great adventure, he said. Then he concluded, "After being on hundreds of university campuses in more than eighty countries and having seen all the great religions of the world firsthand, I know now more than ever that Christ towers over all the movements of history and religion. Absolutely unique! He stands erect among the fallen, clean among the defiled, Saviour of the world, King of kings and Lord of lords!"

What an eloquent way to put it! Christ is the one door of the sheep!

All who ever come before Jesus claiming to announce life apart from faith in Him cannot make themselves the door of the sheep. Actually they are thieves and robbers—whether they are priestly rulers, religious politicians whose hands have been dirtied ever since the time of the Maccabees, or those eager for power and recognition, claiming to be "the Messiah," leading the people astray with false promises, selfishly preying on them, dividing and robbing them. But the sheep have not heard these confusing, alien voices.

So when Jesus says, *"The thief does not come except to steal, and to kill, and to destroy,"* He is speaking to those who are standing before Him at this very moment. They have betrayed their calling to be spiritual leaders in the very way they have thrown out this one who has been healed, and in so doing have rejected the One who has healed him. Their motives to steal and destroy have been unmasked.

The church in every age has had to deal with those who try to crawl over the fence to take over the flock, claiming to be the door. In our day of anxiety and confusion, we confront everything from Eastern mysticism and "thought control" to the Unification Church and the Bahais; they are false prophets promising life, but in the end bringing death.

But with Jesus, there is life abundant. Those who enter by Him *"will be saved"* (v. 9). They are given wholeness as they join the other sheep in the fold. Here they live in liberty, freely going *"in and out,"* led by the One to whom they belong. They have heard the Shepherd call their names. And they are satisfied, for He provides *"pasture."* He shares with them the abundance of His own life.

Is this not what the blind man has been given? The salvation he received is both physical and spiritual. It also gave him freedom from the rigid legalism of the Jews, freedom from the fear of his parents, and the provision of the Shepherd, who has made him one of His flock.

THE GOOD SHEPHERD

11 "I am the good shepherd. The good shepherd gives His life for the sheep.

12 "But he who is a hireling and not the shepherd, one who does not own the sheep, sees the wolf coming and leaves the sheep and flees; and the wolf catches the sheep and scatters them.

13 "The hireling flees because he is a hireling and does not care about the sheep.

14 "I am the good shepherd; and I know My sheep, and am known by My own.

15 "As the Father knows Me, even so I know the Father; and I lay down My life for the sheep.

16 "And other sheep I have which are not of this fold; them also I must bring, and they will hear My voice; and there will be one flock and one shepherd.

John 10:11–16

Jesus again openly identifies Himself, *"I am the good shepherd."* In so doing He lays hold of the rich meaning of Yahweh as Israel's shepherd, their Ruler, Protector, Leader, and caring Companion. We have seen His warm, pastoral concern in calling and healing the blind man. So those who hear His voice and come to Him discover He is *"good,"* the winsome, attractive Shepherd.

Jesus is the good Shepherd because He gives His life for the sheep. This is why He has come. He cares for the sheep daily, watching, feeding, and protecting them. But in the end He must finally deal with their greatest danger, face the mightiest thief, the evil one, who spreads darkness and disorder through his own servants, the false shepherds. So the good Shepherd will give His life at the cross in this last struggle with this enemy and overcome.

Jesus is also the good Shepherd who knows the sheep and they know Him. There is a loving intimacy between Shepherd and sheep. The Shepherd knows the weak and the strong, the stubborn and the submissive ones, the hurts and the needs of every sheep. And the sheep know and trust their Shepherd—every inflection of His voice, the way by which He leads them out to pasture, His courage in the face of danger. He is their Shepherd. This intimate knowing between Shepherd and sheep is rooted in and modeled after the union between Father and Son.

It is in that knowing love for the sheep that the Shepherd lays down His life. The pain and joy and healing of His death is not for a particular flock, but is so universal and far-reaching that other sheep will hear His voice and come. There will be one Shepherd and one flock, not many. As the woman at the well, the impotent man at the pool, and the blind man have heard and come, so finally His voice will be heard throughout the whole Gentile world. Those who are outside will be included.

In these eight years we have served this courageous inner-city congregation we have watched in amazement as the Shepherd has been gathering His flock—many of them, it would seem, sheep not of this fold, but hearing His voice and coming. Out of the wounds of a terrible church split more than twenty years ago, the Lord is creating a new people—a strange, wonderful mixture of the curious, the seekers, and the needy joining with a faithful remnant to go in and out finding pasture.

One of these was Anna—frizzy-haired and anxious, coming forward at the invitation every six or eight weeks in some service of worship to let us know how desperately she wanted to be a part of His flock. Her childhood life had been filled with anger and trouble. Now two of her sons were in the state penitentiary, one for life, and her daughter was in alcoholic treatment. Anna always seemed to call our home during mealtime or late at night, either to vent her hostility, "I'm never coming back to that church again," or to confess her love for all of us, "I don't know what I'd ever do without that church." What joy it was to watch our people, at first cautiously, but then freely, accept her as one of us. Anna has since died, on the operating table, as the surgeon was trying to repair her stomach, badly damaged by a bleeding ulcer. She represents so many needy, dispossessed, neglected people who have come to us in these last years.

When Bob and Pat, who live five miles east of the church, began worshiping with us, I could not resist asking after some weeks, "Why in the world would you attend First Baptist when many of your tennis-playing and social friends belong to a strong, suburban church?" Bob's answer was classic, "We want to be a part of a church that treats Anna the way First Baptist does." And so they joined! As Jesus said, *"They will hear My voice; and there will be one flock and one shepherd"* (v. 16). His death reaches out and claims us all!

It is a different story with the hirelings. They seem so eager to watch the sheep, but are really more interested in their own gain. They want the catching and caring to be at their own convenience from eight to five and will run at the first sign of danger. These are the careless, indifferent shepherds who betray the sheep because their own selfish interests come first. This is the danger from within, which in many ways is more subtle and disastrous than the thieves and robbers who break in from the outside.

Jesus must have had those scathing words of judgment against false shepherds from Ezekiel's prophecy in mind when he spoke of hirelings,

> "Woe to the shepherds of Israel who feed themselves! . . . you slaughter the fatlings, but you do not feed the flock. . . . with force and cruelty you have ruled them. . . . So they were scattered because there was no shepherd; and they became food for all the beasts of the field when they were scattered" (Ezek. 34:2–5).

Later John speaks sadly of Judas, the betrayer, who left the twelve, "he then went out immediately. And it was night" (John 13:30). Then there were those who crept into the believing community creating confusion and spreading doubt by questioning the authority of the historical Jesus and denying the fleshliness of the Incarnate Son of God (1 John 2:18–23; 2 John 7).

When we came home from our midweek service this week the telephone was ringing, which is not an unusual occurrence. After the dear younger couple at the other end of the line had apologized for calling at this hour of the night they poured out their concern. These were thoughtful leaders in their church, not given to gossip. They were angered, puzzled, and hurt because they were convinced their pastor was giving false leadership by his life and words and their concern was not only for themselves but for the whole congregation which seemed to be drifting spiritually more and more. So we talked and prayed. I went to bed after this disturbing conversation with some of their painful words haunting me. "I have lost all respect for this man." "I just can't trust this guy any more." Any pastor can begin with high hopes and possibilities and end up becoming a hireling.

Laying Down His Life

17 "Therefore My Father loves Me, because I lay down My life that I may take it again.

18 "No one takes it from Me, but I lay it down of Myself. I have power to lay it down, and I have power to take it again. This command I have received from My Father."

19 Therefore there was a division again among the Jews because of these sayings.

20 And many of them said, "He has a demon and is mad. Why do you listen to Him?"

21 Others said, "These are not the words of one who has a demon. Can a demon open the eyes of the blind?"

John 10:17–21

It is the nature of love to reach out, to go the limit. So Jesus comes to lay down His life for the sheep as an amazing expression of the love of the Father and Son for each other. Jesus' death is not a last-minute strategy, nor is it an act of desperation. He is not being forced into an unexpected death, nor is His life taken from Him. His whole ministry from the very beginning has moved toward this final act of obedience, this offering of Himself for the sake of the sheep.

And as Jesus has the authority or right to lay down His life, so He has the power to take up His life again. The laying down and the taking up, the cross and the resurrection, are two sides of the one redemptive act. This power to lay down and take up is the same in Father and Son. Here is the mystery of the divine nature of Jesus, who is at one with the Father. What has been agreed upon in the Godhead, in the "counsels of eternity," for the salvation of all men, will be the historical event of both Jesus' death and resurrection. In all this He is utterly obedient to the Father.

These strong affirmations bring a division among the Jews. Again, Jesus is accused of having a demon. But others wonder if someone who has a demon can heal anyone! They cannot ignore the fact that this Man they accuse has caused the opening of a blind man's eyes. The works He does testify to who He is.

THE SHEEP HEAR AND FOLLOW

22 Now it was the Feast of Dedication in Jerusalem, and it was winter.

23 And Jesus walked in the temple, in Solomon's porch.

24 Then the Jews surrounded Him and said to Him, "How long do You keep us in doubt? If You are the Christ, tell us plainly."

25 Jesus answered them, "I told you, and you do not believe. The works that I do in My Father's name, they bear witness of Me.

26 "But you do not believe, because you are not of My sheep, as I said to you.

27 "My sheep hear My voice, and I know them, and they follow Me.

28 "And I give them eternal life, and they shall never perish; neither shall anyone snatch them out of My hand.

29 "My Father, who has given them to Me, is greater than all; and no one is able to snatch them out of My Father's hand.

30 "I and My Father are one."

John 10:22–30

The last scene in Jesus' public ministry takes place at the Feast of Dedication, sometimes called the Feast of Lights, which came three months after the Feast of Tabernacles. It was a time of great hope, for it marked the last national deliverance. It also celebrated the restoration and purification of the temple, particularly the altar, by Judas Maccabeus three years after its desecration by the Greek general Antiochus Epiphanes in 178 B.C. At this feast people hoped for new beginnings. Expectation filled the air. The people wondered, "Would God's divine deliverer come at this time to set His people free?"

The earlier conversations and questions continue here. The lapse of some months is not as important in the sequence as is the theme of the dialogue. It is now winter and the writer notes that Jesus moved to the east side of the temple, to Solomon's porch, to find shelter from the chilling winds. He *"walked,"* that moving way of teaching. Now the Jews press in, surround Him, not so much in hostility, it seems, as to ask Jesus the central, burning question of their existence, *"If You are the Christ, tell us plainly"* (v. 24). These men pondered and discussed continually the manner and time of the Messiah's coming. And in this celebration of restoration and hope, facing this strange Man, whom they could neither disregard nor explain, they must settle the question of His identity once and for all. For if what He was doing and saying was true, then there would emerge a new people which would mean the destruction of Judaism. And this was their whole life. So they were really asking, "How long will You continue to take away our life?"

But Jesus can only be known as the Messiah by spiritual insight, by hearing and seeing as the blind man had, not by verbal or human proofs. He cannot answer their question in the way these religious leaders want it answered. Over and over again He has urged these people to let His works, which have been done in His Father's name, bear witness to who He is. But they will not submit to that kind of evidence and so it is impossible for them to hear His voice and follow Him. They are not His sheep.

Jesus' sheep hear His voice and follow Him. He shared His abundant and eternal life with them so they will never perish. And no enemy, however strong he may seem, can snatch any of the sheep from Jesus' hand, because His Father, who has given them to the Good Shepherd, is greater than all enemies. The mighty sign of that holding power will be Jesus' resurrection from the dead. To be kept in Jesus' hand is to be held by the Father's hand, for they are One.

SANCTIFIED FOR THE WORLD

31 Then the Jews took up stones again to stone Him.

32 Jesus answered them, "Many good works I have shown you from My Father. For which of those works do you stone Me?"

33 The Jews answered Him, saying, "For a good work we do not stone You, but for blasphemy, and because You, being a Man, make Yourself God."

34 Jesus answered them, "Is it not written in your
law, *I said, "You are gods"* '?

35 "If He called them gods, to whom the word of
God came (and the Scripture cannot be broken),

36 "do you say of Him whom the Father sanctified
and sent into the world, 'You are blaspheming,' because
I said, 'I am the Son of God'?

37 "If I do not do the works of My Father, do not
believe Me;

38 "but if I do, though you do not believe Me,
believe the works, that you may know and believe
that the Father is in Me, and I in Him."

39 Therefore they sought again to seize Him, but
He escaped out of their hand.

John 10:31–39

The Jews are greatly incensed by Jesus' declaration that He is one
with the Father. Once again they take up stones. But Jesus knew
that according to the law they had no right to stone Him unless
there was a specific charge! So He wisely and quietly asks them,
"For which of those works do you stone Me?" (v. 32). And He has done
many. They can only answer that it is not for any works, but for
blasphemy because He makes Himself God. This is the first time in
this Gospel the Jews have officially accused Jesus of blasphemy. But
Jesus never "makes Himself anything. Everything that He is stems
from the Father. He is the Word of God who has become man."[3]

Jesus answers them by quoting from Psalm 82:6 in which unright-
eous judges who had given the people the Word of God were called
"gods." If unholy men who held high office were referred to as *"gods"*
because they were vehicles for God's message, then was it blasphemy
for the One whom God had *"sanctified and sent into the world"* to speak
of Himself as the Son of God?

As Moses and Jeremiah and all men whom God set apart for His
unique work had been consecrated, so Jesus, in a more vast, eternal
sense, has been *"sanctified"* by the Father for His awesome mission
in the world. Jesus had come and "pitched His tent" among men to
minister and give His life for the sheep in obedience to His Father.
His risen body was to become the eternal locus of worship, the place
of gathering for His people, in the new age of grace and truth. Surely
Jesus' words about His own consecration spoken in this earthly temple
which had been reconsecrated have a rich meaning for us. So often

He uses a significant physical celebration or event to illuminate a much greater, spiritual truth.

If these Jews cannot believe in Jesus, then they should at least test the credibility of His works, accept them for what they are, and through that insight, come to know that the Father has sent Him, for the Father is standing behind His works. Therefore He is acting as God's "deputy," as His *saliah*,[4] which in Jewish thought meant that He had the authority of His Sender. Then they might come to know that the Father and the Son dwell in each other. Jesus is carefully making His last open plea to these unbelieving listeners, only asking for an honest investigation of His ministry.

Again they seek to seize Him, but He escapes out of their *"hand"* (v. 39). Surely no human authority, however powerful, can finally take Him. That will be only as the Father allows it. Likewise, no enemy can snatch anyone whom the Son has given eternal life out of the Father's *"hand."*

A HARVEST IN JOHN'S COUNTRY

40 And He went away again beyond the Jordan to the place where John was baptizing at first, and there He stayed.

41 And many came to Him and said, "John performed no sign, but all the things that John spoke about this Man were true."

42 And many believed in Him there.

John 10:40–42

Jesus retreats, leaves this land of unbelief where His own have not received Him, moving to the place beyond the Jordan where John had first baptized. What memories and longings and gratitude must have stirred in Jesus as He returned to the setting where His public ministry had begun. We sense again His deep ties with the Baptizer, who by his faithful witness had prepared for a rich harvest which Jesus now reaps. Everything John had said about Jesus people now know is true—"the Lamb of God who takes away the sin of the world," "the Son of God," "One who baptizes with the Holy Spirit." And many believe. It is a rich time of fulfillment for Jesus before His final struggle.

NOTES

1. Wm. Temple, *Readings in St. John's Gospel,* p. 162.
2. W. B. Westcott, *The Gospel According to John,* p. 215.
3. Raymond E. Brown, *The Gospel According to John I–XII,* p. 408.
4. Ibid., p. 411.

CHAPTER ELEVEN

Loose Him and Let Him Go

John 11:1—12:11

In this last and most dramatic sign, the One who is Life confronts death and overcomes. This event is the doorway through which we enter the passion of Jesus. It is as if the glimpse of splendor seen in the raising of Lazarus is but a foretaste of that greater glory which breaks forth when Jesus steps forth in radiance and power on resurrection morning.

There are interesting similarities between Jesus' first sign at Cana and His last at Bethany. The one was so quiet and the other so awesome. Each takes place within the intimacy of a family circle—the one a wedding and the other a funeral. The central purpose in both miracles was that the glory of God might be manifested: the power of the Father made visible in the action of the Son as He turned water into wine and the tragedy of death into the joy of life. And in each case faith was born or renewed. At Cana Jesus' disciples believed in Him, and at Bethany they were strengthened in their faith.

A FRIEND IS SICK

1 Now a certain man was sick, Lazarus of Bethany, the town of Mary and her sister Martha.

2 It was that Mary who anointed the Lord with fragrant oil and wiped His feet with her hair, whose brother Lazarus was sick.

3 Therefore his sisters sent to Him, saying, "Lord, behold, he whom You love is sick."

4 When Jesus heard that, He said, "This sickness

is not to death, but for the glory of God, that the
Son of God may be glorified through it."

5 Now Jesus loved Martha and her sister and
Lazarus.

6 So, when He heard that he was sick, He stayed
two more days in the place where He was.

7 Then after this He said to His disciples, "Let us
go to Judea again."

8 His disciples said to Him, "Rabbi, lately the Jews
sought to stone You, and are You going there again?"

9 Jesus answered, "Are there not twelve hours in
the day? If anyone walks in the day, he does not
stumble, because he sees the light of this world.

10 "But if one walks in the night, he stumbles,
because there is no light in him."

11 These things He said, and after that He said to
them, "Our friend Lazarus sleeps, but I go that I may
wake him up."

12 Then His disciples said, "Lord, if he sleeps he
will get well."

13 However, Jesus spoke of his death, but they
thought that He was speaking about taking rest in
sleep.

14 Then Jesus said to them plainly, "Lazarus is dead.

15 "And I am glad for your sakes that I was not
there, that you may believe. Nevertheless let us go
to him."

16 Then Thomas, who is called Didymus, said to
his fellow disciples, "Let us also go, that we may die
with Him."

John 11:1–16

There is an intimate tenderness in the announcement brought to
Jesus that Lazarus, *"he whom You love,"* is sick (v. 3). Each of the people
in the home is identified. According to the account in Luke 10:38–
42 Jesus had enjoyed the hospitality of this home and during that
final, costly week it became His place of retreat (Matt. 21:17; Mark
11:11–12). We are made keenly aware here of the precious gift these
three loving friends were to Jesus, which underlines the deep need
all of us have for caring, understanding friends.

But if Jesus loved this family so dearly, how strange that He would
stay in this place two more days, unhurried and seemingly uncon-

cerned. Was there any ministry here more urgent than the need of His dear friend? But Jesus knew that His work of life at Bethany done in His own time would bring greater glory to His Father than if He hurried off to Bethany immediately.

It was after finishing whatever He was about that Jesus said to His disciples, *"Let us go to Judea again"* (v. 7). He does not say He wants to go to Bethany, but to unbelieving Judea, which will now become the place of His suffering and death. Little wonder His disciples, who are now calling Him "Rabbi," recall the last attempt of the Jews to stone Him and ask if He really is planning to go there again.

But there is an appointed time, the twelve hours of daylight, when work is to be done. This is a time when a man does not stumble because the sun is shining. When darkness comes no work can be done. So Jesus will finish the mission the Father has given Him during His appointed time before the darkness of opposition closes in! He knows what He must do and what God's timetable is. And no one, not even the needs of this beloved family at Bethany, can change that agenda.

How wise we are if we know that each of us has his own day of opportunity, a time for God's work. Night will come when we can no longer work.

And a part of that work for Jesus is to call Lazarus back to life. Jesus here speaks of his death as sleep, for physical death is merely an incident in the presence of the One who is Life. The disciples, still so earthbound, misunderstand and think that Jesus is speaking of that healing sleep which comes after the crisis and fever have passed. He would then become well. Would this not make the trip to Judea unnecessary?

Now Jesus bluntly states the simple fact, *"Lazarus is dead"* (v. 14). He is *"glad,"* not that Lazarus has died, but for the sake of His disciples whose faith will be strengthened when they see God's power manifested through His action. Now the time has come. *"Let us go"* (v. 15). They are not going to view a lifeless body; Jesus says they are going *"to him."*

It is then that Thomas, called Didymus, which is Greek for twin, speaks up. He is a realist who wants to be certain of all the facts before he makes a move (see John 20:24), and he says in effect to the rest of them, "We may as well go along and die with Him. It looks as if Jesus is going to Judea regardless of what we say. We know there will be trouble. But we've come this far, and we may as well go all the way." Perhaps there is a mixture of heroism and self-pitying desperation in his response.

LAZARUS IS DEAD

17 So when Jesus came, He found that he had already been in the tomb four days.

18 Now Bethany was near Jerusalem, about two miles away.

19 And many of the Jews had joined the women around Martha and Mary, to comfort them concerning their brother.

20 Then Martha, as soon as she heard that Jesus was coming, went and met Him, but Mary was sitting in the house.

21 Then Martha said to Jesus, "Lord, if You had been here, my brother would not have died.

22 "But even now I know that whatever You ask of God, God will give You."

23 Jesus said to her, "Your brother will rise again."

24 Martha said to Him, "I know that he will rise again in the resurrection at the last day."

25 Jesus said to her, "I am the resurrection and the life. He who believes in Me, though he may die, he shall live.

26 "And whoever lives and believes in Me shall never die. Do you believe this?"

27 She said to Him, "Yes, Lord, I believe that You are the Christ, the Son of God, who is to come into the world."

28 And when she had said these things, she went her way and secretly called Mary her sister, saying, "The Teacher has come and is calling for you."

29 As soon as she heard that, she arose quickly and came to Him.

30 Now Jesus had not yet come into the town, but was in the place where Martha met Him.

31 Then the Jews who were with her in the house, and comforting her, when they saw that Mary rose

up quickly and went out, followed her, saying, "She
is going to the tomb to weep there."

32 Then, when Mary came where Jesus was, and
saw Him, she fell down at His feet, saying to Him,
"Lord, if You had been here, my brother would not
have died."

John 11:17–32

There is no question that Lazarus has died. Twice it is stated that
his body has been in the grave four days. There was a Jewish belief
that the soul of the departed hovered around the body for three
days hoping to return, but when decomposition set in it would leave.
Lazarus may well have been dead by the time the messengers arrived
with the word that he was ill—there had been a days' journey for
them to the Jordan country, then Jesus' staying on two days before
taking the day's journey to Bethany. By the time He arrived the
body had begun to decay.

The proximity of Bethany to Jerusalem made it possible for many
of the *"Jews"* to join Martha and Mary in this time of mourning,
not enemies of Jesus, but friends of the family. This short distance
also meant that the startling news of Lazarus's resurrection could
be quickly carried to the disturbed, angry enemies of Jesus, who
would then begin immediately to plot how they might kill Him.

How differently the two sisters respond to the death of their brother
and the coming of Jesus. Martha, practical and realistic, the activist,
hurrying out to meet Jesus when she heard He was near. She could
not stay around the house mourning. How consistent with the picture
in Luke's Gospel where she is bustling around the kitchen preparing
the meal for their guest, impatient with Mary sitting at Jesus' feet
(Luke 10:38–42). How often I have been called to a home where
death has come and someone—a mother or a sister or a friend—in
the midst of the hushed grief will say, "Well, let's get some coffee
on." That was the spirit of Martha.

She expresses great faith in Jesus when she meets Him. It is simply
a fact, she declares, that if He had been with them her brother would
never have died. And even now she is certain that whatever Jesus
asks for, God will give. One wonders what she really meant, for
later conversation reveals she did not expect Lazarus to be raised.

When Jesus makes the general statement that her brother will rise again, her reply indicates she accepted the traditional Jewish belief in the resurrection at the last day. This is doctrine she had learned at the feet of the rabbis. Yes, she trusts Jesus, but she has not grasped the wonder of the life that is in Him. She does not yet understand who He really is. So often we know the Bible verses or the orthodox doctrine, little realizing the majestic, life-giving Presence the words reveal.

In verse 25 Jesus declares the Source of Lazarus's resurrection with His statement, *"I am the resurrection and the life"* . . . now! Resurrection, the defeat of death, is an event, a reality within Jesus who is Life. It is impossible for death to prevail in His presence! And this is not a concept or a doctrine, but a personal reality. One who clings to Him, is united with Him in faith, is living eternally now, as well as at the end. He will pass through an incident called physical death, but he cannot die eternally because He has put His trust in the One who is Life. So Godet says, "Jesus means therefore: In me the dead lives, and the living does not die."[1]

Then Jesus asks Martha directly if she believes this (v. 26). And while it appears she has not understood the total meaning of what Jesus has said, she accepts Him. She confesses He is the Christ, the Son of God, who has come from God Himself into the world. This means that Jesus stands with her in the presence of death, knowing with her its pain and terror, but offering life which can turn sorrow and separation into joy and wonder.

How vividly I recall being stopped almost abruptly in a hospital corridor by a doctor friend. He was eager to tell me that if he hadn't believed in life everlasting before, he did now. He had just returned from a small Minnesota town where he had attended the funeral service for the son of his beloved former pastor, Alvin Rogness, now president of Luther Seminary. Paul, after two years at Oxford as a Rhodes Scholar, was struck down by a truck ten minutes from his home. In a moment of time, this gifted life had been snuffed out.

The funeral service was a great, triumphant affair. But it was at the cemetery that this doctor had experienced the power of the resurrection anew. Paul's father conducted the committal service for his own son, sharing the living words of Scripture, then offering prayer, and finally leading the people in the favorite hymn of the family: "Abide with me! Fast falls the eventide; the darkness deepens, Lord, with me abide! When other helpers fail and comforts flee, help of the helpless, O abide with me!" As the great congregation began to sing those strong, hopeful words, more and more of the people became so overwhelmed by the occasion and the presence of the Lord that they could no longer sing. And finally it was the clear voice of the father at the head of the grave that stood out, "Heaven's morning breaks and earth's vain shadows flee; In life, in death, O Lord, abide with me!"[2]

Is not this what Martha will discover because she trusts the One who is life?

Now she calls her sister Mary. This intuitive, introspective woman, who wondered and brooded over the meaning of so many things, was now *"sitting in the house"* crushed with the loss of her brother. But why did Martha tell her secretly? Did Jesus want to see her alone? Was there fear even of these Jews who had come to mourn with them? When Martha speaks of Jesus as *"Teacher"* (v. 28), she is using a common term used by His close friends.

Now Mary rises quickly to go to Jesus, who is waiting for her where He had met Martha. That is an interesting detail which could only have been included by an eye witness. Her friends assume she is going out to the tomb to weep and join her, which meant there would be a large crowd of witnesses at the burial place. All of them will become bearers of the news, either as friends or enemies of Jesus.

Hardly a word is spoken as Mary meets Jesus. She can only fall at His feet in adoring worship. Even though, like Martha, she believes Jesus has come too late, she is overcome with gratitude. Jesus has come. How tenderly Jesus meets each of these sisters, who are so different! He meets one with words of life and the other with wordless acceptance. So He meets each of us, where we are with our needs and with what little faith we have.

THE WORD OF LIFE

33 Therefore, when Jesus saw her weeping, and the Jews who came with her weeping, He groaned in the spirit and was troubled.

34 And He said, "Where have you laid him?" They said to Him, "Lord, come and see."

35 Jesus wept.

36 Then the Jews said, "See how He loved him!"

37 And some of them said, "Could not this Man,

who opened the eyes of the blind, also have kept this man from dying?"

38 Then Jesus, again groaning in Himself, came to the tomb. It was a cave, and a stone lay against it.

39 Jesus said, "Take away the stone." Martha, the sister of him who was dead, said to Him, "Lord, by this time there is a stench, for he has been dead four days."

40 Jesus said to her, "Did I not say to you that if you would believe you would see the glory of God?"

41 Then they took away the stone from the place where the dead man was lying. And Jesus lifted up His eyes and said, "Father, I thank You that You have heard Me.

42 "And I know that You always hear Me, but because of the people who are standing by I said this, that they may believe that You sent Me."

43 And when He had said these things, He cried with a loud voice, "Lazarus, come forth!"

44 And he who had died came out bound hand and foot with graveclothes, and his face was wrapped with a cloth. Jesus said to them, "Loose him, and let him go."

John 11:33–44

Confronted by uninhibited weeping, the loud, unrestrained wailing of Mary and her friends, Jesus *"groaned in the spirit and was troubled"* (v. 33). He shuddered with grief and anger, even audibly like the snorting of horses. Who can fathom the depth of Jesus' human emotions at this moment? He is face to face with death, the stronghold of Satan. Not only is He confronting the power of darkness, but He is surrounded by unbelieving grief.

Now He begins to move toward His direct encounter with death by asking for directions, the only time He does so in this Gospel. *"Where have you laid him?"* (v. 34). And their response, *"Come and see,"* is reminiscent of the same invitation Jesus extended to His first disciples at the beginning of His ministry. However, they found life and light, and this invitation can only lead to a grave.

Now Jesus weeps quietly (v. 35). And His tears here are like those He sheds over the unbelieving city which will reject Him, missing its day of opportunity, its only hope for peace and healing, and so finally be destroyed (Luke 19:41). This crowd wrongly assumes that Jesus weeps because He loved Lazarus whose death is so final. And knowing about His healing of the blind man, they wonder why He could not have kept His friend from dying. Jesus grieves at the tomb because of the darkness which blinds the people to the Truth. They cannot see who it is that has come and what God will do through Him.

What a lesson Jesus' tears are for our churches. We are so unbelieving and sterile, so unconcerned and indifferent. How bereft we are of honest emotion. We can neither laugh nor cry. When was the last time we stood with Jesus before death and unbelief and wept?

Then Jesus takes over! What a difference that makes! When He gets to the tomb He simply commands that the stone be removed from the cave. Here the gruesome finality of death is made vividly clear again. But Martha, who has expressed such loving faith in Jesus, protests. The body will stink. Her brother has been in the tomb four days. What can anyone, even Jesus, do with a decomposing body?

But Jesus reminds her she will see the glory of God if she will believe. As the shining radiance of God's power will be seen here at this tomb, so in a few days His greatest splendor will break forth at another tomb. So often God has chosen to reveal His majesty unexpectedly in lowly, broken, needy places—like the simple and joyful worship service with Chaplain Ralph Allen and eight prisoners at the Sedgwick County Jail in which I recently took part. We met in a small, crowded room which also serves as the library for this badly overpopulated jail. A cross had been put on the table and the room then became a chapel. Among those eight eager, attentive men who were present—this is all that are allowed to attend because of space and security—were two accused of murder and three of armed robbery. To my dying day I shall never forget the enthusiastic, somewhat off-key singing of these words from the simple chorus, "Jehovah Jirah."

> My God shall supply all my needs
> According to his riches in Glory.
> He gives His angels watch over me
> Jehovah Jirah cares for me.

The glory of God had filled the place and I went on my way rejoicing.

In spite of Martha's misgivings, the people obey Jesus' command and the stone is removed. And in the midst of the stench of death and the unbelieving crowd, Jesus lifts His eyes toward "home" and offers a vibrant, believing prayer. One can sense the intimacy and union between Father and Son and the warm gratitude that the Father has already heard and answered. Jesus constantly abides in His Father's will, so all He does is a prayer. Jesus longs that all who have heard him conversing with His Father, these wondering, grieving people, will know that He has been sent by His Father.

Then there is the cry, the loud shout, *"Lazarus, come forth!"* (v. 43). The prayer and the act of obedience now become one. The Greek word for *shout* or *cry* is used only eight times in the whole Bible, and six of these times in John's Gospel. Four times the word is used in the eighteenth and nineteenth chapters (John 18:40; 19:6; 19:12; 19:15), when the crowd cries out for the crucifixion of Jesus. Theirs is the cry of death. His is the shout of life. John states it tersely, *"And he who had died came out."* Miracles of life do not need verbal embroidery. God spoke and something happened. The dead man heard the voice of the Shepherd and came to life.

Now Lazarus comes forth, still bound in the old grave clothes. And Jesus gives those in the crowd an incredible opportunity to participate, *"Loose him, and let him go"* (v. 44). Surely taking off these grave clothes could have been part of His miracle, but in His amazing humility, Jesus allows some in the crowd—could it have been Martha and Mary, or some new believers?—to be part of His work.

For thirty years as a pastor of three different congregations I have watched Jesus call men and women out of spiritual death into new life. I have never lost the wonder and excitement of that kind of resurrection. But then I have also seen loving, caring people reach out and welcome these people, helping them meet new friends and develop new habits, calling forth the gifts in them and encouraging them in discovering their ministry. They are taking off the grave clothes. This is part of the miracle. Joe McAuley in Ottawa, Jan Pay in Sioux Falls, and Jerold Hayes in Wichita represent an amazing procession of people called out of the tomb to discover a new family of hope eager to help set them free. But is not this the calling of a living, Spirit-filled congregation? *"Loose him, and let him go."*

THE PROPHECY OF CAIAPHAS

45 Then many of the Jews who had come to Mary, and had seen the things Jesus did, believed in Him.

46 But some of them went their way to the Pharisees and told them the things Jesus did.

47 Then the chief priests and the Pharisees gathered a council and said, "What shall we do? For this Man works many signs.

48 "If we let Him alone like this, everyone will believe in Him, and the Romans will come and take away both our place and nation."

49 And one of them, Caiaphas, being high priest that year, said to them, "You know nothing at all,

50 "nor do you consider that it is expedient for us that one man should die for the people, and not that the whole nation should perish."

51 Now this he did not say on his own authority; but being high priest that year, he prophesied that Jesus would die for the nation,

52 and not for that nation only, but also that He would gather together in one the children of God who were scattered abroad.

53 Then from that day on they plotted to put Him to death.

54 Therefore Jesus no longer walked openly among the Jews, but went from there into the country near the wilderness, to a city called Ephraim, and there remained with His disciples.

55 And the Passover of the Jews was near, and many went from the country up to Jerusalem before the Passover, to purify themselves.

56 Then they sought Jesus, and spoke among themselves as they stood in the temple, "What do you think—that He will not come to the feast?"

57 Now both the chief priests and the Pharisees had given a command, that if anyone knew where He was, he should report it, that they might seize Him.

John 11:45–57

"Many of the Jews" who have seen what Jesus has done now *"believed"* (v. 45). This forces the religious authorities to act. The Sanhedrin is

called into session with the chief priests, the Sadducees, taking the lead. In the face of Jesus' decisive action these men seem confused, wondering *"what shall we do?"* But if something is not done quickly the whole populace will come to believe in Him, which will surely become a threat to Rome. Then they *"will come and take away both our place and nation,"* crush what little freedom is left and destroy them as a people.

In the midst of this discussion Caiaphas, the high priest, makes a broad, sweeping statement. He was the high priest *"that year,"* the fateful year of God's mighty saving act! He is contemptuous of the naive, indecisive talk in the Council. Do these men not realize that it is expedient that one man should die so that the *"people,"* God's chosen ones, and the *"nation,"* the civil organization, will not perish? Here is a key saying, a prophetic utterance, from the mouth of an enemy. Caiaphas so speaks his own thoughts "that he pronounced a sentence of God unconsciously."[3] By a mysterious irony he interpreted the true meaning of the death of Jesus, "though in a way directly opposite to that which he apprehended."[4]

Jesus' death, arranged by Caiaphas and his fellow council members, was not only for the salvation of Israel, but for all God's children scattered abroad. Not only those separated geographically, but those divided culturally and spiritually. All mankind, Jew and Gentile, slave and free, male and female, would be drawn to Jesus, "lifted up," partaking in a common life with Him and with one another. This *"gathering together"* is John's way of speaking of the church (v. 52). God's dispersed are to be gathered into one family by Jesus as He gathered up the fragments at the feeding of the five thousand. "It is scarcely accidental that John's description of redeemed Jews and Gentiles gathered into one echoes the terminology of the eucharistically oriented multiplication of the loaves (John 6:13) where the fragments are gathered together."[5]

Now the decision is made, and the Council begins to make deliberate plans to kill Jesus. He no longer walks openly but withdraws to Ephraim, apparently a wild country northeast of Jerusalem, to remain *"with His disciples"* (v. 54). One wonders about the conversations, the teachings among these men during these last quiet days.

When the people begin arriving in Jerusalem to purify themselves before the Passover, they look for Jesus in the temple. Undoubtedly many recall times when they had heard Him teaching so boldly within the temple confines. Now, the people assumed that He probably would not be coming for the Passover because the word was out that if anyone knew where He was it was to be reported to the authorities who were eager to seize Him.

ANOINTING IN BETHANY

1 Then, six days before the Passover, Jesus came to Bethany, where Lazarus was who had been dead, whom He raised from the dead.

2 There they made Him a supper; and Martha served, but Lazarus was one of those who sat at the table with Him.

3 Then Mary took a pound of very costly oil of spikenard, anointed the feet of Jesus, and wiped His feet with her hair. And the house was filled with the fragrance of the oil.

4 Then one of His disciples, Judas Iscariot, Simon's son, who would betray Him, said,

5 "Why was this fragrant oil not sold for three hundred denarii and given to the poor?"

6 This he said, not that he cared for the poor, but because he was a thief, and had the money box, and used to take what was put in it.

7 Then Jesus said, "Let her alone; she has kept this for the day of My burial.

8 "For the poor you have with you always, but Me you do not have always."

John 12:1–8

In the meantime Jesus comes to a dinner party in Bethany. This feast of thanks, in which Lazarus, Martha, and Mary are involved, may well have taken place in the home of Simon the Leper if this is the same occasion recorded in Matthew 26:6–13 and Mark 14:3–9.

Martha is in her customary place of serving while Lazarus, never more fresh and alive, is at the table with Jesus. Even now one can almost hear the joy and soft laughter of their animated conversation as they eat and drink. It is Mary who kneels and anoints Jesus' feet, generously pouring out costly perfumed oil that was equivalent to the wages of a year's work, and then wiping His feet with her hair (v. 3). It is a symbol of consecration for that divine work which

Jesus was about to do. An early preparation for His death. Also a pledge of honor reserved for royalty. In a few days Jesus will enter Jerusalem as an anointed King.

The fragrance of this generous gift, so gratefully poured out, fills the house with far more than its sweet smell. It brought the warm, pervasive glow of love. One can always tell when a home has become a place of hospitality and caring because the smell of fragrant love poured out fills the air.

This act of love is so extravagant that Judas, who obviously feels it has been a waste, asks piously why this money could not have been given to the poor (v. 5). He asks this not because he cares, but because he is a selfish thief. Apparently Judas was gifted in handling money, so he had been given the responsibility for the common pot, which became his undoing. How often we go astray in the area of our strength. The gifted preacher can succumb to his ego, the brilliant accountant become an embezzler, or the empathetic counselor give in to adultery.

While Mary is giving her best in preparing for His death, the greed of Judas will cause Jesus' death. In Jewish thought, preparation for death was an act of mercy, a greater "good work" than justice, which was almsgiving for the poor. So Jesus commends Mary, not because He is indifferent to the poor, but because she has done a generous work of kindness preparing for His own death.

Destroying the Evidence

9 Then a great many of the Jews knew that He was there; and they came, not for Jesus' sake only, but that they might also see Lazarus, whom He had raised from the dead.
10 But the chief priests took counsel that they might also put Lazarus to death,
11 because on account of him many of the Jews went away and believed in Jesus.

John 12:9–11

People come to Bethany, not only to see Jesus, but to see the man He has raised from the dead. It is a procession of the curious. And they believe! So the *"chief priests"* take counsel on how even Lazarus can be put to death (v. 10). He is another evidence of Jesus' lifegiving power which is bringing men to faith. And this must be put to an end. One can feel both the fear and the paranoia of the hierarchy.

NOTES

1. Frederic Louis Godet, *Commentary on John's Gospel,* p. 740.
2. Rev. H. F. Lyte, "Abide With Me," 1847.
3. W. B. Westcott, *The Gospel According to John,* p. 175.
4. Ibid.
5. Raymond E. Brown, *The Gospel According to John I–XII,* p. 443.

CHAPTER TWELVE

A King on a Donkey's Colt

John 12:12–50

NATIONAL LIBERATOR OR SAVIOR?

12 The next day a great multitude that had come
to the feast, when they heard that Jesus was coming
to Jerusalem,

13 took branches of palm trees, went out to meet
Him, and cried out:

> "Hosanna!
> *'Blessed is He who comes in the name of the*
> *LORD!'*
> The King of Israel!"

14 Then Jesus, when He had found a young donkey,
sat on it; as it is written:

> 15 *"Fear not, daughter of Zion;*
> *Behold, your King is coming,*
> *Sitting on a donkey's colt."*

16 His disciples did not understand these things at
first; but when Jesus was glorified, then they
remembered that these things were written about Him
and that they had done these things to Him.

17 Therefore the people, who were with Him when
He called Lazarus out of his tomb and raised him from
the dead, bore witness.

18 For this reason the people also met Him, because
they heard that He had done this sign.

19 The Pharisees therefore said among themselves,
"You see that you are accomplishing nothing. Look,
the world has gone after Him!"

John 12:12–19

Lazarus has been raised from the dead! The word is out! There
are witnesses who have seen it. Now the One who raised him is
on His way to Jerusalem in spite of all the earlier threats from high
places. This must be the Messiah. He is coming to take over. One
can feel the excitement building!

Even while visiting villages in India or Africa on missionary tours
I have been utterly overwhelmed by the crowds, young and old,
running out breathlessly to meet us. We shrink back embarrassed.
How can anyone greet us in this way! We are only men—forgiven
sinners as they are. Ah, but they are coming with gratitude and joy.
We represent the people who first shared the good news with them,
bringing salvation and healing. This is why they shout and sing and
wave branches. So we join in the celebration.

But can anyone grasp the frenzied, bottled up emotions let loose
by these crowds welcoming Jesus to Jerusalem? Those who accompany
Him are eager to tell anyone who will listen the amazing things they
have seen. And people in the city, a great host who have come for
the feast, have heard He is coming and they surge out to meet Him,
and there is a mingling of crowds.

What mighty hopes and expectations they have. If Jesus has raised
a man from the dead, surely He can set them free from the shackles
of Rome. He has come to occupy the throne of David. This Jesus
is their "national liberator," so everything they do has political over-
tones. Even the palm branches are a sign of Maccabean nationalism.
For when Judas Maccabeus rededicated the temple altar in 164 B.C.
after the desecration by the Syrians, the Jews came bringing palms
to the temple. They were victors! And later when his brother Simon
conquered the Jerusalem citadel in 142 B.C. the Jews took possession
carrying palm fronds.

Even the phrase *"went out to meet Him"* is a "normal Greek expression
used to describe the joyful reception of Hellenistic sovereigns into
a city."[1] And the shout *"Hosanna"* which means "save now" is an
acclamation of praise greeting Jesus as a conqueror. There is even a
political innuendo in the cry, *"Blessed is He who comes in the name of the
Lord!"* because the words *"The King of Israel!"* are added (v. 13). Their

hopes and ambitions for Israel are man-centered and nationalistic. These people have misunderstood the meaning and implications of the raising of Lazarus as did the crowd of five thousand whom Jesus fed. They are about to acclaim Jesus as the king who will overthrow Rome and set them free.

Jesus answers the pressure and false expectations of this frenzied crowd with a prophetic, but simple, act. He *"found a young donkey"* and *"sat on it"* (v. 14). Yes, He is coming as Messiah. John's words from Zechariah 9:9, which speak of the long-expected Chosen One, make this clear, *"Behold, your King is coming, sitting on a donkey's colt."* Had Jesus come to fulfill the earthly, nationalistic ambitions of these people He would have ridden a horse, as a warring liberator. But He comes on a donkey, an honored animal in that day, as a Man of Peace.

Not even the disciples understood what this all meant until much later when they were enlightened by the Spirit and they saw it through the crucifixion and resurrection.

Raymond Brown has made the suggestion that the first part of this quotation, *"Fear not, daughter of Zion,"* may well have come from the prophecy of Zephaniah 3:16.[2] This would be another of John's compound quotations, using two passages to open up a world of larger meaning. Who then is the Messiah? "The Lord your God in your midst, the Mighty One, will save. . . . I will gather those who sorrow. . . . I will deal with all who afflict you; I will save the lame" (Zeph. 3:17–19). The raising of Lazarus is not a sign of nationalistic glory for Israel, but a promise that when the Messiah comes He will share the gift of healing and life with all the people!

But do we not often have false, unholy expectations of what Jesus will do for us—be our errand boy and satisfy our needs; help make our way easy and comfortable; be on our side wherever we decide to fight, be that Lebanon or El Salvador or some other place? But all our perverted, self-centered hopes are radically altered by this One who comes riding on a young donkey.

The frustrated, impatient Pharisees are now on the defensive. But in their angry discussion they unknowingly reveal how universal the mission of Jesus has really become. For as they accuse one another of accomplishing nothing in the face of this dramatic turn of events, they are forced to admit, *"Look, the world has gone after Him!"* (v. 19).

DEATH THAT BRINGS A RICH HARVEST

20 Now there were certain Greeks among those who came up to worship at the feast.

21 Then they came to Philip, who was from Bethsaida of Galilee, and asked him, saying, "Sir, we wish to see Jesus."

22 Philip came and told Andrew, and in turn Andrew and Philip told Jesus.

23 But Jesus answered them, saying, "The hour has come that the Son of Man should be glorified.

24 "Most assuredly, I say to you, unless a grain of wheat falls into the ground and dies, it remains alone; but if it dies, it produces much grain.

25 "He who loves his life will lose it, and he who hates his life in this world will keep it to eternal life.

26 "If anyone serves Me, let him follow Me; and where I am, there My servant will be also. If anyone serves Me, him My Father will honor.

John 12:20–26

Now the Greeks come. The "other sheep, not of this flock" have heard the voice of the Shepherd. The children of God, who are scattered abroad, are being gathered. These are God-fearing Gentiles, possibly proselytes, who have come for the feast. They seek out Philip because they can identify with him. His name is Greek and he comes from a predominantly Gentile area. He is the easiest for them to approach, one of their own "social network." Incidentally, those personal, family, and neighborhood ties are at the heart of most lasting evangelism. They address Philip with respect as they make their request known, *"Sir, we wish to see Jesus"* (v. 21). It is not a matter of looking at Him or meeting a "celebrity," but of visiting with Him, getting to know Him.

Philip, who seems a bit slow and indecisive throughout this Gospel, is not quite certain what he ought to do. So he shares the hopes of these people with Andrew, the one who is so often the introducer or "middleman." Together they take this request to Jesus who at first seems to ignore it.

However, the visit of these Greeks indicates a crucial moment is here. Jesus' hour of glory has come! So often He has said it will come. Now it is here. The coming of the Gentiles, who represent a waiting world, is the sign that the time to lay down His life has come.

His own death, in "the economy of salvation," is like the parable of the grain of wheat which must die if there is to be a harvest. There is no fruit apart from the death and burial of the seed. It is the same with Jesus, who speaks here of His own unique death. There will be no "multiplication of life" without His being cast into the ground.

This will be the glorification of the Son of Man (v. 23). But He is not using this designation as the Jews commonly understood it (Dan. 7:13–14), as the undefeatable world conqueror sent by God. He is not the tremendous figure held on leash by God until the day when He would destroy all enemies. No, while Jesus is the mighty Son of God, He comes, lowly and meek, to be crucified that sin and death might be destroyed.

The disciple is also involved in this harvest. He does not cling with a passion to life in this world, but gives it up, hates it, lets it go, and paradoxically discovers eternal life. He can only share in the resurrected life of his Lord if he dies with Jesus.

This becomes a life of service, following Jesus, learning to be obedient to Him. He will then be with Jesus wherever He is, in this world or in heaven. "To serve Jesus, that is to live according to the sequence obedience-death-life, is to live the life that is honored by God."[3]

So Jesus is not ignoring the Greeks. They will come to "see Jesus" through the faithful witness and ministry of obedient disciples who have lost their lives to serve Jesus wherever He is. Thus Jesus will be universalized in a great harvest.

We catch glimpses of His harvest with June Sutton and Loren Noren in the high rise apartments of Hong Kong; with Michael Zhidkov in the amazing Moscow Baptist Church; with Daniel Fountain in a public health ministry in Vanga, Zaire; or even here in Wichita as we seek to minister in the inner city with our new friends the Southeast Asians, and the poor and emotionally damaged who come our way, as well as the middle-class suburbanites—streams of joyful worshipers, rejoicing in healing and salvation, becoming salt and light in the midst of the world.

FOR THIS PURPOSE

27 "Now My soul is troubled, and what shall I say? 'Father, save Me from this hour'? But for this purpose I came to this hour.

28 "Father, glorify Your name." Then a voice came from heaven, saying, "I have both glorified it and will glorify it again."

29 Therefore the people who stood by and heard it said that it had thundered. Others said, "An angel has spoken to Him."

30 Jesus answered and said, "This voice did not come because of Me, but for your sake.

31 "Now is the judgment of this world; now the ruler of this world will be cast out.

32 "And I, if I am lifted up from the earth, will draw all peoples to Myself."

33 This He said, signifying by what death He would die.

34 The people answered Him, "We have heard from the law that the Christ remains forever; and how can You say, 'The Son of Man must be lifted up'? Who is this Son of Man?"

35 Then Jesus said to them, "A little while longer the light is with you. Walk while you have the light, lest darkness overtake you; he who walks in darkness does not know where he is going.

36 "While you have the light, believe in the light, that you may become sons of light." These things Jesus spoke, and departed, and was hidden from them.

John 12:27–36

The Man who was weary at a well and wept before a tomb does not go automatically or casually to the cross. The flesh shrinks from this awesome death. Here the anguish, the longing of Jesus to avoid the cross, is boldly recorded.

But there is no turning back from the decision made in the counsels of eternity. Jesus has come in loving obedience to the Father's will and every move of His ministry has been a response to that plan. That faithfulness has brought Him to this hour. And there will never be a harvest, the Greeks will never know, unless Jesus completes

His mission. For this purpose He has come! So the trembling, questioning cry, *"Father, save Me from this hour,"* is answered by the Son's decisive prayer of obedience, *"Father, glorify Your name"* (vv. 27–28). That name has been entrusted to Jesus and now in His last, costly act He will lift that name up above all other names.

Then, as at His baptism and His transfiguration, the Father's voice is heard. His name has been glorified throughout all of Jesus' ministry, from the Jordan to Bethany, and now in this hour He will glorify it again. This is a sign of the Father's approval. Are we not often hesitant and indecisive in seeking to obey our Father? We see through a glass darkly and hear so indistinctly even though we are eager to be faithful. But then as we take a feeble step of faith with what light we have and move out we are affirmed and blessed by the One we seek to obey.

After weeks of struggle, with so much uncertainty and inner debate, Ruth and I finally yielded to what seemed to be the inner pressure of the Lord. We left our great, exciting family in Sioux Falls, a church we had been a part of for sixteen years, to cast our lot with a needy, hopeful congregation in Wichita. As they had said, "All we have is a huge building and lots of problems." At first we were so certain we were to turn down this invitation to continue our ministry in Sioux Falls. Then I heard the unexpected word of the Lord through a Catholic priest. It was then I became fearfully aware that God wanted us to move to a "new country." When I came home and shared this sudden turn of events with Ruth she simply picked up a book and pointed to a chapter she had been reading that day. It was entitled "The Joy of Obedience" from Catherine Marshall's book *Something More.* We read together through tear-filled eyes and, as we prayed, we knew we had both heard the Father's voice. He will always let us know, sooner or later.

That voice could have been a moment of awakening for this crowd, making them aware of the grave importance of this hour. But they are confused, incapable of hearing the voice of the Father, as they have been unable to hear the word of His Son. So now the speech of God for them is only sound, thunder or perhaps angels!

But the judgment of God will be known in what is to take place. The cross is always a time and place of crisis and decision, where darkness and evil are unmasked and overcome, but also where faith and life are released.

I vividly recall leaving Nickerson Field in Boston a couple of years ago with thousands of other hushed, thoughtful people. We had just heard Billy Graham preach a powerful sermon on the cross. There had been an unusual spirit of God's nearness during the service even though a soft drizzle had fallen during most of it. At the climax, hundreds had come forward to stand quietly and pray and receive encouragement in their decision. As we were leaving, nearing the edge of the field, I heard someone say, "Billy's always best when he preaches on the cross." Why not? That is the pivotal point, the center of it all, the place of judgment and life.

In this hour of struggle, as Jesus moves into enemy territory, the *"ruler of this world"* is driven "out of his former domain . . . his office and power."[4] The Son of Man has come to reclaim all that his greatest enemy has usurped. So as Jesus is *"lifted up"* from the earth on the cross (John 3:14; 8:28), and through His ascension to His place of power, the evil one is *"cast out"!* A "new Monarch" has come who will draw *"all men"* to Himself. Here is Jesus' answer to the Gentiles!

All this has upset and baffled *"the people."* They had welcomed Jesus as the Messiah of the Jews, assuming that He would reign as a permanent King here on earth. Then what did Jesus mean talking about His dying? He has shattered their assumptions. So when they ask, *"Who is this Son of Man?"* it is their last opportunity to hear.

But Jesus does not answer them directly. He repeats language He has used before in John 7:33, 9:4, and 11:9–10 in saying the Light will be with them now only for a short time. They must either believe in Him, walk in the Light, and become sons of light, or darkness will overtake them as they stumble on toward their destruction.

Jesus leaves these men directly after He has confronted them with the ultimate choice between light and darkness. Jesus illustrates dramatically the passing of the light as He hides Himself.

HARDENED HEARTS, BUT A REMNANT

37 But although He had done so many signs before them, they did not believe in Him,
38 that the word of Isaiah the prophet might be fulfilled, which he spoke:

"Lord, who has believed our report?
And to whom has the arm
of the LORD been revealed?"

39 Therefore they could not believe, because Isaiah
said again:

40 *"He has blinded their eyes and*
hardened their heart,
Lest they should see with their eyes
And understand with their heart,
Lest they should turn,
so that I should heal them."

41 These things Isaiah said when he saw His glory
and spoke of Him.

42 Nevertheless even among the rulers many
believed in Him, but because of the Pharisees they
did not confess Him, lest they should be put out of
the synagogue;

43 for they loved the praise of men more than the
praise of God.

John 12:37–43

Here at the conclusion of Jesus' public ministry John is compelled
to ponder the darkness of unbelief which engulfs His people. *"Although*
He had done so many signs before them, they did not believe in Him" (v. 37).
What tragic words! John has witnessed Jesus facing the stubborn
misunderstanding and angry rejection of the very ones who should
have accepted Him at every turn. All this has been a fulfillment of
those words in the prologue, "He came to His own, and His own
did not receive Him" (1:11).

John emphasizes the repeated opportunities his own countrymen
have had to know who Jesus is and why He has come by quoting
from Isaiah. They have neither heard nor understood His teaching
from the Father. *"Who has believed our report?"* And they have belittled
and spurned His mighty works of provision and healing. *"To whom*
has the arm of the Lord been revealed?"

Then in verse 40 John refers to the words the Lord spoke to Isaiah
when He called him to be a prophet. The longer Isaiah would faithfully call his people home, the more their eyes would be blinded
and their hearts hardened. This is a mysterious and dark passage.

The repeated rejection of the Lord, although He graciously deals with His people, is an old and sad story.

There is no neutral ground when God calls. Once Jesus appears and makes His claim men must decide. Who can fathom, in this moral warfare, the evil that moves men away from the Light? Rejection moves at its own pace from misunderstanding, to ridicule, then to anger, and finally death. Their ears cannot hear and their hearts are hardened.

The Hebrews, who had such a profound understanding of a sovereign God, were not afraid to say that He is ultimately responsible for this hardening. There is nothing outside His control, even our choosing to turn against Him. This misuse of our freedom, our spurning of His initiative, is finally His responsibility. Otherwise He would not be God.

And John is reminding us that this awesome rejection of Jesus by His own should not surprise us either. Is this not what Isaiah, who saw the glory of Jesus long ago, had said would happen? If we take Scripture seriously, then we see that this was a predicted spiritual fact.

Does this mean that the door is closed? That this unbelief of the Jewish people was predetermined before Jesus ever came? No, paradoxically this rejection does not mean that! For there is a *"nevertheless"* in verse 42. *"Even among the rulers many believed in Him."* At this very time, in the shadow of the cross, there is a remnant. Some have heard His voice, even here. Fearful and tentative, yes. But their faith, however hidden, was a courageous act, not unlike that which I have known among fellow believers in the Soviet Union. These who came to believe were *"rulers"* in the midst of those who were plotting Jesus' death.

And they were anxious lest they be put out of the synagogue, for they at this stage *"loved the praise of men more than the praise of God."* Before we are too critical of them we need to deal with our own timidity, our own fear of social pressures. Who knows but what some of these were not among the five hundred who saw Jesus after He was raised from the dead (1 Cor. 15:6) and later were among those in the upper room when they received a "holy boldness."

John is writing, not only for non-believers, Greek and Hebrew, but for those who have come to believe in Jesus and are now struggling with the issue of being ostracized from their synagogues and cut off from the only life they have known. This is a word of encouragement and challenge for them from a fellow Jew.

215

FAITHFULNESS TO THE FATHER'S WORD

44 Then Jesus cried out and said, "He who believes in Me, believes not in Me but in Him who sent Me.

45 "And he who sees Me sees Him who sent Me.

46 "I have come as a light into the world, that whoever believes in Me should not abide in darkness.

47 "And if anyone hears My words, and does not believe, I do not judge him; for I did not come to judge the world but to save the world.

48 "He who rejects Me, and does not receive My words, has that which judges him—the word that I have spoken will judge him in the last day.

49 "For I have not spoken on My own authority; but the Father who sent Me gave Me a command, what I should say and what I should speak.

50 "And I know that His command is everlasting life. Therefore, whatever I speak, just as the Father has told Me, so I speak."

John 12:44–50

Jesus now cries out a clear, strong word in the face of the unbelief of the people. We have here a brief summary of the person of Jesus and what His mission has been through the word He has spoken.

Throughout His ministry He has been eager to give His Father the glory. So He makes it plain that faith is not to finally rest in Him, but in His Father who sent Him and commissioned Him. We are not saved by forming a "Jesus cult," but by believing in His Father. Likewise seeing Jesus is seeing the Father since the Son abides in the Father and the Father in the Son. So salvation, being brought from darkness into light, comes from this faith and sight!

Neither are the words Jesus speaks, bringing light to all who believe, given on His own authority. They come by command of the Father and they are the source of either judgment or life. Jesus has not come to judge, but to save! But His words, which come from the Father, bring judgment, both in this present moment and at the last day. That word, which will shortly be the act of the Son on the cross, will divide and condemn, but also bless and heal.

NOTES

1. Raymond E. Brown, *The Gospel According to John I–XII*, pp. 461–462.
2. Ibid., p. 462.
3. Sir Edwyn Hoskyns, *The Fourth Gospel*, p. 424.
4. Frederic Louis Godet, *Commentary on John's Gospel*, p. 787.

CHAPTER THIRTEEN

A Place in Him

John 13:1—16:33

Jesus, knowing that *"His hour had come,"* gathers His chosen ones for a meal (v. 1). It is a tender, but painful moment. He is like an elder brother with His family, unburdening His heart and sharing with them the meaning of the momentous events which are to take place. He also lovingly reassures these men that He will not leave them as orphans, but that they can only have the resources and power of His inner Presence after He is lifted up in death and resurrection.

All through the conversation (chaps. 13–16) He uses phrases that refer to relationships such as "you ought to wash one another's feet," "love one another as I have loved you," "I will come to you," "abide in Me and I in you." The focal point of this section is the Greek word *monē*, translated "dwelling place" or a "place for you" (14:2, 23). That "place" is not a geographic location, but it means "abiding" in Jesus, welcoming the Helper He sends as a "guide," being at home with the Father. Raymond Brown concludes a section dealing with the relational suggestiveness of this word, "In using *monē* John may be referring to places (or situations) where the disciples can dwell in peace by remaining with the Father."[1] So it seems this is the theme that runs through this whole section of intimate teaching.

I heard an echo of this in a visit Ruth and I had recently with a dear older friend who is now struggling with her health. Since she had come to the health center several months before, someone had been moved into her efficiency apartment, and when we visited her, she was facing the prospect of being moved again. As she shared this with some pain, she finally said, "Well, I guess they'll be moving me again, but wherever I am, there it will be home." She is at peace, for she has found a place of dwelling more permanent than any earthly setting, a *monē*. Likewise, Jesus is reassuring His disciples—

218

then and now—that He will be their "place" regardless of what happens.

THE WASHING

1 Now before the feast of the Passover, when Jesus knew that His hour had come that He should depart from this world to the Father, having loved His own who were in the world, He loved them to the end.

2 And supper being ended, the devil having already put it into the heart of Judas Iscariot, Simon's son, to betray Him,

3 Jesus, knowing that the Father had given all things into His hands, and that He had come from God and was going to God,

4 rose from supper and laid aside His garments, took a towel and girded Himself.

5 After that, He poured water into a basin and began to wash the disciples' feet, and to wipe them with the towel with which He was girded.

6 Then He came to Simon Peter. And Peter said to Him, "Lord, are You washing my feet?"

7 Jesus answered and said to him, "What I am doing you do not understand now, but you will know after this."

8 Peter said to Him, "You shall never wash my feet!" Jesus answered him, "If I do not wash you, you have no part with Me."

9 Simon Peter said to Him, "Lord, not my feet only, but also my hands and my head!"

10 Jesus said to him, "He who is bathed needs only to wash his feet, but is completely clean; and you are clean, but not all of you."

11 For He knew who would betray Him; therefore He said, "You are not all clean."

John 13:1–11

There are unique marks of the Passover which characterize this last meal Jesus eats with His disciples—sacrifice, farewell, and even celebration—even though it is eaten before the actual Passover. Jesus loves these men, *"His own,"* to the uttermost! That unconditional and eternal love will bring Him to the cross, the way by which He departs to again be with His Father. And the instrument of His death is at the table with Him. For the intention of betrayal has already entered the heart of Judas, who is now under the dominion of the devil.

In the midst of the silent struggle going on during the meal, the purpose of God is being worked out. The Father has not become a bystander, removed from the evil which is closing in on His Son. He is with Him and has given Him authority and power to finish the work for which He has come. *"The Father had given all things into His hands"* (v. 3). Therefore, Jesus is a free man, knowing who He is, why He has come, and what will be the end of His journey.

As the supper ends, Jesus, who is completely in command of the situation, acts out the significance of His own death. How vividly the details of Jesus' deliberate moves stand out: *"Jesus . . . rose from supper and laid aside His garments, took a towel and girded Himself. After that, He poured water into a basin and began to wash the disciples' feet, and to wipe them with the towel"* (vv. 4–5). This is far more than a courteous gesture by which He is attempting to give His disciples an ethical lesson in serving. Hoskyns has written, "The washing of the disciples' feet rests upon and interprets the death of the Lord."[2] The words "laid aside" (v. 4) and later when He had "taken" [His garments] (v. 12) are identical to those He uses when He earlier speaks of His own death as the Good Shepherd: "I lay down my life that I may take it again" (John 10:11, 15, 17, 18). This is an act of incredible humility when Jesus voluntarily does the menial work of a slave, but far more, it is a parable in action of the sacrifice of His own life.

These men respond in stunned silence. No one speaks until Jesus comes to Peter. He calls the One who stoops before him, *"Lord,"* and asks in amazement, *"are You washing my feet?"* Jesus makes it plain that *"after this"* he will know why. His death and resurrection will give meaning to this act of washing.

Then Peter draws back in embarrassed pride and emphatically refuses to let Jesus wash his feet. How can a sinful, stubborn man such as he accept this lowly gesture of grace? Is not this the problem with most of us? We are great achievers, eager to work our way up, but fearfully unwilling to accept the gift of the One who kneels before us.

But if Peter will not accept the washing, Jesus says *"you have no part with Me"* (v. 8). His rejection of this gift is infinitely more significant than refusing the offer to have his dusty feet washed. He is spurning Jesus' personal gift of cleansing in His blood. The washing of Peter's feet points to Jesus' saving example on the cross. It is more than an act of humility to be imitated. If he does not accept this gift, he cannot receive all that Jesus has to give him. Raymond Brown has pointed out that the Greek expression *eichein meros,* which is translated here "part of Him," means more than having fellowship with Jesus. *Meros* has the same meaning as the Hebrew *beleq,* the word which describes the heritage which God has promised Israel.[3] So in rejecting Jesus' offer of washing Peter is turning away from his "heritage," giving up those riches that can only be his through Jesus' sacrificial death.

In response Peter goes to the other extreme. If this footwashing means receiving all the benefits of Jesus' death, then why not wash the whole body? The more washings, the better. But Peter has missed the point of what Jesus has said. It is the foot washing that is important, because it symbolizes Jesus' death. More washings do not add to the "once for all" saving work of Jesus on the cross.

There is one present who is not changed by the footwashing. Judas has not opened himself to the ministry of Jesus. He has removed himself from the sphere of His love by becoming the tool of the devil's hatred.

THE TEACHING

12 So when He had washed their feet, taken His garments, and sat down again, He said to them, "Do you know what I have done to you?

13 "You call me Teacher and Lord, and you say well, for so I am.

14 "If I then, your Lord and Teacher, have washed your feet, you also ought to wash one another's feet.

15 "For I have given you an example, that you should do as I have done to you.

16 "Most assuredly, I say to you, a servant is not greater than his master; nor is he who is sent greater than he who sent him.

17 "If you know these things, happy are you if you do them.

18 "I do not speak concerning all of you. I know whom I have chosen; but that the Scripture may be

fulfilled, 'He who eats bread with Me has lifted up his heel against Me.'

19 "Now I tell you before it comes, that when it comes to pass, you may believe that I am He.

20 "Most assuredly, I say to you, he who receives whomever I send receives Me; and he who receives Me receives Him who sent Me."

John 13:12–20

Jesus accepts it when His disciples address Him with respect as *"Teacher and Lord,"* for they are under His authority. If then He has washed their feet as an example and they are "part" of Him, they are under obligation to do to one another what He has done to them. They have a debt. They *"ought to"* wash one another's feet, which means laying down their lives for one another. They are to enter into the sacrifice of the cross in their relations with one another.

Bickerings, jealousies, and competitiveness have frequently crept in among these men. Each man is so utterly different; there is much about each one that "rubs the others the wrong way." But Jesus has chosen them and called them to be a new community. But this is an impossibility unless they first allow Jesus to wash their feet!

So it is with us. How often we are exasperated or angered by someone we call a brother or a sister. And a wall, a distance, comes between us. How embarrassing or difficult it is then to go to them and wash their feet, to say, "I have not understood," or "Will you forgive me?" or "I affirm and bless you in the name of the One who has washed my feet." I have spent some costly moments, after being inwardly pushed and prodded by the Spirit, before I would finally go nervously to the one I had hurt or offended to confess and ask for forgiveness.

I had such a luncheon a week ago with a dear friend whom I had hurt because of some careless, rather pontifical comments I had made in the Sunday announcements. This friend was gracious enough to write me sharing her honest feelings. We were a bit stiff at first, but then we shared our differences in love, and we both left laughing with joy and gratitude. Much of the sickness in the institutional church has been caused by our unwillingness to wash one another's feet.

When we do what Jesus has shown and taught us, and not only

approve and admire it, we will be *"happy"* because we will be nearer Him (v. 17).

But there is one in Jesus' band who has cut himself off from all life. He neither hears nor intends to obey, for he has rejected his calling and turned against his Friend. Jesus quotes a poignant passage from Psalm 41:9, saying this is a fulfillment of a prophecy. The one who has broken bread with Jesus, a sacred, intimate ritual of friendship, has now lifted up his heel against Him, which is "a metaphor derived from the lifting up of a horse's hoof preparatory to kicking."[4]

The treachery of Judas, which will precipitate Jesus' death, will shatter this small group. So Jesus warns them that, however overwhelming the darkness of defeat will become, they can still believe, because He will always be the "I AM" (v. 19).

As Jesus has been sent to live and die as a slave, so we are sent as His slaves to live out this "footwashing" style of life. And as we go as a "part" of Him, Jesus will be received as will His Father. Here is the missionary theme which runs all through this Gospel. As He has been sent by the Father, so He sends us.

DIPPING THE BREAD

21 When Jesus had said these things, He was troubled in spirit, and testified and said, "Most assuredly, I say to you, one of you will betray Me."

22 Then the disciples looked at one another, perplexed about whom He spoke.

23 Now there was leaning on Jesus' bosom one of His disciples, whom Jesus loved.

24 Simon Peter therefore motioned to him to ask who it was of whom He spoke.

25 Then, leaning back on Jesus' breast, he said to Him, "Lord, who is it?"

26 Jesus answered, "It is he to whom I shall give a piece of bread when I have dipped it." And having dipped the bread, He gave it to Judas Iscariot, the son of Simon.

27 Now after the piece of bread, Satan entered him. Then Jesus said to him, "What you do, do quickly."

28 But no one at the table knew for what reason
He said this to him.

29 For some thought, because Judas had the money
box, that Jesus had said to him, "Buy those things
we need for the feast," or that he should give
something to the poor.

30 Having received the piece of bread, he then went
out immediately. And it was night.

John 13:21–30

Jesus is *"troubled"* in the depths of his being. He has "lost" Judas
and is painfully aware of His destiny. Jesus now is facing Satan in
the presence of death. Earlier He has spoken generally of the betrayer.
Now He becomes specific, *"One of you will betray Me"* (v. 21). It is a
solemn, frightening moment. There are only twelve possibilities. A
shiver of perplexed fear runs through the little group as they *"look
at one another"* (v. 22).

Here John, the writer of the Gospel, emerges as one *"whom Jesus
loved"* although his name is never mentioned. He is *"leaning on Jesus'
bosom"* on the couch in the common eating arrangement of that day.
As the Son is in the Father's bosom, so the faithful disciple is in
the bosom of the Son, a sure "place." Peter, who is apparently at
some distance, encourages John with a nod to ask Jesus, *"Lord, who
is it?"* Jesus then replies, *"It is he to whom I shall give a piece of bread
when I have dipped it"* (v. 26). All this must have been a very quiet
exchange in the midst of the wondering disciples.

Now Jesus makes His move! He dips the bread and gives it to
Judas who is near Jesus, perhaps to His immediate left, since he is
the treasurer of the group. Judas is the first to receive food, a sign
of honor. This is love's last appeal! Jesus is reaching out to him as
a friend. It must have been a long, intense moment of struggle when
Jesus gave Judas the bread. The stakes were so high. One wonders
if Judas could look into Jesus' eyes.

But at that moment *"Satan entered him"* (v. 27). He is now his complete
master. There is no turning back. The thought of betrayal has given
birth to the act. It is almost as if Jesus releases Judas when He commands him quietly, *"What you do, do quickly."* The disciples, still wondering, miss the whole point of Jesus' words. After all, Judas is the
treasurer and he may have some urgent business among the poor
at Jesus' behest.

Judas *"went out immediately. And it was night"* (v. 30). Are there any more tragic words in all human experience? The door is closed. Judas, under cover of darkness, both physical and spiritual, will make his deal and set into motion the evil forces that will destroy Jesus. His hour has come!

THE NEW COMMANDMENT

31 So, when he had gone out, Jesus said, "Now the Son of Man is glorified, and God is glorified in Him.

32 "If God is glorified in Him, God will also glorify Him in Himself, and glorify Him immediately.

33 "Little children, I shall be with you a little while longer. You will seek Me; and as I said to the Jews, 'Where I am going, you cannot come,' so now I say to you.

34 "A new commandment I give to you, that you love one another; as I have loved you, that you also love one another.

35 "By this all will know that you are My disciples, if you have love for one another."

36 Simon Peter said to Him, "Lord, where are You going?" Jesus answered him, "Where I am going you cannot follow Me now, but you shall follow Me afterward."

37 Peter said to Him, "Lord, why can I not follow You now? I will lay down my life for Your sake."

38 Jesus answered him, "Will you lay down your life for My sake? Most assuredly, I say to you, the rooster shall not crow till you have denied Me three times."

John 13:31–38

With Judas' departure, the little band is purged of that evil element. The hour of Jesus' glory has now come! One of the church fathers called it "humble glory." Here Jesus refers to Himself for the last time in this Gospel as the *"Son of Man,"* identifying Himself as the "suffering servant" of Isaiah 53:1–3. Giving glory to God has been at the center of Jesus' life and mission (John 2:11; 11:4; 17:4; 17:10). And through His obedience, the Father has glorified the Son. The glory Jesus has with the Father in eternity has been revealed in His earthly ministry and will break forth with power in that hour of His death and resurrection and His return to the Father. It is glory past, present, and future!

The sense of a family gathering at Passover is now evident as Jesus calls these men *"little children"* (v. 33). He is tenderly preparing them for His departure which will so shortly take place. They will seek for Him in pain and wonder after He is gone. But they will not be able to come where He is going. This is a journey He must make alone! Earlier Jesus made it clear to the Jews that their unbelief had barred the door so they could never join Him. But with His disciples the door is open. Jesus and His Father will subsequently return to these men.

But Jesus' band of followers are not to live on in a scattered vacuum clinging to some memories after He is gone. He gives them a new commandment, *"that you love one another; as I have loved you"* (v. 34). This was not an optional extra thrown in, but a command to be obeyed. And only in keeping it would the Spirit of Jesus flood these men and draw them together in a living community stronger than life or death. This commandment of love is new because it is based on a new covenant sealed with these disciples in His own blood. The old command, "you shall love your neighbor as yourself" was based on Mosaic law, not on grace (Lev. 19:18). This love is a gift shared freely by Jesus. He is the only Source of a love that needs no other motivation.

The distinguishing mark of discipleship is not programs or signs, wonders or eloquence or ecclesiastical power, but Christ's love in us that allows us to love one another. This does not mean these men were to become a self-centered, ingrown clique. That may be caused by sentimentality, but not by Christ's love shared among His people. The world will always confront Christ and have to deal with Him if His people love one another as He has loved them.

One wonders if Peter heard this radical command of Jesus. He is still brooding over where His Lord is going when He leaves. Jesus again states that he cannot follow Him now, but afterward he will. Surely He is speaking prophetically, for at the end of his earthly discipleship, Peter will join Him through a martyr's death. But Peter, who does not understand, insists that he will lay down his life for Jesus' sake (v. 37). He will do the work of the Good Shepherd. How stubbornly presumptuous he is. The disciples are not without sin simply because Judas has left. Are not all of us guilty at times of the sin of pride, trying to play the Savior, making ourselves into "little Messiahs," insisting we can do His work?

Little does Peter realize that at the very outset of the struggle he will deny Jesus, not once, but three times. How well Jesus knows him, as He does us. And He still loves us with a love that will not let us go.

Preparing a Place: Departure and Return

1 "Let not your heart be troubled; you believe in God, believe also in Me.

2 "In My Father's house are many mansions; if it were not so, I would have told you. I go to prepare a place for you.

3 "And if I go and prepare a place for you, I will come again and receive you to Myself; that where I am, there you may be also.

4 "And where I go you know, and the way you know."

5 Thomas said to Him, "Lord, we do not know where You are going, and how can we know the way?"

6 Jesus said to him, "I am the way, the truth, and the life. No one comes to the Father except through Me.

7 "If you had known Me, you would have known My Father also; and from now on you know Him and have seen Him."

8 Philip said to Him, "Lord, show us the Father, and it is sufficient for us."

9 Jesus said to him, "Have I been with you so long, and yet you have not known Me, Philip? He who has seen Me has seen the Father; so how can you say, 'Show us the Father'?

10 "Do you not believe that I am in the Father, and the Father in Me? The words that I speak to you I do not speak on My own authority; but the Father who dwells in Me does the works.

11 "Believe Me that I am in the Father and the Father in Me, or else believe Me for the sake of the works themselves.

John 14:1-11

When we arrived at the lovely, cozy home of Doug and Jackie Lowman they were a bit nervous. Entertaining a Baptist pastor and his wife for dinner was a novel experience for them. But when we sat down to eat, Doug's spontaneous, fresh prayer set us all at ease. As he said afterwards, "You know, this is all new to me." And we all kidded Jackie good-naturedly when she brought in her surprise dish, a new recipe she had picked up from a TV program, and it was delicious.

The whole evening turned out to be a celebration! We had a friendly laugh about Jackie's delightful southern hillbilly drawl. As Doug said, "You ought to hear the family when they get together. You can hardly understand them!" But they also trusted us enough to share some of their pain. They had both been married before and had children scattered throughout the South, mainly in Tennessee and Kentucky.

But they were most eager to talk about the new things the Lord had been doing in their lives. They had been baptized together seven weeks before and none of us will ever forget how Doug had whispered "I love you" to Jackie in the baptistry just before they were immersed. They had come to Christ—she a "fallen away" Baptist and he a drifting, indifferent Roman Catholic—through the tender, patient influence of Peter and Barbara Fleming, who had recently given themselves anew to Christ.

Now the Lowmans were getting a great kick out of being in a Bible study group. And they were "soaking up" everything they could learn at the church. They were amazed how specifically God had answered their prayers, and were grateful that God had given them such concern for some of their unreached family, as well as the neighbors across the street. Doug spoke of a couple of his fellow employees at the V.A. Hospital, where he is a dentist, who seemed to be floundering. He wondered if the Lord wasn't nudging him to reach out to them. It was so refreshing to hear their honest, direct questions about the Bible and the Christian life.

All we could do as we were leaving was embrace one another and give thanks and praise to the One who had made it all possible! Ruth and I drove home rejoicing! The Lowmans had entered that "place" that Jesus had gone to prepare. For all His disciples—not only in the next world, but in this world right here in Wichita, Kansas. All that Jesus had promised His disciples in their last tender visit a few hours before His death was being fulfilled in the lives of these two.

Yes, Jesus' disciples were troubled. They needed to be reassured by this One whom they loved, but often could not understand. He had spoken of one among them being His betrayer and that He would be leaving them, going where they could not come. These disciples were gripped by that same fearful emotion that Jesus had experienced when He faced death at the tomb of Lazarus and when He spoke of Judas betraying Him (John 11:30, 13:21).

The only remedy for this dread of death and separation, which is the stronghold of Satan, is faith in God, who is firm and cannot be shaken. If they have this faith in God they will have faith in Jesus. And in being united with Him in faith they will conquer the world through the victory of Jesus (John 16:33).

This is far more than a "pep talk" by Jesus. He is on His way to being reunited with His Father in glory. Through His death and resurrection, His leaving them, He will open the way for these men to live in union with Him and His Father. This will become their "place" of dwelling, their *monē*. His Father's house is great and spacious, an eternal place of dwelling with many rooms. The Son's work will prepare a place for each of them in that home. But He will return and make His home with His followers here. The dwelling place Jesus speaks of here, *"I will come again and receive you to Myself,"* is the *"monē"* in this present life. For the disciple who is united with Jesus, home, his place, is wherever Jesus is—here or in the Father's house.

When Thomas still insists that they do not know where Jesus is going and asks how they can know the way, Jesus declares His great conclusive *"I am."* For all of the "I am's" of the Gospel—"water," "bread," "light," "resurrection and life"—are caught up in Jesus' saying, *"I am the way"* (v. 6). There is no other door to life with the Father. Jesus is the one gate by which men may enter His Father's fold. He is the Way because in Him the truth of the Father is revealed, not in concepts or ideals, but through coming to know Him. To know Jesus is to know His Father. So life comes through this truth.

But Philip is not satisfied. He asks for some further sign, some mystical appearance that will finally prove they have really seen the Father. We can almost sense a pained disappointment in Jesus' answer. After all this time and in all the experiences they have shared, does Philip still not know? Everything Jesus has said and done has been shared out of His life in the Father. Why doesn't Philip carefully investigate the works He has done and let that lead him to knowing who He is? He will then see the Father through the Son.

GLORY IN WORKS AND PRAYER

12 "Most assuredly, I say to you, he who believes in Me, the works that I do he will do also; and greater works than these he will do, because I go to My Father.
13 "And whatever you ask in My name, that I will do, that the Father may be glorified in the Son.
14 "If you ask anything in My name, I will do it.

John 14:12–14

The Father will continue the work of His Son through His disciples. After His return in resurrection power the Son will manifest Himself through these who are united with Him in faith. Their works will glorify the Father in a continuing harvest.

It is only as these disciples pray in the name of Jesus, in union with Him, that glory will come to the Father. And the mighty work begun in Jesus will continue and expand. The test of all Christian prayer is whether it is in the name of Jesus, offered out of our life in Him, and gives glory to the Father. Can we be trusted with the name of Jesus as He was with the Father's name? So much of what we do in the church is temporary and frenzied. It may win compliments and approval from other church people, but it does not give glory to God, nor does it last.

THE GIFT OF THE HELPER

15 "If you love Me, keep My commandments.
16 "And I will pray the Father, and He will give you another Helper, that He may abide with you forever,
17 "even the Spirit of truth, whom the world cannot receive, because it neither sees Him nor knows Him; but you know Him, for He dwells with you and will be in you.

230

18 "I will not leave you orphans; I will come to you.

19 "A little while longer and the world will see Me no more, but you will see Me. Because I live, you will live also.

20 "At that day you will know that I am in My Father, and you in Me, and I in you.

21 "He who has My commandments and keeps them, it is he who loves Me. And he who loves Me will be loved by My Father, and I will love him and manifest Myself to him."

22 Judas (not Iscariot) said to Him, "Lord, how is it that You will manifest Yourself to us, and not to the world?"

23 Jesus answered and said to him, "If anyone loves Me, he will keep My word; and My Father will love him, and We will come to him and make Our home with him.

24 "He who does not love Me does not keep My words; and the word which you hear is not Mine but the Father's who sent Me.

25 "These things I have spoken to you while being present with you.

26 "But the Helper, the Holy Spirit, whom the Father will send in My name, He will teach you all things, and bring to your remembrance all things that I said to you.

John 14:15–26

Jesus has great concern for these "little children." He will not leave them *"orphans"* with no one to care for them (v. 18). So He assures these fearful disciples that he will ask the Father to give them a *"Helper,"* the Paraclete (v. 16). Jesus speaks of this gift immediately after He has encouraged His disciples to ask for anything in His name and He will give it that glory may be given the Father.

We have no single word in our language that can express the rich, powerful meaning of "Paraclete," the English translation of the unique title John uses for this Holy Companion. *Para* in the Greek means "alongside," and the root of *kletos* is "to call." So this *"Helper"* whom Jesus will send will be alongside the disciples as Jesus has been, "calling out" as an "encourager," a "counselor," an "advocate," a "witness," and as a "judge." "Paraclete" means all this and even more.

And He is given to His disciples. The Paraclete comes into the world as Jesus was sent into the world. He is the promised gift of the Father, sent at the Son's request. But He is given only to those who have received the Son, loved Him, and kept His commandments. These are the conditions which determine His being given. The Paraclete is not given to the world which neither sees nor knows Him. As it has been blind and deaf to Jesus, so the world does not know the Paraclete has come.

This Paraclete will come after a *"little while,"* after Jesus has passed through the anguish and darkness of the cross and after the disciples have fled in fear, bereft and orphaned (v. 19). Then in the glory of His resurrected, ascended power Jesus will send this Paraclete. In fact, it is necessary that Jesus depart before the Father can send this One. His coming rests on Jesus' completed work of salvation.

The Paraclete will remain forever with the disciples. He will *"abide"* with them continuously as He makes His home with them. They will be His place, His *monē.* The words used here are intensely personal and relational.

And while He dwells in each disciple personally, He also abides with them corporately. He is the One who gathers them and makes them one. These friends of Jesus, His "little children," will become the body in whom He dwells through the Paraclete. And as Jesus had a ministry in the flesh in the midst of the world, so His disciples, and all who will come to believe because of their witness, will continue to expand that ministry in the power of the Spirit.

There is a rich meaning in the coming of the Paraclete. The Father will give *"another Helper"* who will abide with these disciples forever (v. 16). This means that in His earthly ministry, *Jesus* has been the Paraclete. But Jesus also says *"I will come to you"* (v. 18). His resurrected life will be shared through the Paraclete with those disciples. And the Father will also come, for Jesus says later, *"If anyone loves Me, he will keep My word; and My Father will love him, and We will come to him and make Our home with him"* (v. 23). The Persons of the Godhead come in the Paraclete to abide, encourage, empower, and witness through the disciples. No wonder the disciples will never be orphans.

Jesus repeatedly emphasizes that the Paraclete is the *"Spirit of truth"* (v. 17). He will enlighten and open up the words and works of Jesus. There are many things Jesus has said and taught during His earthly ministry which the disciples have not grasped. All this will be made plain to them when this "Teacher" comes. He will also bring to mind things Jesus has said which would otherwise be forgotten (v. 26).

But the Paraclete is always under the authority of Jesus, clarifying, making clear His teaching and ministry. He comes in Jesus' name to unfold Jesus' meaning for all men. This is crucial, for there are always those who insist the Spirit is taking us beyond Jesus to "newer and deeper truth." If it is not modern-day Gnostics, then it may be the Unification Church or some guru who claims to have a new revelation of the truth. Here is the danger of centering on experience which is not under the authority of the Word. The Paraclete is subject to Jesus! Hence, Spirit-guided Bible study within the believing community under the Lordship of Jesus is important.

PEACE AND THE EVIL ONE

27 "Peace I leave with you, My peace I give to you; not as the world gives do I give to you. Let not your heart be troubled, neither let it be afraid.

28 "You have heard Me say to you, 'I am going away and coming back to you.' If you loved Me, you would rejoice because I said, 'I am going to the Father,' for My Father is greater than I.

29 "And now I have told you before it comes, that when it does come to pass, you may believe.

30 "I will no longer talk much with you, for the ruler of this world is coming, and he has nothing in Me.

31 "But that the world may know that I love the Father, and as the Father gave Me commandment, so I do. Arise, let us go from here."

John 14:27–31

For the Greeks, peace was the absence of war, but for the Hebrews it was a positive blessing growing out of a right relationship with God. So when Jesus leaves peace with these men He is giving them one of the fruits of the great gift of salvation. This positive word of farewell is greater than all their troubles and fears.

I shall always remember the beautiful greeting that Sheldon Louthan would inevitably speak when he came in or went from our midst. He would say, "Shalom" softly, with a glowing smile on his face. This compassionate Quaker had come to encourage and help troubled families and individuals as a part-time pastoral associate on our staff. In the months he was with us we all came to love him deeply.

When he was killed with four others in a tragic small plane accident last Thanksgiving, all of us on the church staff spoke of the meaning of that greeting. Sheldon had shared Christ's peace with us. And now he had heard the Father greet him, "Shalom," as he came to the place that had been prepared for him.

Jesus now urges the disciples to rejoice at His going, not to cling to Him possessively (v. 28). Real love always releases those we care about! It is a perversion, love turned into selfishness, when we attempt to hold on to those we claim to love. Jesus is returning to His Father who sent Him. Even though Father and Son are one, Jesus has submitted Himself to the Father as His Messenger. In this sense, the Father is greater than the Son.

The moment is drawing nearer when the betrayer and the soldiers, who are servants of the evil one, will come to get Jesus. He will go with them only because He is obeying His Father, not because the ruler of this world has any power over Him.

When Jesus says, *"Arise, let us go from here,"* He is ending this part of the discourse (v. 31), but He is also moving with these men to the place where the betrayer will come.

JOY AND HATRED: THE DEPTH OF THE RELATIONSHIP

1 "I am the true vine, and My Father is the vinedresser.
2 "Every branch in Me that does not bear fruit He takes away; and every branch that bears fruit He prunes, that it may bear more fruit.
3 "You are already clean because of the word which I have spoken to you.
4 "Abide in Me, and I in you. As the branch cannot bear fruit of itself, unless it abides in the vine, neither can you, unless you abide in Me.
5 "I am the vine, you are the branches. He who abides in Me, and I in him, bears much fruit; for without Me you can do nothing.
6 "If anyone does not abide in Me, he is cast out

as a branch and is withered; and they gather them
and throw them into the fire, and they are burned.

7 "If you abide in Me, and My words abide in
you, you will ask what you desire, and it shall be
done for you.

8 "By this My Father is glorified, that you bear
much fruit; so you will be My disciples.

John 15:1–8

As Jesus and His disciples leave the upper room and move toward
the Garden of Gethsemane they pass the temple. Here one of the
chief ornaments is a "golden vine with a cluster as large as a man."[5]
This decoration becomes the basis of a visual parable. Jesus' intimate
relationship with these men cannot be stated in precise, theological
terms. So, as He has done all through His ministry, He uses the
motif of a vine and its branches to illustrate spiritual truth. His union
with these men is as alive as the relationship of the vine to its
branches.

Jesus is the *"true vine"* (v. 1). In the Old Testament writings, Israel
had frequently been spoken of as the vine which Yahweh loved and
tended. But over and over again, waywardness and corruption had
made God's people barren (Isa. 5:1–7). Now it is Jesus who is the
real vine, the Chosen One from God.

His Father owns the vineyard and cares for it. And as with any
responsible vineyard owner, His one primary purpose in growing a
vineyard is that it will bear fruit. So the branches that bear no fruit
"He takes away" (v. 2). When they become dry and lifeless He casts
them out to be burned (v. 6). Here is the final judgment on those
who no longer *"abide"* in the vine.

Once these branches had beautiful green leaves and seemed to
flourish, but then the Source of life was cut off, and now they are
barren and dead. Is not Judas, who has walked with Jesus for these
years, even now working out the details of Jesus' death? And there
will be those who begin in belief but eventually have the spirit of
the "antichrist" because they perverted the truth (1 John 2:18–19).
So much of synagogue life, once the center of faith, has become
hardened and legalistic—dead! So selfish interests, unconfessed sins,
a careless disregard for the truth, or a bitter, unforgiving spirit can
block the flow of life from the vine. Gradually the branch dies. It
is then taken away and burned.

But the *"vinedresser"* also prunes those sprouts and leaves which would hinder the branches from bearing fruit in any way. Generally in the month of August the little shoots that would take life from the vine would be pinched off. The fruit-bearing branches must get all the nourishment. Are not those experiences in life we call troubles—the hurts and disappointments and defeats—the Father's way of pinching off those excess leaves that seem so attractive, but bear no fruit? And does not the *"vinedresser"* call us to strong discipline and obedience, the rearrangement of our priorities so that time and talent and resources are at His disposal instead of being drained off in peripheral interests? The *"vinedresser"* has only one criteria for pruning: Will the branches bear more fruit?

Those disciples are not perfect, but they have been made *"clean,"* for the unnecessary leaves have been cut off (v. 3). The *"word"* which Jesus has spoken has pruned them so they might bear much fruit. Each one has been searched and cleansed, prepared for ministry. But this small community has also been pruned, for one among them has left. The life and spirit in Jesus' word has confronted Judas and judged him, and he has gone out!

This being made *"clean"* is as painful as yesterday and as fresh as today. For yesterday was a tangled, unproductive day when I found myself running to meet deadlines, even being scheduled to meet two people at the same time. When I tried to pen some comments and insights about this beautiful chapter in John early in the morning I found myself pushing impatiently, writing words, but little more. When I got to the office my faithful secretary, so eager to serve, was obviously upset by my confused attempt to get half a dozen things done at once.

Later in the afternoon I hurried off in the rain to meet Gottfried Osei-Mensah, executive of the Lausanne Committee for World Evangelization, coming in from Los Angeles to spend the weekend with us. In spite of my feeling that this had been a somewhat wasted day I became aware immediately of the deep peace and joy in this dear brother's life as soon as I met him. So while we sat having a cup of coffee and a snack, getting acquainted, I found myself blurting out some of the frustration and confusion of the day to this new friend. To which Gottfried quietly replied, "Yes, the evil one always tries to get us into this state of affairs." What a word from the Lord that was! I saw then what had been happening. I had lost much of the day to the evil one at the very time I was trying to write about "abiding in Christ."

There was a wedding that evening, a surprisingly blessed event even though the florist did not show up with the flowers. And as Ruth and I drove slowly home, talking over some of the mixed experiences of the day, I found the burden lifting. In the strange mystery of His grace, the battle was again the Lord's. He had taken over. And as I awakened this morning, far more open and relaxed, and turned once again to this powerful, yet somewhat disturbing chapter, I became suddenly aware that He had been making me *"clean"* through His word, that without Him "I can do nothing."

This fruit that the disciples bear is not what they do, but the life of Jesus in them. It is His character reproduced within them and shared with others in love. This cannot come to pass without the disciple abiding in Jesus, making his home in Him as Jesus makes His home in the disciple. His life is shared with the disciples as their life is given to Him.

So Jesus can categorically say *"without Me you can do nothing"* (v. 5). No amount of ingenious planning or restless activities or sponsoring of "spiritual" events on our own can produce this fruit. This is like trying to tie imitation fruit on living branches. It is like Peter's earlier self-centered boast, "I will lay down my life for Your sake" (John 13:37).

LOVE AND JOY IN UNION

9 "As the Father loved Me, I also have loved you; continue in My love.

10 "If you keep My commandments, you will abide in My love, just as I have kept My Father's commandments and abide in His love.

11 "These things I have spoken to you that My joy may remain in you, and that your joy may be full.

12 "This is My commandment, that you love one another as I have loved you.

13 "Greater love has no one than this, than to lay down one's life for his friends.

14 "You are My friends if you do whatever I command you.

15 "No longer do I call you servants, for a servant does not know what his master is doing; but I have called you friends, for all things that I heard from My Father I have made known to you.

16 "You did not choose Me, but I chose you and
appointed you that you should go and bear fruit, and
that your fruit should remain, that whatever you ask
the Father in My name He may give you.
17 "These things I command you, that you love one
another.

John 15:9–17

The union between Jesus and His disciples is not an external arrangement, but an internal, personal relationship. Jesus defines this
union, gives it content and substance, by a "triad of love." The Son
loves these disciples as the Father loves Him. This is the love that
has sought them out, called them into life, and which now holds
them and sends them out into the world to continue His mission.
What an awesome, yet tender reality. But these frail, struggling men
are then to love one another as Jesus loves them. This is not an
option, but a command. It is an impossibility unless they abide in
His love.

This love is not a vague, sentimental feeling that comes and goes,
but a tough reality that is always revealed in obedience. The Son
shares in and shows forth His Father's love by absolute obedience
to all His commands, which takes Him now to the cross. The disciples
can only abide in the love of Jesus, then, if they keep His commandments. Love and obedience are two sides of the same reality.

This does not mean these disciples are called to a grim, cheerless
existence. On the contrary, if they abide in the love of Jesus by
obeying His commands, they will remain in His joy! Jesus' joy will
be in these men constantly, not sporadically (v. 11). G. K. Chesterton
called this joy "the gigantic secret of the Christian." And when Malcolm Muggeridge, brilliant man of the world, first encountered Mother
Teresa in Calcutta among her "destitute and dying," he could not
explain the "luminous quality" he saw in this little, plain woman.
This turned out to be far more than a TV assignment for Malcolm
Muggeridge, for eventually it was that joy which drew him to Christ,
who always shares His joy with those who obey Him.

It is a mystery and challenge to our earthbound way of thinking
that the nearer Jesus came to the cross the more joy became a part
of His vocabulary. How strange this sounds to affluent, comfort-seek-
ing Americans who confuse joy and happiness. Joy is an unexpected
gift growing out of our intimate relationship with this One we love

and serve. While happiness, even though it is frantically sought as some kind of product that can be possessed, turns out to be a disappointing illusion. Happiness is like the pot of gold at the end of a rainbow that does not exist.

No, the more deeply we enter into a loving, obedient union with Jesus the more *"full"* will be our joy, like the melody that comes out of the creative discipline and struggle of an artist who gives himself to the instrument.

Jesus' command to His disciples now becomes very specific. They are to love one another as He has loved them (v. 12). This does not mean tolerating or being nice to one another, but is a call to enter into the mystery of His own death. As these men have heard Jesus say the Good Shepherd "lays down" His life for the sheep and watched Him lay down His garments to wash their feet, so they are to lay down their lives for one another, not only in physical death if need be, but in a caring openness for one another that reveals Jesus.

Jesus has opened the way for this new kind of relationship among these men, calling them *"friends,"* not *"servants"* (v. 15). His love has broken down the wall which separates the master from the slave, the rich from the poor, the one who comes first from the one who comes last. Because these disciples are His friends, Jesus has opened His heart to them, showing the purpose of His coming, holding nothing back. And in the end, the *"greater love"* of His death will completely liberate them so they can give themselves with abandon as *"friends."* They will remain His friends if they do whatever He commands them.

He has *"chosen"* these men to continue His mission (v. 16). The initiative is His, not theirs. He has appointed them, trained them, and prepared them to go and bear much fruit. The word *"appointed"* in verse 16 is the same verb Jesus uses when He speaks of "laying down His life." It is His death then that will empower these disciples to carry out their work in His name. "The Lord divested Himself of life that He might invest them with the apostolate to the world. He set aside His life and set them to their work."[6] And those disciples who will join them because of their witness in the years to come throughout the world will *"remain."* They too will bear fruit.

There is no mission, no fruit borne, without prayer in Jesus' name (v. 16). This is no hit-and-miss surface asking, but a life of intercession for the mission in union with Jesus. His will and purpose then become the disciples' will and purpose. Leighton Ford and Gottfried Osei-Mensah of the Lausanne Committee for World Evangelization have shared with some of us the amazing harvest now being reaped in many parts of God's mighty vineyard. However, we have been reminded again and again that it is where the church is living in prayer—in Romania, East Africa, El Salvador, and particularly in South Korea—that the harvest is the greatest!

It may well be that the most desperate need of the American church is the recovery of fervent, believing prayer in the name of Jesus.

The Hatred of the World

18 "If the world hates you, you know that it hated Me before it hated you.

19 "If you were of the world, the world would love its own. Yet because you are not of the world, but I chose you out of the world, therefore the world hates you.

20 "Remember the word that I said to you, 'A servant is not greater than his master.' If they persecuted Me, they will also persecute you. If they kept My word, they will keep yours also.

21 "But all these things they will do to you for My name's sake, because they do not know Him who sent Me.

22 "If I had not come and spoken to them, they would have no sin, but now they have no excuse for their sin.

23 "He who hates Me hates My Father also.

24 "If I had not done among them the works which no one else did, they would have no sin; but now they have seen and also hated both Me and My Father.

25 "But this happened that the word might be fulfilled which is written in their law, 'They hated Me without a cause.'

John 15:18–25

The disciples will be hated by the world as Jesus has been hated. It is the nature of the world to hate as it is the nature of the disciple to love. And these are mutually exclusive. So as the disciples are known for their love, the world is known for its hatred.

These men are not of the world, for Jesus *"chose them out of the world"* not to leave the world, but to continue His mission in the world as a new community of love. And the separation of the disciples from the world makes them objects of its hatred. The world loves only its own, those who conform to its spirit, accept its values, and worship its false gods. Jesus underlines the sharp line of suspicion the world draws between itself and the disciples by speaking of the world five times in two sentences (v. 19).

When a handful of us from our church in Wichita journeyed to Koinonia Farm in Americus, Georgia, to work and learn for a few days, we saw the bullet holes in one of the buildings and heard the story of community ostracism. For this radical, healing community of love, trying to be totally faithful to Jesus was a challenge and a threat to that hostile community, even though it was so well "churched." That same enmity was revealed when a senior high girl, who was a new Christian in our youth group, wept openly because her non-believing mother was insisting she could no longer come to church. "The implacable hatred of the world for the friends of Jesus is the sign of the verity of that friendship."[7]

So the disciples will be treated as their Master. They will be persecuted as He has been persecuted. But it is also true that those who have kept the word of Jesus will keep the words of His disciples. He is the Source of their authority.

This hatred of the world is sin grounded in their ignorance of God for which they have no excuse. They do not know the Father even though the whole of Jesus' life and ministry, all His work, has been a revelation of His Father. Therefore, their hatred is directed at God the Father, not only at His Son. Here again we see the union of Father and Son in another context.

Their hatred is actually a fulfillment of "their" Scripture. For the very law they boastfully claim to possess and obey prophesies their own sin.

PREPARATION FOR PERSECUTION

26 "But when the Helper comes, whom I shall send
to you from the Father, the Spirit of truth who proceeds
from the Father, He will testify of Me.

27 "And you also will bear witness, because you
have been with Me from the beginning."
16:1 "These things I have spoken to you, that you
should not be made to stumble.

2 "They will put you out of the synagogues; yes,
the time is coming that whoever kills you will think
that he offers God service.

3 "And these things they will do to you because
they have not known the Father nor Me.

4 "But these things I have told you, that when
the time comes, you may remember that I told you
of them.

John 15:26—16:4a

In the face of this humiliation and persecution, the disciples will
be in the world as witnesses to Jesus. Their intimate companionship
with Him *"from the beginning"* is the ground for their witness (v. 27).
However, their authority does not rest simply on the memories of
what He has done. For the hatred of the world will be countered
by the strong witness of the Paraclete who is coming to dwell with
the disciples. He is the Spirit of truth and can only declare the truth
that is in Jesus. He does not have an independent witness of His
own, but "conducts Christ's case for Him before the world."[8] The
Paraclete is under the authority of Jesus and will only magnify the
truth that is in Him. The Spirit is grieved and offended when anyone
claims that in their experience the Spirit has led them into new truth
"beyond Jesus."

So the Paraclete will enlighten the meaning of the teaching and
works of Jesus which the disciples have heard and seen as His compan-
ions. Every disciple is called to be faithful and sensitive in making
his witness to Jesus. The word he speaks for Jesus will always have
the unique stamp of his personality on it. But it is the Spirit who
guides and empowers him so that the witness to Jesus is true!

Jesus is saying these things to prepare His disciples for their time
of persecution. He will not be with them in the flesh when they
are cast out of the synagogues and even put to death. And how
humiliating and confusing that will be, for those who hate and kill
them will be utterly convinced they are doing the work of God
(v. 21). How important then that these disciples remember Jesus'

words of preparation so they will not stumble when the darkness of persecution comes.

Once again John is giving a powerful word of encouragement to fellow believers who are being cast out of synagogues by their own family and friends in the name of devotion to God and who are increasingly facing death at the hands of the Caesars, so jealous of their own power. And in our day, the suffering church in Uganda, Ethiopia, the Soviet Union, and in Central America has been heartened and renewed by those strong words of Jesus given us through John.

THE HELPER AND VICTIM: THE WORK OF THE HELPER

4 "And these things I did not say to you at the beginning, because I was with you.

5 "But now I go away to Him who sent Me, and none of you asks Me, 'Where are You going?'

6 "But because I have said these things to you, sorrow has filled your heart.

7 "Nevertheless I tell you the truth. It is to your advantage that I go away; for if I do not go away, the Helper will not come to you; but if I depart, I will send Him to you.

8 "And when He has come, He will convict the world of sin, and of righteousness, and of judgment:

9 "of sin, because they do not believe in Me;

10 "of righteousness, because I go to My Father and you see Me no more;

11 "of judgment, because the ruler of this world is judged.

12 "I still have many things to say to you, but you cannot bear them now.

13 "However, when He, the Spirit of truth, has come, He will guide you into all truth; for He will not speak on His own authority, but whatever He hears He will speak; and He will tell you things to come.

14 "He will glorify Me, for He will take of what is Mine and declare it to you.

15 "All things that the Father has are Mine. Therefore I said that He will take of Mine and declare it to you.

John 16:4b–15

As the disciples become increasingly aware of the nearness of Jesus' leaving, that His physical presence will no longer be with them, they are overwhelmed with sorrow. It fills their hearts. But they do not ask where Jesus is going. If they knew the purpose of His leaving, the goal of His journey, they would not grieve.

So Jesus attempts to say things to them now which earlier they could not hear or grasp. If He stayed on with these disciples in the flesh the Paraclete would not come (v. 7). He is the One who will be the indwelling Presence, uniting them with Jesus in His glory. But this Helper can only come to the disciples when Jesus has finished His atoning work and returned to the Father. His leaving these men is to their advantage.

The Paraclete will come to actively *"convict"* the world through the witness of these men (v. 8). He will expose the sin of the world. It is the rejection of Jesus which is at the root of all the world's sin. If there is no faith in Jesus, self-centeredness, hatred, and immorality, all concrete signs of unbelief, will take over.

This Advocate will also bring to light the righteousness of Jesus while He unmasks the unrighteousness, the false justice, of the world. In crucifying Jesus the world judges Jesus, this innocent One, guilty. But the Father vindicates Him, declares Him the righteous One, by raising Him from the dead. His return to the Father rebukes the unrighteousness of the world. So the world is convicted of righteousness when Jesus is lifted up by the Spirit.

And the Paraclete will make it clear that the prince of this world is judged, for Jesus will meet the devil at the cross and dethrone him through His resurrection. While the evil one continues to thrash around and the struggle goes on, his power has been destroyed. In the power of the Spirit the Apostles will go forth to boldly announce that Jesus is Lord and that the devil has been overthrown.

But there are other things Jesus cannot say to these disciples now, for they cannot *"bear them"* (v. 12). They are spiritually unprepared to handle them. Furthermore, these are truths which can only be grasped and understood after Jesus' crucifixion and resurrection. Then the Paraclete will come as the Teacher to illuminate all of Jesus' teachings. He will share only the truth He hears from Jesus, for the Spirit is under His authority.

The Paraclete comes to each humble and seeking disciple eager to teach all that is in Christ. What a gift! And as each one submits to this Spirit of truth, he grows in spiritual wisdom and is increasingly conformed to the image of Christ. Over and over again, particularly in small, informal Bible study groups, I have listened in gratitude as a "technically untrained" person has excitedly shared some deep spiritual truth which was obviously the word of the Lord, guided and taught by this One who has come to interpret Jesus!

"And He will tell you things to come" (v. 13). This is far more than a blueprint or schedule of "last things," but a spirit of wisdom and discernment for every new opportunity. There is no way these disciples can know the strange and demanding situations into which Jesus' mission will take them in the years ahead. But the Spirit will give them understanding and illuminate the truth about Jesus in each of these situations. Philip was later to meet a seeking Ethiopian on a desert road who was reading from Isaiah but could not understand it (Acts 8:26–38). The eunuch said, "How can I [understand it], unless someone guides me?" "Then Philip opened his mouth, and beginning at this Scripture, preached Jesus to him." And the eunuch believed and was baptized. This is the constant work of guidance and discernment of the Spirit within the obedient disciple. And Peter, who was so Jewish in every way, is cast into utterly new and uncomfortable circumstances, almost being forced by the Spirit to witness to Cornelius, the Roman centurion, and his entire family. And the Lord, through the guidance of His Spirit of truth, opened a great door to the Gentile world and enlarged Peter's vision mightily. The primitive church in Jerusalem could never remain a Jewish sect after that (Acts 10—11:18).

This is true in our day. Our ministry here with "internationals" has been an amazing illustration of this "guiding ministry" of the Spirit. Who would have thought that fifteen thousand Southeast Asians, most of them refugees, would end up here in Wichita in the heart of America? And when we were called by a National Ministries staff member in Valley Forge asking on short notice if we could help resettle one family from a refugee camp in Thailand we nervously agreed to do our best. So in a week we tried to get ready to accept Bounchop and Douangmala Vilaythong and their three children, hurrying about to find housing, work, and furniture. Little did we realize that God was opening a door into a fascinating new ministry. But the Holy Spirit did!

That was the first of twenty-five families totaling 131 people coming from Laos, Cambodia, and Viet Nam that our church helped sponsor. Everyone seemed to have an aunt or a mother or a cousin that wanted to come to the U.S. At first there were a handful of volunteers in our church who appropriately called themselves the "No Longer Strangers Task Force," working out all the arrangements. Then a simple Sunday school was launched with fourteen or fifteen of our people becoming teachers. None of us will ever forget the enthusiastic, almost raucous, singing of "Hallelujah, Praise the Lord," in Chinese, Thai, and English lifted up to God by these people in those beginning days. Heavenly music!

Then we suddenly became aware that right in our midst was a gifted, compassionate Thai couple, San and Sineerat Jittawait, whom God had prepared in a very remarkable way to lead out and pastor this spiritually hungry group of people. Then worship services three Sundays a month were started, and a Saturday night Bible study and prayer time. Now almost every week we are hearing stories of life-changing conversions as these people are coming out of the old superstitions and bondage into Christ's new way. We had no manual or organization chart that would fit this unexpected situation. Only the guidance of the Spirit who gave wisdom to His people.

It is the Father who takes all things that are the Son's—wisdom and truth for all His people—and pours them out through the Paraclete that Jesus may be glorified. Here again we see the eternal, living intimacy within God through His ministry.

SORROW BECOMES JOY

16 "A little while, and you will not see Me; and again a little while, and you will see Me, because I go to the Father."

17 Then some of His disciples said among themselves, "What is this that He says to us, 'A little while, and you will not see Me; and again a little while, and you will see Me'; and, 'because I go to the Father'?"

18 They said therefore, "What is this that He says, 'A little while'? We do not know what He is saying."

19 Now Jesus knew that they desired to ask Him, and He said to them, "Are you inquiring among yourselves about what I said, 'A little while and you will not see Me, and again a little while and you will see Me'?

20 "Most assuredly, I say to you that you will weep

and lament, but the world will rejoice; and you will
be sorrowful, but your sorrow will be turned into joy.

21 "A woman, when she is in labor, has sorrow
because her hour has come; but as soon as she has
given birth to the child, she no longer remembers the
anguish, for joy that a human being has been born
into the world.

22 "And therefore you now have sorrow; but I will
see you again and your heart will rejoice, and your
joy no one will take from you.

John 16:16–22

When Jesus speaks of a *"little while"* and these disciples will not
see Him, and a *"little while"* and they will see Him, there is a confused
wondering among them. What does He mean by this *"little while"*?

Jesus is not speaking of linear time, the measurement of hours or
days or weeks, but of crisis time, *kairos,* time that is heavy with decision, judgment, and opportunity.

A week ago the phone rang and when I answered our oldest son
greeted me jubilantly, "Good morning, Grandpa." The weeks of waiting were over, for a seven-pound son had been born to Elaine and
Randy. So "Grandma Ruth" came on and we wept and laughed together with the new father, celebrating the coming of Joel Stephen.

But a week earlier when they called, they had reported that, after
visiting the doctor, the baby might come a week or two later than
expected. So there was a mounting concern, an added *"little while."*
Elaine is quite a small person and was even then having some difficulty
walking. But then the time came, and the pain of the night became
the joy of the morning!

The *"little while,"* the time from birth pangs to the coming of life,
is like the "leaving" and "returning" of Jesus. The separation of His
death will "give birth" to the joy of His coming in the morning of
His resurrection. How beautifully Jesus likens His own passion to
the pain and joy of childbirth. Again He has reached deep into the
imagery of the Old Testament prophets and uses a picture with which
His people were familiar. For the joy of the coming Messianic age
and the promise of resurrection are like the birth of a child (Isa.
26:17–21; 66:7–8, 13–14; Jer. 22:23; Hos. 13:13–15).

Jesus' crucifixion, His act of sacrifice, which brings such sorrow, will become the source of a joy which can never be taken away. With the coming of the Paraclete, Jesus will abide with all His disciples forever.

How different is this joy from the world which takes savage delight in putting Jesus to death but in the end is judged by that very death.

REVOLUTION IN PRAYER

23 "And in that day you will ask Me nothing. Most assuredly, I say to you, whatever you ask the Father in My name He will give you.

24 "Until now you have asked nothing in My name. Ask, and you will receive, that your joy may be full.

25 "These things I have spoken to you in figurative language; but the time is coming when I will no longer speak to you in figurative language, but I will tell you plainly about the Father.

26 "In that day you will ask in My name, and I do not say to you that I shall pray the Father for you;

27 "for the Father Himself loves you, because you have loved Me, and have believed that I came forth from God.

28 "I came forth from the Father and have come into the world. Again, I leave the world and go to the Father."

John 16:23–28

Jesus' atoning death will revolutionize the praying of these disciples. All through Jesus' earthly ministry they have asked all kinds of anxious, earthy questions to satisfy their curiosity or their needs, but they have not asked in His name. But when the Paraclete unites them with Jesus, they are to ask in Jesus' name, not fearfully or anxiously, but confidently in love, for their whole status has been changed. "It is on the grounds of all that the Son is and does that these men receive gifts from the Father."[9] Jesus encourages the disciples to keep on asking, and as the Father shares all that the Son can give them, the joy of the resurrection will fill them. They are now in the Father's presence.

Repeatedly, the Jews have urged Jesus to speak plainly, and His disciples have not understood the meaning of the images He has used such as the Shepherd and the sheep, the Vine and the branches, and now the pain and joy of childbirth. This has been a figurative language, with hidden meanings. But how can One from above speak plainly to those who are earthbound? The mystery of Jesus' hidden teaching will only begin to disappear when they are born from above. Then the Paraclete will bring enlightenment to all that Jesus has taught and make it plain.

It is in this knowing, this being taught by the Spirit, that the incredible reality of prayer is opened up for the disciple. Then the disciple knows he is loved as the Father loves Jesus. In this intimate relationship the disciple is in the presence of the Father. The Christian's prayer now is Jesus' prayer. As John Calvin puts it, "We have the heart of God as soon as we place before Him the name of the Son."[10]

All this rests on what Jesus has done in becoming one with men and also His being one with the Father. So in a magnificent summarizing statement, Jesus says that in coming into the world He "has established a bond of union with His fellow men; leaving the world, He returns to reestablish in its fullness His union with the Father."[11] It is only when His hour is completed, His journey of descent and ascent is finished, that the disciples can welcome the Paraclete and know complete union and joy with Jesus. Then Jesus will speak to them *"plainly"* about the Father and they can pray in His name.

PEACE IN TRIBULATION

29 His disciples said to Him, "See, now You are speaking plainly, and using no figure of speech!

30 "Now we are sure that You know all things, and have no need that anyone should question You. By this we believe that You came forth from God."

31 Jesus answered them, "Do you now believe?

32 "Indeed, the hour is coming, yes, has now come, that you will be scattered, each to his own, and will leave Me alone. And yet I am not alone, because the Father is with Me.

33 "These things I have spoken to you, that in Me you may have peace. In the world you will have tribulation; but be of good cheer, I have overcome the world."

John 16:29–33

The disciples rush ahead impetuously and boast that *"the hour"* has already been fulfilled and that they now hear Jesus speaking plainly. They no longer need to raise any further questions for they insist they now understand and believe that He is from God.

No wonder Jesus has earlier called them "little children" for their faith is incipient and immature. Thus He must deal with all of us. There is no way these disciples can know all they claim, for Jesus' work is not completed and the Spirit of truth has not yet come.

So Jesus tells them how immature they are and what will take place. Under the impact and fury of the attack of the Jews, which is soon to come, these men will all be scattered, each running to his own place of hiding (v. 32). A sad word, for after spending these years of intimate life together they will leave Jesus alone when trouble comes. John, the beloved, who leaned on Jesus' breast and will later stand with His mother at the cross, honestly reports the cowardice and fear of all the disciples. But Jesus is not alone. His Father will be with Him, as He has been throughout all eternity as well as through His earthly ministry.

There is a word of triumphant hope at the conclusion of the discourse, a great sense of encouragement for those weak, needy men, and for all those who confront the hostile rejection of this world. In Jesus they will have peace, one of the fruits of salvation, even though in the world they will experience hatred and persecution. What a contrast! In Jesus there is peace; in the world, tribulation. That peace is only possible because in union with Jesus the disciples will share in His victory over the world.

NOTES

1. Raymond E. Brown, *The Gospel According to John XIII–XXI*, p. 619.
2. Sir Edwyn Hoskyns, *The Fourth Gospel*, p. 437.
3. Raymond E. Brown, *The Gospel According to John XIII–XXI*, p. 565.
4. Leon Morris, *The Gospel According to John*, p. 622.
5. Earl F. Palmer, *The Intimate Gospel*, p. 129.
6. Sir Edwyn Hoskyns, *The Fourth Gospel*, p. 478.
7. Ibid., p. 479.
8. Leon Morris, *The Gospel According to John*, p. 684.

9. Ibid., p. 708.

10. John Calvin, *The Gospel According to St. John, Part Two 11–21, and the First Epistle of John,* p. 170.

11. Schlatter, as quoted in Raymond E. Brown, *The Gospel According to John XIII–XXI,* p. 735.

CHAPTER FOURTEEN

The Prayer

John 17:1–26

I have read Jesus' moving prayer scores of times and have even tried to pray it! But never, until now, have I caught the depth and tenderness of it—more because of a beautiful time of prayer with our church leaders than because of my attempt to ferret out some worthwhile comments that might be of some help.

We had been going through one of those "flat" times in our church life—no major crisis, but a time of dullness and spiritual apathy, it seemed. So after some weeks of pondering our situation and a bit of conversation with Roger Fraley, the chairman of our Diaconate, I sent out a pastoral letter inviting about seventy or eighty of our people to come together for a time of prayer and open conversation. I made the invitation as gentle as possible so that no one would feel guilty if they were not able to come. People were asked to come at 7:00 A.M. on a Saturday, not the usual time for prayer in our church.

As I drove down to the church that snowy morning, a quiet spirit of anticipation came over me. "There may be only a handful because of the snow and the early hour," I thought, "but we'll have a good time together." But as I drove into the parking lot there were more cars on hand than I had expected.

And there was a good deal of laughter and friendly banter going on about the time and the snow as I walked into Fellowship Hall. Eventually, fifty-six people showed up, almost all of them on time. It was obvious they were eager for something. So after a few minutes of coffee and rolls we settled down for our meeting, which turned out to be a surprising affair. I shared with these dear people my burden for our church. We were not in a noticeable crisis, but we seemed to be in a time of spiritual lethargy and indecisiveness, spending too much time on peripheral, institutional matters. Surely the Lord had something deeper and better for us.

A hush seemed to come over the group as we turned to John 17 to spend a few moments with Jesus' prayer for Himself and His church. I am certain it was my own struggle in those last few weeks to lay hold on the meaning of this prayer that had given me a sense of dissatisfaction with ordinary church life, but also a renewed vision of what the Lord expected the church to be. Could we not have a renewed understanding of Jesus' will for our church in the light of His prayer? The glory He longs to manifest among all His people? The Name we have been given to bear as we keep His word? The mission for which He has sanctified us by His own sacrifice? And that holy unity He calls us to which reflects the oneness of the Father and the Son?

There were some comments, made very briefly, because people were eager to pray. So we divided up into groups of fours and fives to praise God, to ask for His forgiveness, and to ask that Jesus' prayer for our particular church might be answered. It was a holy, cleansing, and joyous time, like quiet music filling the air to the glory of God. Following this there was some further discussion and another time of free, open prayer. People left with shining faces, drawn together in the love of the Father and the Son. I know now as never before it is in praying, not simply in discussion, that we learn the meaning of Jesus' prayer for the church.

The Glory of the Father and Son

1 Jesus spoke these words, lifted up His eyes to heaven, and said, "Father, the hour has come. Glorify Your Son, that Your Son also may glorify You,

2 "as You have given Him authority over all flesh, that He should give eternal life to as many as You have given Him.

3 "And this is eternal life, that they may know You, the only true God, and Jesus Christ whom You have sent.

4 "I have glorified You on the earth. I have finished the work which You have given Me to do.

5 "And now, O Father, glorify Me together with

> Yourself, with the glory which I had with You before
> the world was.
>
> *John 17:1–5*

In the closing words of His discourse Jesus has made it clear that His disciples will be scattered, leaving Him alone. But He will not be alone, for He lives in constant communion with His Father. And His disciples will not be lost permanently. Jesus will have victory over the world, which they will share with Him, and they will return to be a continuing community of witness through whom Jesus will be glorified.

So between His teaching and His death, Jesus prays. He enters into holy work, offering Himself to His Father with all His people, those present and those to come, that glory may come to His Father.

This is an intimate prayer. When Jesus lifts His eyes upward toward "home" to commune with the One who sent Him, He uses a tender family greeting, *"Father"* (v. 1). The whole prayer is spoken out of that living union which He has had with the Father throughout eternity.

This is a word and a deed offered up at a particular time and place in the presence of His disciples, but it is also a continuing priestly intercession for all His people for all time.

In this final hour, an hour which has been anticipated all through Jesus' ministry (John 2:4; 4:21, 23; 5:25; 7:30; 8:20) He will share in the glory of God. That glory is always initiated from above. It moves from the Father through the obedience and love of the Son to those who believe in Him, that it may return to the Father. All through Jesus' earthly ministry men have seen that glory revealed through His teaching and signs.

In His incarnation the Son of God has been given authority over all flesh. So He has touched and transformed the common and the earthy—water has been turned into wine, a stormy sea has been quieted, the eyes of a blind man have been opened, and Lazarus has been raised from the dead. Through these signs, these acts of power in which the majesty of God has been revealed,[1] the disciples have come to know and trust the only true God and Jesus Christ whom He has sent. In verse 3 is a simple definition of faith in the midst of prayer. It is those who know that Jesus has come from God who receive eternal life. They are a gift from the Father to the Son.

Jesus has finished this work through which the glory of the Father has been revealed. But often it has been seen partially and dimly because the glory has been hidden, veiled in flesh.

So now Jesus makes a simple request—that the glory which He has had with the Father throughout all eternity might now be revealed in Him directly and openly; that in being broken open on the cross and being raised from the dead, the majesty and splendor of His Father might shine forth in power, not through signs, but in the reality of Himself! And this request is not made for His own sake, but that He might share this glory with His Father and manifest it among His disciples.

The Men with a Name

6 "I have manifested Your name to the men whom You gave Me out of the world. They were Yours, You gave them to Me, and they have kept Your word.

7 "Now they have known that all things which You have given Me are from You.

8 "For I have given to them the words which You gave Me; and they have received them, and have known surely that I came forth from You; and they have believed that You sent Me.

9 "I pray for them. I do not pray for the world but for those whom You have given Me, for they are Yours.

10 "And all Mine are Yours, and Yours are Mine, and I am glorified in them.

11 "And now I am no longer in the world, but these are in the world, and I come to You. Holy Father, keep through Your name those whom You have given Me, that they may be one as We are.

12 "While I was with them in the world, I kept them in Your name. Those whom You gave Me I have kept; and none of them is lost except the son of perdition, that the Scripture might be fulfilled.

13 "But now I come to You, and these things I speak in the world, that they may have My joy fulfilled in themselves.

14 "I have given them Your word; and the world

has hated them because they are not of the world, just as I am not of the world.

15 "I do not pray that You should take them out of the world, but that You should keep them from the evil one.

16 "They are not of the world, just as I am not of the world.

17 "Sanctify them by Your truth. Your word is truth.

18 "As You have sent Me into the world, I also have sent them into the world.

19 "And for their sakes I sanctify Myself, that they also may be sanctified by the truth.

John 17:6–19

Now these disciples who are with Jesus are drawn into His prayer. They are affirmed and blessed as a people in whom Jesus is glorified. For they are men who bear a name. The Father has called them out of the world and given them to the Son. As Jesus has received and kept them, He has given them the Father's name and revealed to them the nature of God.

Jesus has held nothing back. All the things His Father has given Him, the Son has shared with the disciples. As they have received His word and known it is from God, they have believed He was sent by God. As they have come to know Jesus is "Bread from heaven" and "the Light of the world," the "Water which springs everlasting" and "the Resurrection and the Life," they have been given His name, "I AM," Yahweh, the Lord Himself!

It is through these men the Father has chosen to reveal His glory. And it is for the circle of believers, this cleansed and believing "little church," that Jesus the Lord now prays.

He prays for these eleven men He is leaving, not for the world. He loves the world and came to save it (John 3:16) and neither His love nor His purpose has changed, even though the world has turned away and rejected Him. It is as these men faithfully manifest His glory and love that the world will be confronted and called to believe.

The Son appeals to His Father to keep this body of men in His name, lest they abort the mission. Addressing the Father as *"Holy"* here emphasizes His divine separation from the world. It is in bearing this name that these men are marked off from the world. They are to be holy as He is holy (Lev. 19:2). Sharing this relationship with the Father and the Son is the basis of this unity, not a common human interest or way of thinking. While Jesus has been with these men He has been able to keep all of them in this unity except for the one who is lost, the son of perdition (v. 12). Even here Scripture is fulfilled because it is through the betrayal of Judas that Jesus has come to His hour of glory!

For Jesus to ask that these men be full of His joy (v. 13) does not mean they will escape tribulation and hostility. This would mean taking them out of the world. No, they will remain and be hated, just as Jesus has been, because they are *"not of this world."* To bear the name, to be with Jesus, marks them as aliens in the world. And this provokes trouble; for when they are faithful to the word Jesus has given them, the world reacts with hostility.

So Jesus asks that they be kept from the evil one (v. 15). For he will break in as a thief and destroy this small band, stealing them one by one, unless they continue to be guarded by the word of Jesus.

These men are being sent into the world. As Jesus has been sent by the Father, so they are sent by the Son. His mission will be their mission. So Jesus asks that they be sanctified, set apart, and consecrated for their special task (v. 17). It is the truth of Jesus' word, which is the whole message of God's love and glory as it is revealed in the words and teaching of Jesus, which will equip them for this mission. They have already been called and made clean by that word. Now they are sanctified by it; they belong to Jesus. Union with Him gives them authority and power for the mission.

Now Jesus sanctifies Himself, offers Himself to the Father as the Victim for the sacrifice (Heb. 10:10). He is the perfect Lamb, the only One who can take away the sin of the world (John 1:29). So He offers Himself for those whom God has given Him. The Victim becomes their Priest. The sanctification of the disciples for their mission rests in the completion of Jesus' work on the cross. "The power of Jesus' words to His disciples in sanctifying them is grounded in the efficacy of His own death."[2]

HIS PRAYER FOR THE COMING CHURCH

> 20 "I do not pray for these alone, but also for those
> who will believe in Me through their word;

21 "that they all may be one, as You, Father, are
in Me, and I in You; that they also may be one in
Us, that the world may believe that You sent
Me.

22 "And the glory which You gave Me I have given
them, that they may be one just as We are one:

23 "I in them, and You in Me; that they may be
made perfect in one, and that the world may know
that You have sent Me, and have loved them as You
have loved Me.

24 "Father, I desire that they also whom You gave
Me may be with Me where I am, that they may behold
My glory which You have given Me; for You loved
Me before the foundation of the world.

25 "O righteous Father! The world has not known
You, but I have known You; and these have known
that You sent Me.

26 "And I have declared to them Your name, and
will declare it, that the love with which You loved
Me may be in them, and I in them."

John 17:20–26

Jesus' prayer is not only for these who are gathered with Him.
He reaches out and includes all those who will come to believe in
Him through *"their word,"* that they may know the glory and love
of the Father and the Son. This is His prayer for the church that is
to come.

He prays that all His people throughout all time may be one. Jesus
asks that their unity may be rooted in *"Us"* (v. 21), reflecting that
eternal oneness which the Father and Son know in dwelling in one
another. This unity of His disciples is not institutional or organized,
but a living, organic oneness which flows from the action of the
Father.

This gift of unity is not a forced conformity, but an expression
of the creative diversity within the Godhead. As there is only one
"true God" who manifests Himself through the differing functions
of Father, Son, and Spirit, so the loving unity of the body of believers
is expressed through a rich variety of gifts and ministry. The whole
family of God is a beautiful montage of differing cultures and tem-
peraments, colors and gifts, offered to God in worship and ministry
that He may be glorified.

This unity is not simply mystical and spiritual, but it is revealed in a particular fleshly company of disciples. As the love of Christ is perfected among God's people in a deepening unity which is visible, the world is challenged. The church then becomes God's call to the world. All men will come to know Jesus has been sent by God through the witness of a fleshly company of forgiven sinners who love one another as the Father loves the Son and as He loves His people. This is Christ's body in the world. And "what the Incarnate Son of God had once been to the Jewish people, the church is now to the world—the incarnate love and glory of God."[3]

This unity of Jesus' people is a gift, a living place, into which believing disciples are called. But there are particular times when its meaning stands out with sharp clarity.

None of us who were present will ever forget—every detail is etched in my memory—the service of reconciliation between First Baptist and Metropolitan Baptist churches more than twenty years after an angry division. Fellow believers, some of whom had not met together or spoken to one another in years, had come together to worship. And as we sang "Great Is Thy Faithfulness" that night four years ago and turned to greet one another in the crowded sanctuary, many people embraced and their tears of joy and gratitude were mingled. Surely the angels sang at this defeat of the evil one. And the next day on the street people stopped some of us saying they had heard the "good news." The message we proclaimed had become more credible.

As Jesus prayed for His original disciples (v. 6) and then for those who would come to believe through their word (v. 20) so now He anticipates the coming of those who will be with Him forever in glory (v. 26). Jesus *"desires"* that the church militant, God's people on mission, may be with Him in glory. In this final place, this eternal *monē*, all his disciples will behold in all its fullness the glory He had with the Father before *"the foundation of the world"* (v. 24). The faithful disciples will be united with Jesus in the love of the Father because they have been united with Him on earth. The church on mission has become the church eternal.

Even here as Jesus prays, *"O Righteous Father,"* we become aware that there are those who have never known Him (v. 25). They have rejected the overtures of a loving God who now has become their Judge. But the final doxology is that those who know Jesus now apprehend His love and are "transformed from glory to glory."[4]

NOTES

1. Raymond E. Brown, *The Gospel According to John XIII–XXI,* p. 751.
2. Sir Edwyn Hoskyns, *The Fourth Gospel,* p. 502.
3. Ibid., p. 505.
4. John Marsh, *Saint John* (Philadelphia: The Westminster Press, 1968), p. 570.

CHAPTER FIFTEEN

The Hour

John 18:1—19:42

THE ARREST

1 When Jesus had spoken these words, He went out with His disciples over the Brook Kidron, where there was a garden, which He and His disciples entered.

2 And Judas, who betrayed Him, also knew the place; for Jesus often met there with His disciples.

3 Then Judas, having received a detachment of troops, and officers from the chief priests and Pharisees, came there with lanterns, torches, and weapons.

4 Jesus therefore, knowing all things that would come upon Him, went forward and said to them, "Whom are you seeking?"

5 They answered Him, "Jesus of Nazareth." Jesus said to them, "I am He." And Judas, who betrayed Him, also stood with them.

6 Then—when He said to them, "I am He,"—they drew back and fell to the ground.

7 Then He asked them again, "Whom are you seeking?" And they said, "Jesus of Nazareth."

8 Jesus answered, "I have told you that I am He. Therefore, if you seek Me, let these go their way,"

9 that the saying might be fulfilled which He spoke, "Of those whom You gave Me I have lost none."

10 Then Simon Peter, having a sword, drew it and struck the high priest's servant, and cut off his right ear. The servant's name was Malchus.

11 Then Jesus said to Peter, "Put your sword into the sheath. Shall I not drink the cup which My Father has given Me?"

John 18:1–11

We come now to the tragedy and joy of Jesus' hour of glory—an hour from which He does not shrink back in fear. But He moves into these events with a calm courage, even anticipation, like a runner eager for a race. This is why He has come. Jesus is the central actor, the prime mover, throughout His arrest, His trials, and His crucifixion, not Judas or Annas or Caiaphas or Pilate, although their judgments and actions may seem to precipitate what takes place.

It is Jesus who *"went out"* with His disciples where there was a garden, and who *"went forward"* to meet His enemies when they came, and who asked that they let His disciples *"go their way"* and not arrest them. And through the interrogation Jesus is really the One who is judging those trying to put Him on trial.

There are suggestive meanings throughout the account of Jesus' arrest. When Jesus *"went out with His disciples"* and crossed the Brook Kidron, He could not help being aware that the stream was dyed red with the blood of the thousands of lambs being sacrificed in the temple for the Passover. A channel carried the waste blood into the Brook.[1] And it was to a garden He came. This would be not only the scene of His arrest, but of His crucifixion nearby and His resurrection. It was in a garden that man first lost his way in disobedience, and now it is in a garden that man is given the possibility of being restored to God's paradise.

Now Judas comes to this place, knowing how frequently Jesus came here, leading a *"detachment of troops,"* which could be as many as six hundred soldiers, as well as officers from the Sanhedrin. Here the Roman "state" and the Jewish "church" are joined in their evil plans. Imagine such a large force coming to arrest this one lone Man with His handful of nervous disciples. There must have been fear that Jesus would pull off some kind of surprise resistance. How ironic that they should come with lanterns and torches to seek the One who is the "Light of the world." When Judas had last left Jesus, he had gone out and "it was night." How could any artificial light guide them in their spiritual darkness?

When Jesus steps forward to meet His captors, asking them who they are looking for, and they answer, *"Jesus of Nazareth,"* He identifies Himself simply and directly, *"I am He"* (v. 5). No wonder His enemies fall to the ground, more before the awesome majesty of who He is than in amazement that He has come to them.

Then Jesus intervenes for His disciples, these weak, frightened men who will be scattered, fulfilling His own prayer, "Those whom You gave Me I have kept" (17:12). One thinks of all those dangerous, dark places in the world, those prison cells and torture chambers in Uganda, Romania, Uruguay, North Korea and elsewhere, where Jesus silently pleads for His own that they may be kept in the Father's house.

It is Peter again who impetuously tries to take things in his own hands by reaching for the sword. He apparently swung wildly trying to split open a man's skull and in the darkness missed, cutting off Malchus' ear. In the face of so many armed men this was a foolhardy act of courage. And as Jesus has Peter put his weapon away He reminds him that He alone must drink the cup of suffering and death which the Father has given Him (v. 11). He is the Shepherd that must be slain for all the sheep. And Peter cannot shield Him from that.

THE TRIALS: JESUS BEFORE ANNAS

12 Then the detachment of troops and the captain and the officers of the Jews arrested Jesus and bound Him.

13 And they led Him away to Annas first, for he was the father-in-law of Caiaphas who was high priest that year.

14 Now it was Caiaphas who gave counsel to the Jews that it was expedient that one man should die for the people.

John 18:12–14

Now Jesus is brought to Annas, a wily, powerful, ecclesiastical politician, who had been high priest from A.D. 6 to 15. He must have been a king maker, because five of his sons had been high priests over the years and his son-in-law, Caiaphas, held the post at this time. Many questions have been raised by the scholars about Jesus being brought to Annas first for what apparently was an informal initial interrogation. Barclay has made the interesting observation that if Annas had a vested interest in the "temple business" and Jesus had cleansed the temple of the money changers earlier, which could have hurt Annas' business, then surely he would have wanted to get Jesus alone where he could deal with Him on his terms.[2]

THE TRIAL OF PETER

15 And Simon Peter followed Jesus, and so did another disciple. Now that disciple was known to the high priest, and went with Jesus into the courtyard of the high priest.

16 But Peter stood at the door outside. Then the other disciple, who was known to the high priest, went out and spoke to her who kept the door, and brought Peter in.

17 Then the servant girl who kept the door said to Peter, "You are not also one of this Man's disciples, are you?" He said, "I am not."

18 And the servants and officers who had made a fire of coals stood there, for it was cold, and they warmed themselves. And Peter stood with them and warmed himself.

John 18:15–18

In the meantime Peter has followed Jesus with *"another disciple"* (v. 15). The intimate details which tell us how Peter got into the courtyard from the *"outside"* indicate that John was present here, but he did not mention his name. His father Zebedee apparently had a prosperous fishing business and his status may well have opened contacts within the high priest's official family. So a name is mentioned or an old favor is spoken of and Peter is allowed to come in. The servant at the door, a girl, asks Peter, who a few minutes before has been swinging a sword, if he is not one of the Man's disciples also. She phrases her question in such a way that a negative answer will be quite natural (v. 17). The evil one will tempt us through innocent-appearing means, very often unexpectedly, making it easy to yield. Peter's response, *"I am not,"* is a contrast to Jesus' identification of Himself, "I am." How often we answer the "yes" of God with our "no." Peter's only comfort after his denial is that he can stay by a human fire.

JESUS QUESTIONED

19 The high priest then asked Jesus about His disciples and His doctrine.

20 Jesus answered him, "I spoke openly to the world. I always taught in the synagogues and in the temple, where the Jews always meet, and in secret I have said nothing.

21 "Why do you ask Me? Ask those who heard Me what I said to them. Indeed they know what I said."

22 And when He had said these things, one of the officers who stood by struck Jesus with the palm of his hand, saying, "Do You answer the high priest like that?"

23 Jesus answered him, "If I have spoken evil, bear witness of the evil; but if well, why do you strike Me?"

24 Then Annas sent Him bound to Caiaphas the high priest.

John 18:19–24

Annas, who is here referred to as the *"high priest"* because of his control of the office, now asks Jesus about His disciples and His teachings. This is the only question the Jewish establishment puts to Jesus during the trials in this Gospel. He must be wondering if Jesus has been fomenting revolution. If this is meant to be a trial, then what Annas is doing is illegal. Jewish law provided strict safeguards for the accused; they could not be asked questions that would incriminate them, and the case had to be established by witnesses which the accuser must bring forth, none of which Annas has done.

In response Jesus declares that none of His teaching has been secret or hidden: *"I spoke openly . . . I always taught in the synagogues . . . in secret I have said nothing"* (v. 20). We sense Jesus' strong authority coming through in His answer. Those who heard Him could testify that He shared the truth openly. In this bold challenge to the high priest Jesus is completely within His rights.

Some officer, perhaps an ordinary guard, strikes Jesus with his hand, another illegal act, like a bully trying to please his master.

Now Annas sends Jesus back to Caiaphas, who may have had quarters in the same building or nearby. In John's record, the official role of the Jewish leaders in the interrogation of Jesus is minimized. And they never pass official judgment on Him. We are not certain, according to this Gospel, that there was even an attempt to call the Sanhedrin together to make any kind of decision. Yet by making the case against Jesus political, by insisting that He is a dangerous challenge to Roman authority, the Jewish leaders force Pilate to pass judgment eventually.

PETER AND THE ROOSTER CROW

25 Now Simon Peter stood and warmed himself. Therefore they said to him, "You are not also one of His disciples, are you?" He denied it and said, "I am not!"
26 One of the servants of the high priest, a relative of him whose ear Peter cut off, said, "Did I not see you in the garden with Him?"
27 Peter then denied again; and immediately a rooster crowed.

John 18:25–27

The drama again moves to Peter, who continues to warm himself by the fire in the courtyard. Now two more chances are given him to confess he is one of Jesus' disciples. Perhaps the people around the fire are wondering how things are going with the Galilean, and one of them turns and asks Peter if he is one of His disciples. Again he answers, *"I am not!"* Then after a relative of Malchus asks if he had not seen him in the garden and Peter denied again, immediately there was the "rooster crow." Some scholars have made the point that this may have been the bugle call that ended the third watch of the night. This would mean Peter's denials came to an end about 3:00 A.M. This has been Peter's trial, the first opportunity in alien territory since those tender moments with Jesus during His teaching and His prayer to confess His Name. But he has been judged and found wanting. He chose the warmth of the fire over the cost of the witness. How much like him we so often are.

"ARE YOU A KING?"

28 Then they led Jesus from Caiaphas to the Praetorium, and it was early morning. But they themselves did not go into the Praetorium, lest they should be defiled, but that they might eat the Passover.
29 Pilate then went out to them and said, "What accusation do you bring against this Man?"

30 They answered and said to him, "If He were not an evildoer, we would not have delivered Him up to you."

31 Then Pilate said to them, "You take Him and judge Him according to your law." Therefore the Jews said to him, "It is not lawful for us to put anyone to death,"

32 that the saying of Jesus might be fulfilled which He spoke, signifying by what death He would die.

33 Then Pilate entered the Praetorium again, called Jesus, and said to Him, "Are You the King of the Jews?"

34 Jesus answered him, "Are you speaking for yourself on this, or did others tell you this about Me?"

35 Pilate answered, "Am I a Jew? Your own nation and the chief priests have delivered You to me. What have You done?"

36 Jesus answered, "My kingdom is not of this world. If My kingdom were of this world, My servants would fight, so that I should not be delivered to the Jews; but now My kingdom is not from here."

37 Pilate therefore said to Him, "Are You a king then?" Jesus answered, "You say rightly that I am a king. For this cause I was born, and for this cause I came into the world, that I should bear witness to the truth. Everyone who is of the truth hears My voice."

38 Pilate said to Him, "What is truth?" And when he had said this, he went out again to the Jews, and said to them, "I find no fault in Him at all.

39 "But you have a custom that I should release someone to you at the Passover. Do you therefore want me to release to you the King of the Jews?"

40 Then they all cried again, saying, "Not this Man, but Barabbas!" Now Barabbas was a robber.

19:1 So Pilate then took Jesus and scourged Him.

2 And the soldiers twisted a crown of thorns and put it on His head, and they put on Him a purple robe.

3 And they said, "Hail, King of the Jews!" And they struck Him with their hands.

4 Pilate then went out again, and said to them, "Behold, I am bringing Him out to you, that you may know that I find no fault in Him."

5 Then Jesus came out, wearing the crown of

thorns and the purple robe. And Pilate said to them, "Behold the Man!"

6 Therefore, when the chief priests and officers saw Him, they cried out, saying, "Crucify Him, crucify Him!" Pilate said to them, "You take Him and crucify Him, for I find no fault in Him."

7 The Jews answered Him, "We have a law, and according to our law He ought to die, because He made Himself the Son of God."

8 Therefore, when Pilate heard that saying, he was the more afraid,

9 and went again into the Praetorium, and said to Jesus, "Where are You from?" But Jesus gave him no answer.

10 Then Pilate said to Him, "Are You not speaking to me? Do You not know that I have power to crucify You, and power to release You?"

11 Jesus answered, "You could have no power at all against Me unless it had been given you from above. Therefore the one who delivered Me to you has the greater sin."

12 From then on Pilate sought to release Him, but the Jews cried out, saying, "If you let this Man go, you are not Caesar's friend. Whoever makes himself a king speaks against Caesar."

13 When Pilate therefore heard that saying, he brought Jesus out and sat down in the judgment seat in a place that is called The Pavement, but in Hebrew, Gabbatha.

14 And it was the Preparation Day of the Passover, and about the sixth hour. And he said to the Jews, "Behold your King!"

15 But they cried out, "Away with Him, away with Him! Crucify Him!" Pilate said to them, "Shall I crucify your King?" The chief priests answered, "We have no king but Caesar!"

16 So he delivered Him to them to be crucified. So they took Jesus and led Him away.

John 18:28—19:16

The Jewish leaders have made up their minds that Jesus must be killed. So Caiaphas has Jesus taken to the Praetorium, probably the fortress Antonia, a remodeled Hasmonean castle which was the center of civil government and served as Pilate's residence whenever he was in Jerusalem. Here the Roman procurator, who served the emperor in Palestine from A.D. 26 to A.D. 35, is brought into the drama. He was responsible to the emperor to keep order among these troubled and restless people in Palestine and see that the taxes for Rome's coffers were collected.

In spite of his authority, Pilate seemed to be a troubled man, trying to make the best of a difficult and very insecure position. Over the years his status had been undermined by these stubborn Jews in a number of incidents. And he had to contend with the wealth and power in the house of Annas and deal with the Sanhedrin which was a well-organized, exclusive group. There was also the constant challenge of radical groups, particularly the Zealots and the Essenes. And the feast of the Passover with thousands of pilgrims crowded into Jerusalem was always an explosive time. It must have seemed like an impossible situation. And he could not help wondering about his standing with Caesar, who had developed a special relationship with Herod. Several of his decisions over the past few years had been reversed because of Herod's influence.

So when this strange man Jesus is brought to his quarters in the wee hours of the morning by these Jews, he must have been suspicious. They had already made up their minds that Jesus must be killed by Roman authority, but yet will not contaminate themselves by entering the unclean house of a Gentile. Surely Pilate felt the pressure of their tainted self-righteous motives. No wonder he tells them to take care of the whole affair, to judge the Man by their own laws (18:31).

But when they say that if Jesus had done no evil they would not have brought Him here and they have no authority to put Him to death for His wrong, the whole affair takes on a more serious note! Pilate now will listen, and here he becomes directly involved. In speaking of Jesus' being put to death, the Jews have unknowingly fulfilled His prophecy of His own crucifixion (12:32).

Then Pilate has Jesus brought into the Praetorium. As the lowly Galilean and the proud Roman face each other, we have one of the most intense and provocative encounters in all Scripture. As the certainty of Jesus' innocence becomes increasingly clear to Pilate, the struggle in his own soul intensifies. One can feel the vacillation and uncertainty in Pilate as he moves back and forth, in and out, from the quiet, probing conversation with Jesus in the Praetorium to the angry political pressure of the Jews outside who are demanding the death of the Man he faces.

As Pilate genuinely tries to save Jesus from execution one way or another, the pressure of the scribes and chief priests for Jesus' blood keeps building until finally he succumbs to their threats and *"delivered Him to them to be crucified"* (19:16). Pilate does not have the inner resources to withstand his own anxious desire to stay in the good graces of his powerful "friend," Caesar. But do we not all struggle with our unholy compromises? Raymond Brown has put it tellingly, "Many are those who can find mirrored in Pilate their own tragic history of temporizing and indecision."[3]

So we become aware throughout the dialogue that the eternal truth of an everlasting kingdom confronts the political power of Rome. And the Jews capitulate to this power, for in the end they renounce all loyalty they may have to the expected Messiah and shout, *"We have no king but Caesar!"* (19:15). They have thrown aside their deepest spiritual aspiration for the blood of Jesus in succumbing to the power of this world.

The central issue in this struggle is the kingship of Jesus. Pilate's first question to Him is, *"Are You the King of the Jews?"* (18:33). If Jesus is a king, then maybe He is a threat to Rome. When Pilate insists this is the charge the Jews have brought against Jesus, he goes on to ask, *"What have You done?"* (18:35). In other words, he wonders if Jesus is making plans to launch some kind of a revolution. Jesus does not answer the question, but He speaks a simple, yet profound word about His *"kingdom,"* which is not centered in Jerusalem and in which there are no plans to overthrow Rome. If that were the case, Jesus' disciples would have physically resisted arrest in the garden, which is the way of all earthly kingdoms (18:36). No, His kingdom comes from above. It is spiritual and everlasting with no geographic boundaries. Yet it challenges and judges every earthly power. Otherwise, Jesus would not be standing before Pilate.

Now when Pilate asks Jesus directly, *"Are You a king then?"* He answers, *"You say rightly"* (18:37). That is the only purpose for which He has come and has been the dominating passion of His whole ministry. Jesus has come to reveal the truth of an everlasting kingdom, to make it plain by word and deed and life that His loving Father is the gracious sovereign over all life. And everyone who hears and accepts that truth hears Jesus.

While Pilate cannot understand the truth of Jesus' talk about an everlasting kingdom, he does seem to relax a bit. This Man is not the threat the Jews are trying to make Him out to be. But there is no point in discussing harmless philosophical abstractions about truth. That is simply a waste of time. In the world of politics and armies and power it is results that count.

So since Pilate finds no fault in Jesus he goes out to the Jews and makes a proposal which he hopes will free Him. He appeals to a little-known custom that someone be released at the time of the Passover. So there is a choice to be made between Barabbas, a robber and a man of revolution, and Jesus, the Man of peace. Are we not always choosing between Jesus and Barabbas? But they *"all cried,"* as we do so often, for the blood of the innocent Man, and Barabbas is released. One wonders if Pilate was surprised by this response. He had been so sure his offer would be a way out.

Pilate now subjects Jesus to the physical cruelty and sarcastic taunts of his soldiers, thinking this may satisfy the accusers. While the scourging and the twisted crown of thorns, the purple robe and the shouts of derision are all a mockery of Jesus' kingship, yet at a deeper level, the kingdom level, He is being proclaimed King. It is part of John's inspired genius that he makes it clear here that this humiliation in Pilate's court is Jesus' hour of glory. He is a King suffering for the salvation of His people.

Pilate may have sensed something of the regal majesty of Jesus in the midst of this degrading sport, for he again says, *"I find no fault in Him"* (19:4). Then Jesus *"came out,"* truly a King appearing before His subjects. Pilate may have referred to the bruised, bleeding Man scoffingly, *"Behold the Man!"* I vividly recall my first visit to the Louvre in Paris and being drawn to a stirring, yet simple, painting of the face of Jesus, the crown of thorns pressed down on His brow and the streaks of blood coursing down His cheeks—all so realistic. But it was the compassionate, pain-filled eyes that held me. The words *Ecce Homo* below, Latin for "Behold the Man!", still haunt me from time to time. The suffering Lamb of God stands before us.

A beloved friend comes to mind. Clarence Jordan is the founding father of Koinonia, an interracial farm near Americus, Georgia. He was a strong, gentle, and big man who suffered much abuse because he was utterly convinced that Jesus had called him to a life of non-violence and peace-making. That is what reading the New Testament had done for him. When I once asked him how he had gotten along with people of the surrounding community during the Second World

War with his pacifist style of life, Clarence said quietly, "Well, when I went to town to buy groceries I would get pushed in the gutter once in awhile. But I'd walk there for a spell and then get up on the sidewalk again." Clarence was a servant of the King!

But this is not enough for the *"chief priests and officers"* (19:6). Their strident cry, *"Crucify Him!"* only becomes louder. Now Pilate tries again to push Jesus off on the Jews, *"You take Him and crucify Him."* Now they get to the heart of their charge, saying Jesus is a blasphemer. *"He made Himself the Son of God"* (v. 7). This is why He ought to die according to Jewish law. Of course, Jesus never *"made"* Himself to be anything. He *is* the Son of God!

Now Pilate is afraid. He is superstitious and naive about spiritual matters. *"King"* is one thing, but this *"Son of God"* business sounds like something he can't explain. But now when he anxiously asks Jesus, *"Where are You from?"* he is raising the central question of Jesus' whole ministry. Who is He and what is the source of His authority? In every encounter, in every teaching, as the "Word became flesh," the question of Jesus' identity is the issue.

But Jesus *"gave him no answer"* (v. 9). There is no way He can make this spiritually darkened man understand. There is a veiled threat in Pilate's impatient response to Jesus' silence. Isn't this strange Man aware that His fate—to live or to die—is in Pilate's hands? Oh, if Pilate only knew how limited his authority is. The only power he has comes from above. But Pilate is ignorant. It is the one who has *"delivered"* Jesus to Pilate, who has talked about God and studied the prophecies of the Messiah's coming and presumes to be a spiritual leader, that has been guilty of the greater sin (v. 11).

There is now a kind of desperation in Pilate's trying to release Jesus. He is being cornered by the insistent pressure of these Jews. They are aware of Pilate's hunger for power, his desire to be identified with Caesar's "in crowd," even though the emperor may have barely known Pilate's name. The Jews then say, *"If you let this Man go, you are not Caesar's friend. Whoever makes himself a king speaks against Caesar"* (19:12). The charge against Jesus then is political insurrection. "There was a brief and terrifying moment for Pilate when the people thought he was a friend of Jesus."[4]

This cannot be, for then he will lose all face with Rome. So now Pilate has been forced to action. He sits down in his place of judgment—both the Aramaic and Hebrew names are given for the platform or bench in v. 13. And at the sixth hour, late morning, when the sheep were being killed for the Passover on this day of Preparation, Pilate announces, *"Behold your King!"*

And when the Jews cry out again for blood, Pilate very shrewdly makes his last move. *"Shall I crucify your King?"* he asks, which forces these people to openly declare their allegiance. How tragic it is that they cry, *"We have no king but Caesar!"* (v. 15).

With powerful understatement John writes, *"So he delivered Him to them to be crucified."* The Jews had not received Jesus as He came offering Himself, teaching and healing, but now they *"take"* Him to crucify Him. In these last strange, dark happenings, God has prepared the way to reveal His greatest glory.

THE CRUCIFIXION: THE KING ON HIS THRONE

17 And He, bearing His cross, went out to a place called the Place of a Skull, which is called in Hebrew, Golgotha,

18 where they crucified Him, and two others with Him, one on either side, and Jesus in the center.

19 And Pilate wrote a title and put it on the cross. And the writing was:

> JESUS OF NAZARETH,
> THE KING OF THE JEWS.

20 Then many of the Jews read this title, for the place where Jesus was crucified was near the city; and it was written in Hebrew, Greek, and Latin.

21 Then the chief priests of the Jews said to Pilate, "Do not write, 'The King of the Jews,' but, 'He said: "I am King of the Jews." ' "

22 Pilate answered, "What I have written, I have written."

23 Then the soldiers, when they had crucified Jesus, took His garments and made four parts, to each soldier a part, and also the tunic. Now the tunic was without seam, woven from the top in one piece.

24 They said therefore among themselves, "Let us not tear it, but cast lots for it, whose it shall be," that the Scripture might be fulfilled which says:

> *"They divided My garments among them,*
> *And for My clothing they cast lots."*

Therefore the soldiers did these things.

John 19:17–24

John uses remarkable restraint in giving us his account of Jesus' crucifixion. His language is lean. The facts are simply stated without embellishment. Words here can in no way add to the meaning of God's gracious and costly deed!

Jesus, *"bearing His cross, went out,"* as Isaac bore the wood for the burnt offering (Gen. 22:6). We catch here again the initiative of the Lamb of God as He moves out to offer Himself as the sacrifice for the sins of the world. He went to *"the Place"*—this is His *monē* that we may be made secure in Him— *"of a Skull, which is called in Hebrew, Golgotha."* Our word "calvary" is from the Latin *calveria*, which also means "skull."[5]

The King is between two others that are being crucified with Him. The cross is His only earthly throne.

Every criminal was identified by a placard over his head on the cross listing the crimes for which he was being executed. How ironic that the procurator, a pagan, should proclaim the kingship of Jesus to the many Jews who passed. Jesus was a King so universal that it was announced in the three major languages of that day. This is surely a sign that this "grain of wheat" which was falling into the ground would "bear much fruit." And what Pilate had written he refused to change in spite of the protests of the chief priests. In a strange way, Pilate has had the last say.

It was the custom that the soldiers involved in a crucifixion would get the garments of the one put to death. John is very specific in pointing out that each soldier involved got one of Jesus' four garments and that lots were then cast for His seamless tunic. Even in this gambling, Scripture is fulfilled. This tunic was a priestly garment worn next to the body like that which Aaron had been instructed to wear when he went into the holy place to make sacrifice (Lev. 16:4). The early Christians were quick to point out that there was rich symbolism in John's statement, *"Now the tunic was without seam, woven from the top in one piece."* This seemed to mean that "Jesus' death will not destroy the unity of the people whom He has gathered together."[6]

CARE FOR HIS MOTHER

25 Now there stood by the cross of Jesus His mother, and His mother's sister, Mary the wife of Clopas, and Mary Magdalene.

26 When Jesus therefore saw His mother, and the disciple whom He loved standing by, He said to His mother, "Woman, behold your son!"

27 Then He said to the disciple, "Behold your mother!" And from that hour that disciple took her to his own home.

John 19:25–27

As there were four unbelieving soldiers at the cross, so there were four believing women standing by with fear and sorrow—the mother of Jesus, whose name is never mentioned in this Gospel; His mother's sister, who was undoubtedly Salome, the mother of the sons of Zebedee; Mary the wife of Clopas—this could have been the Cleopas on the Emmaus road (Luke 24:18)—and Mary of Magdala. These friends did not leave in Jesus' hour of desolation. Surely strength and comfort were shared with Jesus in this act of faithful companionship. Most people do not wish to be alone in the moment of death.

Jesus now reaches out in His hour of death and cares for His mother as she cared for Him in His boyhood years. How tenderly the "word made flesh" in family life is revealed here. When Jesus calls her *"woman"* He is not using a cold, formal word, but a warm term of respect. It is to John the disciple, and his mother's nephew, that He gives the responsibility for her care. This act may also be saying that God's chosen people must find their home with those who have come to believe through the ministry of Jesus, that the true destiny of Israel is to be found in the fellowship of the church.

ALL THINGS ARE ACCOMPLISHED

28 After this, Jesus, knowing that all things were now accomplished, that the Scripture might be fulfilled, said, "I thirst!"

29 Now a vessel full of sour wine was sitting there; and they filled a sponge with sour wine, put it on hyssop, and put it to His mouth.

30 So when Jesus had received the sour wine, He
said, "It is finished!" And bowing His head, He gave
up His spirit.

John 19:28–30

Here is the heart of the Gospel. Jesus has completed all the work
His Father has given Him. He has left nothing undone. And every
detail of His ministry has been the fulfillment of Scripture, even
His cry of thirst. Both the work and the word come from His Father.
Jesus is a man of flesh. And in this hour of need, He voices the
physical thirst of every man. And the soldiers show some spark of
kindness by sharing some of their sour wine with Him.

But there is also a rich symbolism beyond the physical cry. Jesus
had told Peter earlier in the Garden that He must drink the cup
which His Father had given Him (John 18:11). Drink every dreg of
suffering to the bottom of the cup. And in this cry of weakness, as
the Psalmist had prophesied, Jesus has come to the lowest point of
His descent—but also to the moment of His being lifted up. In both
of the Psalms which speak so eloquently and specifically of the anguish of Jesus' thirst (22:15; 69:3, 21b) there is also joyful praise
for the Lord has triumphed (22:31; 69:30, 34).

Hyssop was used to lift the wine to Jesus' parched mouth, as hyssop
was used by God's people to sprinkle blood on the doors of their
homes the night in which they were delivered from captivity (Exod.
12:22). Jesus is the Lamb of God whose blood is shed and the one
door by which we must enter. "The Jewish Passover is fulfilled in
the sacrifice of the true Paschal Lamb."[7]

Jesus' last word, *"It is finished!"* is a cry of victory, not of defeat.
He is really in charge! He willingly accepts death because it is the
completion of God's plan. The work of the Incarnate Word has been
accomplished. This is the moment of His glory, not His enemies'.
The verbs are active, *"bowing His head, He gave up His spirit"* (v. 30).
Did Jesus give His spirit to those at the foot of the cross who now
symbolize the new people of God?

HIS SIDE PIERCED

31 Therefore, because it was the Preparation Day,
that the bodies should not remain on the cross on the

Sabbath (for that Sabbath was a high day), the Jews
asked Pilate that their legs might be broken, and that
they might be taken away.

32 Then the soldiers came and broke the legs of
the first and of the other who was crucified with Him.

33 But when they came to Jesus and saw that He
was already dead, they did not break His legs.

34 But one of the soldiers pierced His side with a
spear, and immediately blood and water came out.

35 And he who has seen has testified, and his
testimony is true; and he knows that he is telling the
truth, that you may believe.

36 For these things were done that the Scripture
should be fulfilled, *"Not one of His bones shall be
broken."*

37 And again another Scripture says, *"They shall
look on Him whom they pierced."*

John 19:31-37

It was the Roman custom to leave the bodies of the crucified victims
on the cross as a warning to others. But according to Jewish law, a
dead body was not to remain "overnight on the tree, but you shall
surely bury him that day, so that you do not defile the land which
the Lord your God is giving you" (Deut. 21:22-23). This was particularly true the day before the Sabbath. And on this day of Preparation
before the Passover Sabbath, which was a *"high day"*—here is an
explanatory note for the Greeks again—the Jews are particularly eager
that the legs of the men be broken and the bodies be removed. Pilate
grants their request, and the soldiers break the legs of the other two
who were *"crucified with Him,"* who must have shown some signs of
life.

"But when they came to Jesus," they did not break His legs because
He was obviously dead. Yet a soldier *"pierced His side"* (v. 34). Are
we able to explain this? Was this done casually as soldiers' sport?
Men who live with death can become brutal. Or was he thinking,
"Well, the Man is dead but I'll make doubly certain," as he cut Him
open? Whatever the motive, the thrust of the spear brought forth
blood and water which has become a symbol of God's mysterious
dealings with us.

Whether blood and water coming forth so shortly after death is
miracle or natural occurrence, Jesus is really dead. In the face of

those who would argue that the death of Jesus is an illusion, John is saying this Man of flesh has died! The sacrifice is complete, and now life is offered. Jesus' blood has been shed and now gushes forth a cleansing stream of forgiveness. Likewise the water of the Spirit flows forth as a river of life. The Spirit will now come forth from the depths of Jesus, "rivers of water," as He had earlier promised! (John 7:37–38).

The writer has used two Old Testament prophecies to illuminate the meaning of this event. On the first night of the Passover the most perfect animal from the flock was to be chosen as the Paschal Lamb. And not one of its bones was to be broken when it was sacrificed and its blood was poured as a sign of grace on this night of death (Exod. 12:46). Jesus now has become the perfect Paschal Lamb, shedding His blood to save His people, and none of His bones has been broken.

And as in life, so in death. At the cross Jesus becomes the focal point for those non-believers—the vengeful chief priests, hardened soldiers, and that curious crowd—but also for that handful of believing women and disciples. Some mourn as for the loss of a first-born son. But in the midst of this grief "the Spirit of grace and supplication" is poured out on the "house of David" (Zech. 12:10). From Jesus' opened side flows the blood of forgiveness and the water of His spirit.

And this one who stands by becomes a faithful witness to these happenings through the Spirit. "This is He who came by water and blood—Jesus Christ; not only by water, but by water and blood. And it is the Spirit who bears witness, because the Spirit is truth" (1 John 5:6). The Spirit through the writer is testifying to the truth of all those events. As John the Baptist bore witness at the outset of this Gospel to "the Lamb of God who takes away the sin of the world" (1:29), so now John the beloved bears witness to the completion of the sacrifice of Jesus that men may believe. And he does not make this confession alone, but with the whole company of believers (John 21:24) a testimony which is confirmed by the Lord.

A LAST GIFT

38 After this, Joseph of Arimathea, being a disciple of Jesus, but secretly, for fear of the Jews, asked Pilate

that he might take away the body of Jesus; and Pilate gave him permission. So he came and took the body of Jesus.

39 And Nicodemus, who at first came to Jesus by night, also came; and he brought a mixture of myrrh and aloes, about a hundred pounds.

40 Then they took the body of Jesus, and bound it in strips of linen with the spices, as the custom of the Jews is to bury.

41 Now in the place where He was crucified there was a garden, and in the garden a new tomb in which no one had yet been laid.

42 So there they laid Jesus, because of the Jews' Preparation Day, for the tomb was nearby.

John 19:38–42

Sometimes what is not given in life is given in death. Here two disciples who have been "secret believers," "closet disciples," emerge and publicly ask Pilate for the body of Jesus. Judged and inspired by the "glory" of the cross, they openly confess they are followers of Jesus. By a courageous act, they may have done in death for Jesus what they had not done in life. And Pilate may have been eager to get rid of the body. This has been a troublesome case for him.

These are men of status and wealth, both of them members of the Sanhedrin. Joseph came originally from Arimathea, a Judean town sixty miles from Jerusalem, and Nicodemus, a "ruler of the Jews," had heard of the new birth in a visit with Jesus at night (John 3:1–21).

And they may have been among those rulers who "believed in Him, but because of the Pharisees . . . did not confess Him" (John 12:42). But now, after a long time of silence and fear, they come forth to announce their allegiance.

Every "secret disciple," especially Hebrew believers, who had not yet confessed Jesus openly, being intimidated by those who seemed more powerful, would be encouraged when reading this Gospel by the stand that Joseph and Nicodemus had taken.

Their gift to Jesus was a *"new tomb"* and a dignified, but hasty, burial. After all, they were very much aware that at six o'clock the "high day" of Passover began. The extremely generous mixture of myrrh and aloes, wrapped in the clothes in which the body was buried, underlined again Jesus' kingship. Jesus was buried as a King.

In a garden *"nearby"!* The proximity of Calvary to the garden of resurrection seems to symbolize the small step we take from accepting
the death of Jesus to entering into His life.

NOTES

1. William Barclay, *The Gospel of John, Vol. II* (Philadelphia: The Westminster
Press, revised ed. 1975), p. 221.
2. Ibid., p. 226
3. Raymond E. Brown, *The Gospel According to John XIII–XXI*, p. 864.
4. Earl F. Palmer, *The Intimate Gospel*, p. 158.
5. Leon Morris, *The Gospel According to John*, p. 804.
6. John Marsh, *Saint John*, p. 615.
7. Sir Edwyn Hoskyns, *The Fourth Gospel*, p. 531.

CHAPTER SIXTEEN

From Sight to Faith

John 20:1–31

SEEING WITH EYES OF LOVE

1 On the first day of the week Mary Magdalene came to the tomb early, while it was still dark, and saw that the stone had been taken away from the tomb.

2 Then she ran and came to Simon Peter, and to the other disciple, whom Jesus loved, and said to them, "They have taken away the Lord out of the tomb, and we do not know where they have laid Him."

3 Peter therefore went out, and the other disciple, and were going to the tomb.

4 So they both ran together, and the other disciple outran Peter and came to the tomb first.

5 And he, stooping down and looking in, saw the linen cloths lying there; yet he did not go in.

6 Then Simon Peter came, following him, and went into the tomb; and he saw the linen cloths lying there,

7 and the handkerchief that had been around His head, not lying with the linen cloths, but folded together in a place by itself.

8 Then the other disciple, who came to the tomb first, went in also; and he saw and believed.

9 For as yet they did not know the Scripture, that He must rise again from the dead.

10 Then the disciples went away again to their own homes.

John 20:1–10

The resurrection of Jesus is not a spectacular event with crashing cymbals and blaring trumpets. No, the discovery that He is alive is

281

like the quiet dawning of a new day heralding the defeat of the
night. The risen Christ meets His friends personally and intimately
at unexpected times and places, overcoming their grief and doubt.
They are flooded with joy and peace as they move from sight to
faith.

It is Mary who first comes to the tomb. Love is all she has to
bring. She had sinned much and Jesus had done for her what no
one else could do. He had forgiven and cleansed her. So she comes
in the darkness sometime after 3:00 A.M., only to discover that something has happened. The stone has been removed. I recall the strange
feeling that came over us when we walked into our home after being
gone for some weeks. Someone had been there. One of the chairs
was not in its regular place. Then we noticed a pane of glass in the
back door was broken, and that the small kitchen radio was missing.
That was only the beginning. Thieves had broken in! When Mary
got to the grave, she knew with dismay someone had been there.

When Mary sees the open tomb she assumes the body is gone.
She must get this news to the disciples. So with breathless urgency
she runs to share this disturbing news with Peter, still the leader in
spite of his weakness, and *"the other disciple, whom Jesus loved"* (v. 2).
Can Peter be staying with John who is now caring for Jesus' mother?
We become aware that others have been with Mary at the tomb
when she reports, *"We do not know where they have laid Him."* They are
concerned about the location of a lifeless body, and have no thought
of any other kind of possibility.

When the two disciples hear this news they both take off running
for the tomb to find out what might have happened. But *"the other
disciple outran Peter,"* not because he was younger or stronger necessarily,
but because he is the one who loved more. It is love that brings
the disciple to the tomb first, as it drew Mary to the tomb early.
He does not *"go in,"* but stoops down at the entrance and "peeps
in" seeing nothing but the linen cloths. Obviously there is no body
here.

It is Peter, impulsive and courageous as ever, who goes in all the
way and sees the grave clothes lying there neatly, all in place. "Still
in the folds" is the Greek phrase. Even the head cloths are separated
from the rest of the garments. It is as if the dead one had simply
stepped out into life. Peter sees, but apparently makes no response.

Now John *"went in also; and he saw and believed"* (v. 8). Notice the
sequence. Love has brought John into the tomb, and then with eyes

of love, he sees and understands what physical eyes alone can never penetrate. The empty tomb and the folded grave clothes are quiet evidence for him that Jesus is alive. And John believes! Love has brought him to faith. Later the living Christ will illuminate and open up those Scriptures which testify to His own resurrection, teachings the disciples never understood during Jesus' earthly ministry.

Was it in fear or perplexity or humble gratitude that the disciples *"went away again to their own homes"?* They needed time to reflect and ponder all that had taken place.

GO TO MY BRETHREN

11 But Mary stood outside by the tomb weeping, and as she wept she stooped down and looked into the tomb.

12 And she saw two angels in white sitting, one at the head and the other at the feet, where the body of Jesus had lain.

13 And they said to her, "Woman, why are you weeping?" She said to them, "Because they have taken away my Lord, and I do not know where they have laid Him."

14 And when she had said this, she turned around and saw Jesus standing there, and did not know that it was Jesus.

15 Jesus said to her, "Woman, why are you weeping? Whom are you seeking?" She, supposing Him to be the gardener, said to Him, "Sir, if You have carried Him away, tell me where You have laid Him, and I will take Him away."

16 Jesus said to her, "Mary!" She turned and said to Him, "Rabboni!" (which is to say, Teacher).

17 Jesus said to her, "Do not cling to Me, for I have not yet ascended to My Father; but go to My brethren and say to them, 'I am ascending to My Father and your Father, and to My God and your God.' "

18 Mary Magdalene came and told the disciples that she had seen the Lord, and that He had spoken these things to her.

John 20:11–18

Mary has returned and stands weeping at the tomb. Nothing has changed for her. Although when she stoops and looks in she may be hoping that the body has been returned. There is no body, but she sees an angel at both ends of the place where Jesus had been laid. As there had been two thieves with Jesus at the cross, so now there are two angels at the place of resurrection, a glorious testimony to God's liberating action. Since they are messengers of life, little wonder they should ask Mary about her tears. In her hopelessness she answers, *"They have taken away my Lord, and I do not know where they have laid Him"* (v. 13).

Now she turns and mistakes Jesus for the gardener. Grief can fill us with self-pity and keep us from seeing the truth. Then, as Barclay has said, we can be "facing in the wrong direction."[1] So Mary sees Jesus as a stranger, who now also asks about her grief. Those in glory must often wonder about our tears. They see from such a different vantage point.

Jesus asks then, *"Whom are you seeking?"*—not what, but *"whom?"* And, assuming that this "stranger" may have been involved in moving Jesus' body to a permanent grave, Mary asks if she may have the body to care for it. This is a small way in which she can show her love.

It is then the risen Christ speaks her name—tenderly, but with all the authority of one who has conquered death, *"Mary!"* (v. 16). It is the Shepherd calling one of His sheep, and Mary knows the voice. Then she *"turned"* to Him; she changes directions. It is the movement from grief to joy, from death to life. And in adoration and wonder, she falls at His feet and utters, *"Rabboni!"* This is the title one gives to Jesus at the beginning of faith.

And she clings to Jesus, attempting once again to lay hold on past association, to grasp Jesus as He was before the crucifixion, tabernacled here in flesh, with all its limitations. So Jesus emphatically insists that Mary cannot continue clinging to Him.

In His resurrection Jesus has not only broken the bonds of sin and death, but also the limitation of space and time and the weaknesses of earthly existence. By the power of God He has wrought a new creation, a new order. He is now returning to His Father. Mary is to cling to Him when this journey is completed and He is in perfect union with the Father. Through the Spirit, she will then abide in Christ and *"cling"* to Him as her permanent place of abiding.

Mary is now to go to the *"brethren,"* a new title for the disciples who have become sons and daughters of the Father through Jesus' death and resurrection (v. 17). When Jesus speaks of *"My Father and your Father,"* and *"My God and your God,"* He is defining a whole new standing for believers in the "divine household."

Mary, who is the first to see the Lord, is to be the messenger of His resurrection and ascension. Rather than allowing her to cling to Him, the risen Lord sends her on a mission to tell the others what she has seen and heard. Like Mary, we are sent forth to announce that the body is not in the tomb, for He is with the Father in resurrected glory.

BREATHED ON FOR MISSION

19 Then, the same day at evening, being the first day of the week, when the doors were shut where the disciples were assembled, for fear of the Jews, Jesus came and stood in the midst, and said to them, "Peace be with you."
20 And when He had said this, He showed them His hands and His side. Then the disciples were glad when they saw the Lord.
21 Then Jesus said to them again, "Peace be with you. As My Father has sent Me, I also send you."
22 And when He had said this, He breathed on them, and said to them, "Receive the Holy Spirit.
23 "If you forgive the sins of any, they are forgiven them; and if you retain the sins of any, they are retained."

John 20:19–23

The living Lord who came to Mary now comes to the disciples. These men are gathered in fear behind bolted doors. They are certain that sooner or later the vengeful enemies of Jesus will seek them out. Jesus had sought repeatedly to make it clear to these men that they would know the hatred of the world as He had experienced it (John 15:18, 20; 16:2; 17:14). The servant would not be greater than his master, even in persecution. And it might be coming much sooner than they expected.

How often the contemporary church finds itself behind closed doors, fearful and ineffectual, living on the wrong side of the resurrection. The problems are so vast and the enemy so overwhelming and all the talk about Jesus seems futile. What can be done but hide in the sanctuary discussing how desperate the situation is?

But then Jesus came to these men and *"stood in the midst."* This was no peripheral visit, but an assurance at the center of their lives that He will be with them forever. And His first word, *"Peace be with you"* (v. 19), was far more than a familiar greeting. This gift of peace is the fruit of the salvation He has won on the cross. When He showed these men the nail prints in His hands and the great wound in His side, from which water and blood came, they are *"glad"* (v. 20). Here is the visible evidence of the victory He shares with them in His peace.

This is not another Jesus who has come. These scars are the marks that prove the crucified Jesus is the risen Christ. These wounds are also His credentials in ministering to all suffering humanity. They are scars that the church, His body on earth, must bear if it is to continue the authentic ministry of Jesus.

Now Jesus commissions these men. As He has earlier sent Mary forth with the message of life, so He now sends these disciples. They are given the mission which the Son was given by the Father.

But they cannot begin this mission of healing and peace without the power and energy of Jesus' risen life. So Jesus breathes on these men (v. 22). As God had breathed His life into that first man and He became a living soul, so now His Son shares the intimacy of His own life with His disciples that they may be a new humanity, recreated and empowered for their mission. As Jesus breathes on these men He says, *"Receive the Holy Spirit."* This is a gift to be accepted now, a foretaste of the Person of the Holy Spirit who is yet to come and remain in them permanently after Jesus has returned to the Father.

Then these men are given the authority to continue Jesus' "priestly" work, to carry forward His ministry of forgiveness. Jesus is the only one who can forgive; it is His blood that cleanses the sinner and sets Him free! But these who have been breathed upon are called to be a forgiving, healing people. They are given the right to speak a discerning word of power in Jesus' name that will release the burden of sin. Wherever the breath of the risen Lord is, there is forgiveness. Jesus gives His people the boldness to speak this word in His behalf.

In a gathering of the Lord's people, particularly in small groups, it is good to see someone share a hidden pain, anger, or wrongdoing. It has often been a heavy burden for a long time. Then those on whom Christ has breathed have interceded, given the burden to the resurrected Christ, and in His name have pronounced forgiveness and affirmation, and all have left rejoicing!

Whenever our deacons gather for prayer before serving the Lord's Supper we ask one another if there are any present who stand in need of forgiveness, and every once in awhile there is confession and healing. These are sacred moments which have prepared us to go in to share the bread and cup with new freedom and power.

Too often the institutional church has not been "breathed on" and consequently has lacked the spiritual authority to deal with sin. Then it becomes a "do-good club" enmeshed in a maze of legalisms or simply a friendly collection of people. But there is no loosing of sin.

It is also true that the sins of those who turn from life by rejecting the invitation of the Shepherd are retained as the sins of Judas and the Jewish leaders were. The life of Jesus among His believers will reveal the hardness and rebellion of those who persist in their sinful unbelief.

This authority to speak the word of release and forgiveness or retention and judgment is not given to a spiritually elite group or to specialized clergy, but to all the people who live under the authority of the risen Christ.

DOUBT THAT BECOMES CONFESSION

24 But Thomas, called Didymus, one of the twelve, was not with them when Jesus came.

25 The other disciples therefore said to him, "We have seen the Lord." But he said to them, "Unless I see in His hands the print of the nails, put my finger into the print of the nails, and put my hand into His side, I will not believe."

26 And after eight days His disciples were again inside, and Thomas with them. Jesus came, the doors being shut, and stood in the midst, and said, "Peace be with you."

27 Then He said to Thomas, "Reach your finger
here, and look at My hands; and reach your hand here,
and put it into My side. And do not be unbelieving,
but believing."
28 And Thomas answered and said to Him, "My
Lord and my God!"
29 Jesus said to him, "Thomas, because you have
seen Me, you have believed. Blessed are those who
have not seen and yet have believed."

John 20:24–29

But there is one who was not with them on that first Sunday
evening. Thomas, the twin, had missed that first encounter with Jesus.
Ever the practical realist, he had been so certain they were coming
to Judea to "die with Him" (11:16). So the crucifixion was the end
for Jesus as far as Thomas was concerned. Now which one of Jesus'
disciples would be next? So perhaps had Thomas hidden in fear,
gone off to brood over the failure of Jesus' whole mission, or turned
back to his old ways. Whatever it was that cut Thomas off from
the other disciples gave him occasion to voice his deepest doubts.
Mary had failed to recognize Jesus because of her grief and Thomas
had slipped away from the others because of doubt.

So when the *"other disciples"* seek Thomas out and declare, *"We have
seen the Lord,"* he simply demands proof (v. 25). Unless he can see
and feel Jesus' scarred hands and wounded side, how can he be certain
these others have seen anything more than a mystical apparition? I
have been to the end of that road and have found it to be a lie.
During seminary days I came to a point in my studies where I was
desperately asking the questions of Thomas. If I could not have objective proof—seeing and handling—I would not believe. I felt, perhaps
the resurrection was a subjective, existential, mystical experience
rather than a historical, objective event which kindled faith. How
could anyone be certain that a man of flesh who was actually dead
had been raised again to life? It was a dark night. I lived with my
doubts until I began to become aware that I could not explain the
power of a transformed, living community of believers without knowing that Someone—an actual, living Person—had been the Source of
this life and power. This compelled me to read again the New Testament accounts of Jesus' resurrection as a child would for the first
time. I was grasped by J. B. Phillips's *Ring of Truth*[2] and encountered

the living, resurrected Lord. So I am profoundly grateful to Thomas, who saw his doubts through to the end.

We can all thank God that the *"others"* somehow got Thomas to come to their next "meeting" eight days later. In every generation there are those who have patiently and lovingly built relationships of trust so that they have been able to bring some honest seeker to the "meeting." Sunday evening I was called by a new friend who excitedly reported this had been "one of the greatest days of my life." All day long she had been guided and encouraged by people who reached out to her, first in attending a new Sunday school class, then in a glorious Palm Sunday worship service, and finally at the end of the day in one of our small neighborhood groups. Here she had dared enter into the open sharing and prayer. Someone cared and asked her, and it had been a new beginning.

Again Jesus comes to this meeting—through closed doors—and His greeting this time is, *"Peace to you!"* He offers to them the gift of His presence. It is as if He has come to meet personally with Thomas, to gently deal with His misgivings. And He came to him, not with words or arguments, but offering Himself. "Look and touch, Thomas." *"Do not be unbelieving, but believing"* (v. 27). Jesus' wounds are a sign of His presence. This is not an illusion or a vision, but a real Person! Thomas does not need to touch. He, too, has moved beyond sight to faith. All he can do is fall down before Jesus and cry out in adoration, *"My Lord and my God!"* Twice he speaks the personal *"my,"* "showing that he speaks from a lively and earnest feeling of faith."[3]

He spontaneously gives to Jesus the loftiest title that can come from human lips. Ever since, this has been the central Christological affirmation of the living church. The resurrected Lord is God! The Son is honored just as the Father! (John 5:23).

To Mary and Thomas and the others, sight of the resurrected Lord has been granted. But faith does not finally rest on sight or smell or touch, but on the word and call of the risen Lord! As John believed before he saw the risen Lord, so we believe and trust the witness of those who have seen and believed. We have seen His life revealed in the community of those on whom He has breathed, and as we have heard Him speak our name and responded in trusting faith, we have been born into His family. The Spirit then confirms that we are the children of God, as blessed as those who have seen and believed.

THE PURPOSE

30 And truly Jesus did many other signs in the
presence of His disciples, which are not written in this
book;

31 but these are written that you may believe that
Jesus is the Christ, the Son of God, and that believing
you may have life in His name.

John 20:30–31

There is no way John can put in words all the works of Jesus,
those signs by which the glory and character of God have been revealed, particularly in His resurrection appearances. But he has given
his readers sufficient evidence to believe that Jesus is the "Chosen
One," the very Son of God, and in believing they receive life in
His name.

This is an evangelistic document in which that *"name"* has been
lifted up. For the central issue for both Jews and Greeks throughout
the writing has been the identity of Jesus. And as all men and women
read and ponder and dare believe that Jesus is "I AM," the Christ
of God, they are given life. But those who turn against Jesus in unbelief are condemned to die. So there is the wondrous possibility of
life in reading these words but also the great danger of rejection
and death. We must read carefully and critically, for our lives depend
upon how we read.

NOTES

1. William Barclay, *The Gospel of John, Vol. II,* p. 269–70.
2. J. B. Phillips, *Ring of Truth* (New York: The Macmillan Company, 1967).
3. John Calvin, *The Gospel According to St. John, Part Two 11–21,* and *The First Epistle of John,* p. 211.

CHAPTER SEVENTEEN

Worldwide Mission: Fishing and Tending Sheep

John 21:1–25

FISHING FOR MEN

1 After these things Jesus showed Himself again to the disciples at the Sea of Tiberias, and in this way He showed Himself:

2 Simon Peter, Thomas called Didymus, Nathanael of Cana in Galilee, the sons of Zebedee, and two others of His disciples were together.

3 Simon Peter said to them, "I am going fishing." They said to him, "We are going with you also." They went out and immediately got into the boat, and that night they caught nothing.

4 But when the morning had now come, Jesus stood on the shore; yet the disciples did not know that it was Jesus.

5 Then Jesus said to them, "Children, have you any food?" They answered Him, "No."

6 And He said to them, "Cast the net on the right side of the boat, and you will find some." So they cast, and now they were not able to draw it in because of the multitude of fish.

7 Therefore that disciple whom Jesus loved said to Peter, "It is the Lord!" Now when Simon Peter heard that it was the Lord, he put on his outer garment (for he was wearing only an undergarment), and plunged into the sea.

8 But the other disciples came in the little boat (for they were not far from land, but about two hundred cubits), dragging the net with fish.

9 Then, as soon as they had come to land, they
saw a fire of coals there, and fish laid on it, and bread.

10 Jesus said to them, "Bring some of the fish which
you have just caught."

11 Simon Peter went up and dragged the net to land,
full of large fish, one hundred and fifty-three; and
although there were so many, the net was not broken.

12 Jesus said to them, "Come and eat breakfast."
And none of the disciples dared ask Him, "Who are
You?"—knowing that it was the Lord.

13 Jesus then came and took the bread and gave it
to them, and likewise the fish.

14 This is now the third time Jesus showed Himself
to His disciples after He was raised from the dead.

John 21:1–14

This Gospel does not end with the faith of Thomas in the risen
Lord, "but with a confident statement that Jesus' mission to the world
undertaken at His command and under His authority will be the
means by which many are saved."[1] It is as if John had second thoughts
after seeming to conclude the Gospel by stating the purpose of his
writing (20:31). He must now conclude his testimony by making it
clear that the church has been given an urgent, worldwide mission
by the resurrected Lord. This mission is set forth in the familiar
imagery and setting of fishing and caring for sheep.

How much later this passage may have been written we do not
know, but the language throughout is Johannine. In this last chapter,
he uses such phrases and words as *"after these things"* and *"showed Himself,"* which he used throughout the rest of his book. He also uses
the word *"catch,"* a word not used in the first three Gospels, but
used six times in this Gospel. And Thomas and Nathanael are spoken
of uniquely in this Gospel.

Seven of the disciples have gone back to the well-known haunts
of the Tiberias to fish. Once again the lake is given its Greek name,
for the mission is to the world. These men need time to work things
through. The events of the last days have been overwhelming. Their
whole world has been shaken, and they are baffled and confused.
What can they do next? So when Peter says, *"I am going fishing,"* six
of the other disciples join him (v. 3). Here is something they know
and understand and feel comfortable doing. Even the way they refer
to *"the boat"* rather than *a* boat indicates they have used it before.

But after fishing all night—this is the best time for a good catch—they are empty-handed. It must have been a long, dismal night. One can almost imagine snatches of conversation breaking into long periods of silence. "Where do you suppose He is now?" "What could have gone wrong?" "Why didn't the other four join us?" They may have remembered what Jesus had said earlier, "Without Me you can do nothing" (15:5).

Then there is a figure on the shore they do not recognize who cries out, *"Children"* (or it can be translated "fellows"), *"have you any food?"* How suggestive the physical and spiritual implications of that question are. And when they answer, *"No,"* the "Stranger" commands them to *"Cast the net on the right side of the boat, and you will find some"* (v. 6). How often, like these disciples, we have been fishing on the wrong side, making our own decisions, trying to get things done in our own strength and wisdom, really saying on our own, "I am going fishing."

Now they take such a multitude of fish in their net that they are not able to draw it in. What tremendous, unexpected things happen when they obey the Lord. It is when I surrender this beloved church, which I am so eager to see become a spiritual center of power in the city, to the Lord that His Spirit moves and "fish are caught." The more tightly I seek to control the program, insisting the fishing must be done my way, the more often the net is pulled up empty.

Now John the Beloved must have taken a long look at this Man on the shore only one hundred yards away and in the dawning of this new day recognized Him and joyfully cried out to Peter, *"It is the Lord!"* Again it is the one who sees with love that first recognizes the risen Christ. Jesus has come to show Himself again to the disciples and to call them from their fishing trip to their apostolic mission. Peter, on hearing the good news, hastily covers his body with an outer garment and impulsively plunges into the sea to greet his Lord (v. 7). He cannot meet Jesus in his state of spiritual nakedness, so he seeks to hide his shameful failure in the courtyard. Peter must have been longing to meet with Jesus one more time, hoping for some kind of restoration.

There is a fire glowing on the beach, not the alien fire by which Peter had tried to warm himself earlier, but a flame kindled by the risen Lord who now invites these men to join Him for breakfast.

After the Lord asks for some of the fish which the men have just caught, Peter helps finish hauling in the full net, which has been dragged to the shore by the other disciples. He is still the leader of these men. And every one of the fish has been counted by these fishermen. Yet none of these fish are eaten, for the Lord has already made provision of bread and fish. And why the unusual number of fish—one hundred and fifty-three? Jerome, the church father, has pointed out that this was the perfect catch, for at that time there were only one hundred fifty-three different varieties of fish known in that world. Furthermore, he points out that this was the fulfillment of the prophecy in Ezekiel 47:10, "It shall be that fishermen will stand by it from En Gedi to En Eglaim; they will be places for spreading their nets. Their fish will be of the same kinds as the fish of the Great Sea, exceedingly many."

This may be a fanciful interpretation, but it is an intriguing one. It underlines the worldwide mission Jesus has given to these men. They were first called by Jesus to be "fishers of men." Now that mandate is being renewed and clarified. These disciples are to fish for the souls of men throughout the whole world, to go to all men. This venture will be under the Lord's authority. They are to cast the net on the right side by His command and bring Him the fish.

And in spite of the great catch of one hundred fifty-three, the net has not torn. So the disciples are to remain one. The unity for which Jesus has prayed will be manifested in their apostolic mission.

Now Jesus has breakfast with these men. *"Jesus then came and took the bread and gave it to them, and likewise the fish"* (v. 13). He feeds them as He fed the hungry crowd. As He graciously shares His food with them, their covenant with Him is renewed. They are drawn together in love by His resurrection power after having been scattered. Their unity is restored.

PETER THE SHEPHERD

15 So when they had eaten breakfast, Jesus said to Simon Peter, "Simon, son of Jonah, do you love Me more than these?" He said to Him, "Yes, Lord; You know that I love You." He said to him, "Feed My lambs."

16 He said to him again a second time, "Simon, son of Jonah, do you love Me?" He said to Him, "Yes,

Lord; You know that I love You." He said to him,
"Tend My sheep."

17 He said to him the third time, "Simon, son of
Jonah, do you love Me?" Peter was grieved because
He said to him the third time, "Do you love Me?"
And he said to Him, "Lord, You know all things; You
know that I love You." Jesus said to him, "Feed My
sheep.

18 "Most assuredly, I say to you, when you were
younger, you girded yourself and walked where you
wished; but when you are old, you will stretch out
your hands, and another will gird you and carry you
where you do not wish."

19 This He spoke, signifying by what death he
would glorify God. And when He had spoken this,
He said to him, "Follow Me."

John 21:15–19

But there is still unfinished business. Jesus now draws Peter aside
to deal with him personally. This is a searching time of healing and
restoration. The "backslider" is not only welcomed home, but commissioned by the great Shepherd to care for His sheep. The mission
is not only to evangelize, to catch fish, but to disciple, to feed the
sheep.

The question that Jesus addresses to Simon Peter—and the seriousness of the encounter is underlined by Jesus' use of Peter's full name—
is not concerned with impulsive action, however courageous, but with
Peter's heart, *"Do you love Me more than these?"* This is the most important
question. Does Peter love Jesus unselfishly and unconditionally more
than he cares for fishing with all of its trappings, or anything else?
Peter's immediate response is affirmative, *"Yes, Lord; You know that I
love You"* (v. 15). He makes no reference to any other claims on his
love. But words are not enough, for there is a mission. Converts
are to be cared for. The lambs are to be fed.

Twice more Jesus asks Peter the question, *"Do you love Me?"* without
making reference to any other matters. Each time there is a positive
answer. Finally Peter responds, *"Lord, You know all things"* (v. 17). Jesus
knows Peter's heart, whether his act of repentance has truly brought
him back in undying love. Jesus is not asking about an ascending
or descending scale of love here, but whether Peter loves Him so

deeply and personally that he will faithfully obey Him in the mission which he is being given. It is not a question of how many green leaves come forth in Peter's life, but how much fruit he will bear because he is abiding in Jesus' love. Peter will care for all the sheep—feed the young ones, discipline the stubborn ones, and tenderly watch over the old ones.

There is restoration and healing. Peter is home! Now Jesus predicts that He will die a martyr's death to the glory of God. That eager, untimely offer Peter had made earlier, "I will lay down my life for Your sake" (13:37), will be fulfilled. In following Jesus all the way, Peter will finally be tied down and carried to his death by others. The only security any of us has in following Jesus is His everlasting presence, but that is enough.

THE OTHER DISCIPLE AND HIS WITNESS

20 Then Peter, turning around, saw the disciple whom Jesus loved following, who also had leaned on His chest at the supper, and had said, "Lord, who is the one who betrays You?"

21 Peter, seeing him, said to Jesus, "But Lord, what about this man?"

22 Jesus said to him, "If I will that he remain till I come, what is that to you? You follow Me."

23 Then this saying went out among the brethren that this disciple would not die. Yet Jesus did not say to him that he would not die, but, "If I will that he remain till I come, what is that to you?"

24 This is the disciple who testifies of these things, and wrote these things; and we know that his testimony is true.

25 And there are also many other things that Jesus did, which if they were written one by one, I suppose that even the world itself could not contain the books that would be written. Amen.

John 21:20–25

Peter drops back into his old impulsive ways even here. Seeing John nearby, he wants to know about his destiny. What will his future be? But John, who loves Jesus so deeply, has already obeyed and now is following Him. He needs no further commands. How much like Peter so many of us are. We are so prone to run other people's lives, to work out the arrangements for what a father, a daughter, a pastor, or a deacon should be doing.

But John's future is not Peter's concern. That is all in the hands of the Lord, who could let him live until He returned if He so willed. A rumor got around that John would live until Jesus returned because people misunderstood what Jesus said. So the writer had to clarify what Jesus had really said. What an honest and instructive detail. People then, too, even in the believing community, did not hear correctly and therefore would pass on confusing information which had to be corrected. Times have not changed.

The testimony of *"the disciple,"* the writer John, is true (v. 24). He has given us his witness out of the believing community in which Jesus dwells. And they say *"we know that his testimony is true."* The witness we bear to Jesus is never made alone, but always out of that company who know He is alive. And in a larger sense, we are surrounded and encouraged by all the hosts of heaven.

John has borne witness to an "unlimited Christ." He supposes that if all that Jesus did were recorded there would not be enough books in the world to contain the whole story. Perhaps this is why we need eternity so that we can praise God for all His acts of grace. But John's testimony is complete, all we need to bring us to faith and life.

NOTES

1. Sir Edwyn Hoskyns, *The Fourth Gospel*, p. 550.

Bibliography

Baillie, D. M. *God Was In Christ.* New York: Charles Scribner's, 1948.

Barclay, William. *The Gospel of John, Vol. I.* Philadelphia: The Westminster Press, rev. ed. 1975.

Barclay, William. *The Gospel of John, Vol. II.* Philadelphia: The Westminster Press, rev. ed. 1975.

Barrett, C. K. *The Gospel According to St. John.* London: S.P.C.K., 1955.

Brown, Raymond E. *The Gospel According to John I–XII,* Vol. 29: *The Anchor Bible.* New York: Doubleday & Company, Inc., 1966.

Brown, Raymond E. *The Gospel According to John XIII–XXI,* Vol. 29A: *The Anchor Bible.* New York: Doubleday & Company, Inc., 1970.

Calvin, John. *The Gospel According to St. John, Part One, 1–10,* trans. T. H. L. Parker. Grand Rapids: Wm. B. Eerdmans Publishing Company, 1961.

Calvin, John. *The Gospel According to St. John, Part Two, 11–21,* trans. T. H. L. Parker. Grand Rapids: Wm. B. Eerdmans Publishing Company, 1959.

Forsyth, P. T. *The Cruciality of the Cross.* New York: Eaton and Mains.

Godet, Frederic Louis. *Commentary on John's Gospel.* Grand Rapids: Kregel Publications, 1978.

Griffith, Leonard. *The Eternal Legacy from an Upper Room.* New York: Harper & Row, 1963.

Hendriksen, William. *The Gospel of John.* Grand Rapids: Baker Book House, 1953.

Hoskyns, Sir Edwyn. *The Fourth Gospel,* ed. F. N. Davey. London: Faber and Faber Limited, 1947.

Huckle, John, and Paul Visokay. *The Gospel According to St. John,* Vol. I of *New Testament for Spiritual Reading,* ed. John L. McKenzie (25 vols.) New York: The Crossroad Publishing Company, 1981.

MacGregor, G. H. C. *The Gospel of John,* Vol. 4: *The Moffatt New Testament Commentary.* New York: Harper and Brothers Publishers, 1928.

Marsh, John. *Saint John.* Philadelphia: The Westminster Press, 1968.

Meyer, F. B. *A Commentary on the Gospel of John.* Grand Rapids: Zondervan Publishing House, 1950.

Morris, Leon. *The Gospel According to John.* Grand Rapids: Wm. B. Eerdmans, 1971.

Mowinckel, Sigmund. *He That Cometh,* trans. G. W. Anderson. New York: Abingdon Press, 1954.

Ogilvie, Lloyd John. *The Bush Is Still Burning.* Waco, TX: Word Books, 1980.

Palmer, Earl F. *The Intimate Gospel.* Waco, TX: Word Books, 1978.

Peck, M. Scott. *People of the Lie.* New York: Simon and Schuster, 1983.

Phillips, J. B. *Ring of Truth.* New York: The Macmillan Company, 1967.

Sanders, J. N., and B. A. Mastin. *A Commentary on the Gospel According to St. John,* Vol.

4: *Black's New Testament Commentaries,* ed. Henry Chadwick. London: Adam & Charles Black, 1968.

Schlatter, Adolf. *Der Evangelist Johannes.* Stuttgart: Calwer Verlag, 1930.

Smail, Thomas A. *Reflected Glory.* London: Hodder and Stoughton, 1975.

Temple, William. *Readings in St. John's Gospel.* London: Macmillan & Company, Ltd., 1949.

Westcott, W. B. *The Gospel According to John.* Grand Rapids: Wm. B. Eerdmans, Reprint 1981.